MORPHOLOG

TYPOLOGICAL STUDIES IN LANGUAGE (TSL)

A companion series to the journal "STUDIES IN LANGUAGE"

Honorary Editor: Joseph H. Greenberg
General Editor: T. Givón

Editorial Board:

Volumes in this series will be functionally and typologically oriented, covering specific topics in language by collecting together data from a wide variety of languages and language typologies. The orientation of the volumes will be substantive rather than formal, with the aim of investigating universals of human language via as broadly defined a data base as possible, leaning toward cross-linguistic, diachronic, developmental and live-discourse data. The series is, in spirit as well as in fact, a continuation of the tradition initiated by C. Li *(Word Order and Word Order Change, Subject and Topic, Mechanisms for Syntactic Change)* and continued by T. Givón *(Discourse and Syntax)* and P. Hopper *(Tense and Aspect: Between Semantics and Pragmatics)*.

Volume 9

Joan L. Bybee

Morphology
A Study of the Relation between Meaning and Form

MORPHOLOGY

A STUDY OF THE RELATION
BETWEEN MEANING AND FORM

JOAN L. BYBEE
SUNY at Buffalo

JOHN BENJAMINS PUBLISHING COMPANY
Amsterdam/Philadelphia

1985

Library of Congress Cataloging in Publication Data

Bybee, Joan L.
  Morphology.

(Typological studies in language, ISSN 0167-7373; v. 9)
Bibliography: p. 217
1. Grammar, Comparative and general -- Morphology. 2. Grammar Comparative and general -- Grammatical categories. I. Title. II. Series.
P241.B9   1985   415   85-9201
ISBN 0-915027-38-0 (pb.; U.S.; alk. paper)
ISBN 0-915027-37-2 (hb.; U.S.; alk. paper)
ISBN 90-272-2877-9 (pb.; European; alk. paper)
ISBN 90-272-2878-7 (hb.; European; alk. paper)

PREFACE

This work is concerned with both morphology and morpho-phonemics. The study of morphology approaches morphemes as the (minimal) linguistic units with semantic content, and studies the relations among them. In contrast, morpho-phonemics, as classically defined, studies the relations among allomorphs — the variant phonological representations of a single morpheme. The latter study, it would appear, is a study of form only and has often been approached that way. The present work proposes to demonstrate that in morphology form should not be studied independently of meaning. The meaning of a morpheme and the meaning of the context in which an allomorph occurs determine many properties of their formal expression.

Some readers of this book may be more interested in morphology, while others may prefer to read about morpho-phonemics. Throughout most of the book, the discussion of both subjects is interwoven, but Chapters 3 and 5 are more relevant to those interested in morpho-phonemics, while Part II is less about morpho-phonemics and more about the content of morphological categories of the verb.

Perhaps some readers will wonder how this book relates to my earlier book on Natural generative phonology, since it might appear at first that the current work deals with a different set of issues. Actually, the present work has grown up spontaneously from this earlier work. Natural generative phonology is an attempt at a formal theory which addresses the problem of arbitrariness in morpho-phonemics. Abstract generative phonology approaches this problem by trying to equate morpho-phonemics with phonology, and thereby reduce its arbitrariness. Natural generative phonology responds by treating morpho-phonemics as part of morphology, emphasizing the notion of morphological conditioning. This approach has turned out to be productive, in the sense that it raises questions which seem to me to be more interesting and important than the formal issues of rule order and levels or means of representation that are debated in generative phonology. They are questions of how morphology is acquired, how morphological classes are structured, what determines productivity, what are possible morpho-phonemic changes, and how morphological paradigms are organized.

In the course of my research into these questions, I realized that the data needed to answer them was yet to be gathered. It is data on child language acquisition, on adult language processing, on language universals, and on historical change. I also realized that linguists have set their goals too low in attempting only to account for "competence", and have unnecessarily restricted their database by excluding data on language processing, and by considering data on universals and diachronic change to be somehow "external" when compared to distributional data.

In an attempt to broaden the range of data that I could work with competently, I spent a year (1979 - 1980) at UC Berkeley with the support of a Social Science Research Council Post-doctoral Fellowship, and there I was introduced to the basics of child language research and psycholinguistic experimentation under the guidance of Dan Slobin, an opportunity for which I am extremely grateful. The following year I began to formulate the cross-linguistic hypotheses more clearly, and I am indebted to the National Endowment for the Humanities for a Summer Stipend that allowed me time to begin the cross-linguistic work. The resulting work attempts to pull together psycholinguistic data and cross-cultural comparison into a set of principles that determine certain aspects of the organization of morphology.

The major empirical contribution of the present work is a report on a survey of verbal inflection in fifty languages. This survey was conducted with the help of two people to whom I owe a thousand thanks: Revere Perkins, who composed the stratified probability sample of languages used, and made available to me the reference works on this sample, and Richard Mowrey, who wrote the program that I used for coding and correlating the data. This work was in part possible because of generous contributions to the Department of Linguistics at SUNY/Buffalo from my parents, to whom I owe thanks of many sorts.

The actual writing of most of this book took place while I was a Fellow at the Netherlands Institute for Advanced Study in Wassenaar, during the academic year 1983 - 1984. Many thanks to NIAS for a peaceful year which allowed me time for a better-developed analysis and theory than otherwise would have been possible.

A number of individuals have contributed to the ideas developed in this book, and I thank them for their enthusiastic interactions with me on the topics discussed here. Over many years Henning Andersen has shared with me his many ideas on and interest in morphology and morphological change.

He encouraged me to write this book, and I in turn hope that his will soon come to life. A different song entirely is the one David Zager sings, and his thinking has given me a new slant on some very old problems. I am grateful to the two of them for friendship both in and out of morphology. Many people read drafts of various versions of the chapters of this book — some so long ago that they were not yet reading chapters of a book — but all the comments I received were extremely helpful to me, so I am indebted to Ruth Berman, Eve Clark, Deborah Keller-Cohen, Uli Frauenfelder, Brian Mac-Whinney, Carol Lynn Moder, Blair Rudes, Michael Silverstein, Dan Slobin, and Leonard Talmy. I also have a special thanks for Sandy Thompson, not just for reading drafts of various chapters and offering suggestions, but for being an encouraging and kind friend for many years, and for Bill Pagliuca, who has generously offered both friendship and comic relief, and who has, through a critical reading of the whole manuscript, contributed more than anyone else to an increase in whatever stylistic grace and theoretical cohesion this work might have to offer. The inadequacies that remain here despite the efforts of all my friends and supporters are my own responsibility.

Finally, just one big thank to Brody for dedicating many hours to playing Dungeons and Dragons while I worked, and for saying that the Past Tense of *slay* is *slung*.

Wassenaar, June 1984.

TABLE OF CONTENTS

PART I

MORPHOLOGY AND MORPHO-PHONEMICS

CHAPTER I:
TOWARD EXPLANATION IN MORPHOLOGY

The traditional concern of morphological study has been the identification of morphemes: dividing words into parts and assigning meaning to the parts. This is a descriptive enterprise which assumes that words are indeed divisible into parts. Of course, a number of problems arise from this assumption. On the one hand, words are not always uniquely divisible into discrete parts: at times there are semantic units that seem to have no expression in the word (zero morphs), or parts of the word that do not seem to be associated with any semantic units (empty morphs), or cases where it is simply impossible to find the boundaries between morphemes in the word. On the other hand, morphemes do not always have the same shape in the different environments where they occur. This latter problem, the problem of allomorphy, along with the problem of segmentation, sabotage the ideal of a one-to-one relationship between the semantic units and their phonological expression. Most morphological studies seek to offer means of describing these deviations from the one-to-one correspondence between sound and meaning (for example, Bloomfield 1933, Nida 1946, Matthews 1974 and Aronoff 1976).

The approach offered in this work is quite different. The goal is not to propose a descriptive model of morphology, but rather to propose certain principles in a theory of morphology whose goal is to explain the recurrent properties of morphological systems, including fusion and allomorphy, which are traditionally viewed as problems, in terms of the general cognitive and psychological characteristics of human language users. The first step in this chapter will be to outline a few of the traditional problems of morphology, and to give a general sketch of the approach to these problems taken in the current work, including a mention of the type of hypotheses to be proposed and the nature of the data used to test these hypotheses.

Let us take as a hypothesis (to be revised almost immediately) that the most economical way for sound to relate to meaning is in a one-to-one correspondence, in which each unit of meaning is uniquely and discretely associated with some continuous sequence of the phonological string. The Item and Arrangement model assumes this to be the ideal state (Hockett

1954). This assumption is based on the experience that indeed a large portion of the material in the languages of the world is organized in just this way. We can also assume that there is a basic psychological principle governing language processing that makes this type of correspondence between sound and meaning ideal. The question is whether deviations from this ideal are all aberrations, arbitrary historical residue that interfere with language acquisition and processing, or are some of these deviations themselves based on other psychological principles that also play a role in language processing?

The theory presented here is based on the assumption that many of the properties of morphological systems can be explained, i.e. that the amount of arbitrariness involved in morphological expression is somewhat less than usually supposed. To illustrate that such explanation is possible, let us consider a well-known example. One type of disturbance in the one-to-one mapping of sound and meaning — the occurrence of morphemes that systematically have *zero expression* — is known to correlate highly with other properties of unmarked categories (Jakobson 1939). That is, the distribution of zero morphemes is not random but rather associated with certain members of grammatical categories, in particular, the members that are considered to be basic or conceptually simpler. This suggests a psychological explanation for the occurrence of zero morphemes, and is discussed along with related phenomena in Chapter 3. This case of the correspondence between meaning and morphological expression type is well known. It is the goal of this book to present other similar cases in which the properties of mophological expression correlate directly with aspects of the meaning expressed, illustrating that even in morphology and morpho-phonemics, which would seem to be the most rigid and conventionalized areas of grammar, the relation between meaning and form is not entirely arbitrary.

1. *Morphological fusion*

A major hypothesis developed and tested in this book is the hypothesis that the degree of morpho-phonological fusion of an affix to a stem correlates with the degree of semantic *relevance* of the affix to the stem. The semantic relevance of an affix to a stem is the extent to which the meaning of the affix directly affects the meaning of the stem. This hypothesis, which is developed in Chapters 2, 3, and 4, can be used to arrange inflectional categories on a scale from which various predictions can be made. For instance, the categories of valence, voice, aspect, tense, mood and agreement are ranked for relevance to verbs in that order. From this ranking we can predict the frequency with which categories have lexical, derivational or inflectional expression in the languages of the world, the ordering of affixes, as well as the extent to which the stem and affix have a morpho-phonemic effect upon one another.

The predictions this hypothesis makes for verbal morphology would be rather empty if they were not testable. But indeed, they are testable in a variety of ways. The primary method used in this work is cross-linguistic testing — the application of the hypothesis to a large number of languages. This study has had the advantage of a sampling technique, introduced by Revere Perkins (1980), by which a sample of fifty languages has been chosen in such a way as to prevent the effects of bias due to genetic relations or areal contact. An exhaustive survey of the verbal inflection in these fifty languages is reported on in the present work. Because of the nature of the sample, reliable estimates of the frequency of various morphological phenomena can be made.

The distinction between *derivational* and *inflectional* morphology, which must be treated in any book on morphology, is seen as a gradual rather than a discrete distinction, the basis of which is *relevance*, the same principle that can be used to predict differences among inflectional categories. That is, all morphological categories must be high in relevance, but differences in degrees of relevance yield the derivational / inflectional distinction, as well as the hierarchical relations within these two broad types. Two other factors are identified as important to the derivational / inflectional distinction: the first is the necessity that inflections have full *generality* of applicability to lexical items of the appropriate class. The various causes of the lack of complete generality among derivational morphemes can be attributed to their meanings. At the same time, the necessity of full generality puts certain constraints on the content of inflectional categories. The final contributing factor is the amount of *semantic change* made by the application of the affix to the radical: the greater the difference between the meaning of the derived word and the meaning of the base, the greater the likelihood that the affix is derivational.

2.   *Allomorphy*

Another major problem that morphological theories must deal with is the disturbance in the one-to-one association of sound and meaning due to allomorphy. There are many cases in which a single semantic unit has multiple surface representations. Much is known about the diachronic sources of allomorphy: it is generally understood that natural phonological processes produce alternations in morphemes as they occur in different phonological contexts, and that the alternations remain when these phonological processes lose their productivity. Such residual alternations often appear arbitrary from a synchronic point of view. This apparent arbitrariness has been handled in various ways in descriptive models. In Item and Process models some of the apparent arbitrariness is covered up by re-creating the historical processes that led to the current situation. This necessitates a number of decisions, many of them also arbitrary, concerning what should be the underlying representation of alternating segments. No satisfactory criteria for establishing underlying representations exist in any of the proposed models, suggesting that this approach to eliminating the arbitrariness of residual alternations is unproductive. The Item and Arrangement and Word and Paradigm models avoid the problem of arbitrariness by listing all the alternating variants without trying to structure them in any way that might make them appear less arbitrary. It is argued here that this approach is also inadequate, since it fails to account for the hierarchical relations that do exist among the surface forms of paradigms. The influence of these hierarchical relations is particularly evident in the direction taken by morpho-phonemic or analogical change.

The approach taken here is based on my earlier work (Hooper 1976a) in that a morphophonemic alternation is understood as an alternation, which, when described in terms of features present on the surface (that is, without reference to abstract phonological units) requires reference to morphological, syntactic or lexical information, and cannot be described using only phonological information. In Hooper 1976a it is argued that morpho-phonemic alternations should be approached in terms of the morphology that they represent. One hypothesis that follows from this is that morpho-phonemic alternations in surface forms tend to diagram or reflect the semantic relations among these forms (Andersen 1980). There is considerable evidence that morpho-phonemic alternations diagram two aspects of the organization of paradigms. One is the relation between the *unmarked* or *basic forms* of the paradigm and the more marked or less basic forms. The former are morpho-phonemically simpler or more basic while the latter are morpho-phonemically more complex and derived from the simpler forms (Vennemann 1972, Bybee and Brewer 1980). The other aspect is the *degree of relatedness* among the forms of a paradigm. The more closely related forms are semantically, the more similar they will be in phonological structure (Hooper 1979a). Both of these hypotheses concerning morpho-phonemic diagrams are discussed in Chapter 3, where historical, experimental and cross-linguistic evidence are presented in their support.

The existence of alternations, irregularities and suppletion in morphological expression is possible because of the availability of *rote processing*, even for morphologically-complex forms. It is simply not necessary for human language users to segment every sequence into its minimal parts, because it is possible to acquire, store and access complex chunks of material without segmentation. Rote processing, then, interacts with analytic processing. There are constraints on rote processing, however. Only the relatively more frequent items tend to be learned by rote, and as a consequence irregularities will be maintained only in the relatively more frequent lexical items or forms of a paradigm. The consequences of the interaction of rote and rule processing for a model of lexical and morphological representation are discussed in Chapter 5, where it is argued from various types of evidence that very frequent lexical items and paradigms may have a different type of representation than medium and low frequency items.

3. *Grammatical meaning*

The recurrent theme in this book is that linguistic expression is not entirely arbitrary, rather there is a strong correspondence between the content of a linguistic unit and the mode of expression it takes. This question is approached much as Sapir approached it: we note that there are several possible means of expression — lexical, derivational, inflectional, periphrastic — and we note that there are different types of meaning. Sapir proposed a distinction between "material content" (or lexical meaning) on one end of the scale and "relational content" (or grammatical meaning) on the other end. He argued that material content tends to be expressed in stems or radicals, and relational content in affixes. He emphasized, however, that a given concept may in one language be treated as though it were material, while in another language the same concept appears as relational, making generalization impossible.

It is an interesting phenomenon in our science, that while the difference between lexical and grammatical meaning forms an important part of the intuitive knowledge that linguists use regularly, and is often mentioned in introductory textbooks, the structuralist theories that have dominated linguistics for the past half a century officially deny that there is any relation between the meaning expressed and the mode of expression it takes (Chomsky 1957, Weinreich 1963). This is partly due to the theoretical position that grammar is independent of meaning, a position that is of course not accepted here. Weinreich 1963 further expresses the opinion that, while it might be nice to propose that certain sorts of meaning are always grammatical, and other sorts are lexical, such an activity is ethnocentric, for there might be some, perhaps not yet discovered, language in which everything is done in the opposite fashion.

In the present work it is possible to propose universal correlations of meaning and expression type without running the risk of being ethnocentric, because the study was conducted using an appropriate data base, one that is free of genetic and areal bias, as was mentioned above. The survey of these 50 languages concentrates on verbal inflection, and its results are discussed in many places in the book. However, Part II is given over entirely to a discussion of the meanings expressed by verbal inflection and the details of their expression types in the 50 language sample. Viewed cross-linguistically there are a great many correspondences between meaning and its mode of expression. I have already mentioned the principle of relevance of the meaning of an affix to a stem, the generality of lexical application and the amount of semantic change as factors predicting expression type. In Part II other correlations between meaning and expression are explored.

The mode of expression of inflectional categories — whether they are suffixes or prefixes, what order the affixes occur in, and so forth — can to some extent be seen as a result of the sources from which they develop diachronically. A major source of inflectional markers is full lexical items, which reduce both semantically and phonologically into inflections. The cross-linguistic data show some evidence of a correlation between the degree of semantic reduction and the degree of phonological reduction and fusion. We also see evidence that suggests a parallel diachronic development across languages for particular inflectional meanings.

This evidence is strong cross-linguistic agreement on the mode of expression for certain inflectional meanings, such as imperative, interrogative and negative. In fact, this agreement about the expression of meanings cross-linguistically is stronger than any language-internal regularity in the expression of the so-called "grammatical categories" of mood, tense, aspect, etc. It is striking that an exhaustive survey of verbal inflection reveals that inflectional meanings for verbs do fit nicely into the conceptual categories already identified by linguists. That is, the inflections found could indeed be said to express aspect, tense, mood and agreement in the usual senses of these terms. However, there is very little evidence that these conceptual categories correspond to structural categories as the traditional notion of grammatical category would predict. Rather it seems that each inflection develops more or less independently and may or may not have an expression that parallels other related meanings. The study of inflectional meaning then becomes a study of the means and motivation for the evolution of meaning from lexical to inflectional.

CHAPTER 2:
SEMANTIC DETERMINANTS OF INFLECTIONAL EXPRESSION

1. *Lexical, inflectional and syntactic expression.*

This chapter proposes a set of principles that contribute to an eventual answer to the question of what are the possible inflectional categories in the languages of the world. The hypothesis is set in the larger framework that includes a consideration of what semantic notions can be expressed lexically and syntactically in the languages of the world, although no complete answer to any of these questions is proposed. The proposed principles do, however, make predictions about the behavior of inflectional categories: their frequency of occurrence in the languages of the world, their order of occurrence with respect to a stem, and the morpho-phonemic effect they have on the stem.

In order to state the hypothesis, it is necessary first to define three major ways in which semantic elements may be combined into expression units.

(a) First, two or more semantic elements may be expressed in a single monomorphemic lexical item. This is *lexical* expression. For instance, the lexical item *kill* at some level of analysis combines the semantic elements of 'die' and 'cause'; *drop* combines 'fall' and 'cause'.

(b) In *inflectional* expression, each semantic element is expressed in an individual unit, but these units are bound into a single word. Inflectional expression may be in the form of affixes added to a stem, or in the form of a change in the stem itself, e.g. English regular Past Tense, *walked*, vs. irregular *brought*. Inflectional expression is by definition very general. A morphological category is inflectional if some member of the category obligatorily accompanies the radical element when it occurs in a finite clause. Thus, an inflectional category must be combinable with any stem with the proper syntactic and semantic features, yielding a predictable meaning.

(c) In *syntactic* expression the different semantic elements are expressed by totally separable and independent units, that is, in separate words. Thus *come to know* is the syntactic expression of 'inchoative' and 'know', while *realize* is the lexical expression of the same notions. This type of expression is also often termed "periphrastic" expression.

These three expression types do not constitute discrete categories, but rather mark off areas on a continuum. Intermediate expression types also exist, and are important to the general hypothesis. Between lexical and inflectional expression lies *derivational* morphology. Derivational expression resembles lexical expression in that derivational morphemes are often restricted in applicability and idiosyncratic in formation or meaning. It resembles inflectional expression in that two distinct morphemes are combined in a single word. The hypothesis to be outlined here will contribute to a better understanding of the inflectional/derivational distinction, which is discussed in detail in Chapter 4.

Between inflectional expression and syntactic expression are various types of units that have properties of grammatical morphemes, that is, they belong to a closed class and occur in a fixed position, but which are not *bound* to any lexical item, and thus are not inflections. These units are variously named *clitics*, *particles* or *auxiliaries*. Examples are the cliticized object pronouns of Spanish or French, or the modal auxiliaries of English (*may, can, will*, etc.). These *free grammatical morphemes* resemble inflections in that they make up contrast sets that are obligatory in certain environments, and they have positional restrictions. They resemble periphrastic expressions in that they are not *bound* to lexical stems. Free grammatical morphemes are not studied in the present work, although their existence is recognized by the theory to be proposed.

These expression types form a continuum that ranges from the most highly fused means of expression, lexical expression, to the most loosely joined means of expression, syntactic or periphrastic expression:

lexical - - - derivational - - - inflectional - - - free grammatical - - - syntactic

‹ --

greater degree of fusion

Given these basic types of expression, the question this chapter considers is whether there are any generalizations to be made concerning the *content* of the semantic elements that may be expressed in each of these ways. Since there seem to be few constraints on what may be expressed syntactically, it is more interesting to focus attention on what may be expressed lexically and inflectionally. In fact, the hypothesis of this chapter is concerned primarily with the most constrained expression type — inflectional expression.

When one looks around casually at the languages of the world, one is struck by the fact that the same or very similar inflectional categories appear in one language after another. Verbal systems quite commonly inflect for aspect and/or tense, mood, and person and number agreement with the subject. Somewhat less frequently, it seems, one finds inflectional causatives, negation, voice, and object agreement. For nouns, number, gender or other types of classifiers, case and sometimes deixis are expressed inflectionally. These lists are not exhaustive, of course, but the fact that it is possible to come up with a relatively short list of semantic elements often expressed inflectionally indicates that there must be some general principles governing inflectional expression. The remainder of this chapter is devoted to explicating two of these principles, *relevance* and *generality*.

2.   *Determinants of inflectional expression*

2.1. *Relevance*

A meaning element is *relevant* to another meaning element *if the semantic content of the first directly affects or modifies the semantic content of the second*. If two meaning elements are, by their content, highly relevant to one another, then it is predicted that they may have lexical or inflectional expression, but if they are irrevelant to one another, then their combination will be restricted to syntactic expression. Notice that the hypothesis does not predict that a semantic element *must* have lexical or inflectional expression in a particular language, it only delineates the set of elements that *may* have lexical or inflectional expression. Let us consider some examples. In English we have a lexical item *walk* which means "to go on foot by taking steps". If we add the meaning "through water", we can express both meanings together in one verb *wade*. These two semantic notions may be expressed together in a single lexical item because whether one has one's feet on dry land or in water is quite relevant to the act of walking. In contrast, whether the sky is sunny or cloudy is not usually relevant to the act of walking, so the hypothesis predicts that languages will not have separate lexical items for "walk on a sunny day" vs. "walk on a cloudy day". The latter two combinations would be more likely to have syntactic expression.

Relevance depends on cognitive and cultural salience: no matter to what extent an entity, event or quality is decomposable into semantic features, if it is perceived as discrete from surrounding entities, events or qualities, it can have a lexical item applied to it. So two semantic elements are highly relevant to one another if the result of their combination names something that has high cultural or cognitive salience. If cognition shapes both language and culture, and cultural and linguistic variation is patterned and constrained by cognition, then, we would expect lexicalization patterns to differ across languages, but in a principled and patterned way. This point is illustrated for motion verbs by Leonard Talmy (1980), who identifies three major lexicalization patterns for motion verbs in the languages of the world. In the type familiar from English, but which also occurs in Chinese and Caddo (an Amerindian language), an indication of the *manner* in which the motion takes place is characteristically included in the meaning of a verb. Thus we have motion verbs such as *walk, swim, fly, slide, roll, swirl, bounce, jump* and many more. Romance languages exemplify the type in which the *path* of the motion is included in the meaning of the verb. This pattern is also found in Semitic, Polynesian and Nez Perce. For example, Spanish has motion verbs such as *entrar* 'to go in', *salir* 'to go out', *bajar* 'to go down', *subir* 'to go up', *pasar* 'to go by', *volver* 'to go back', etc. The third, perhaps least common type is found in northern Hokan languages, in Navajo, and in American Sign Language (McDonald 1982). In this pattern, verbs of motion are not distinguished from verbs of location, but rather both are expressed by verb stems whose meaning specifies the kind of object or material being moved or located. Partially comparable English verbs would be *to rain, to spit*, or *to drip*, which give an indication of the type of material that is in motion. These three patterns illustrate a range of variation, yet all within the boundaries laid out by the requirement that semantic elements lexicalized together be relevant to one another. Manner and direction are inherently related to motion, and types of motions can be distinguished on these parameters. Shape or kind of object or material is not as exclusively relevant to motion, and consequently not restricted to motion verbs in the third language type, but applicable also to verbs of location.

In order to apply the relevance criterion to inflectional categories, it is necessary to refer to a distinction made by Sapir 1921 between *material* and *relational* content. Sapir was also interested in the relation between content and expression, and he distinguished two types of concepts: basic, material or concrete concepts "such as objects, actions (and) qualities" which are "normally expressed by independent words and radical elements (and) involve no relation as such", and less concrete or relational concepts which may be expressed by affixes or changes internal to a root (Sapir 1921: 101). In discussing the relevance of inflectional categories, we will be referring to the relevance of the relational concept (expressed by an affix or internal change) to a material concept (expressed by the radical element).

Among inflectional categories, we can distinguish degrees of relevance of the concept expressed inflectionally to the concept expressed by a radical element, in this case a verb stem. A category is *relevant* to the verb to the extent that *the meaning of the category directly affects the lexical content of the verb stem*. For instance, let us compare aspect to person agreement with the subject. Aspect represents different ways of viewing the internal temporal constituency of an action or state (Comrie 1976:3). Since a verb stem describes an action or state, aspect is highly relevant for verbs. Subject agreement is somewhat less relevant to the verb, since it refers to an argument of the verb, and not to the action or state described by the verb itself. Two general predictions emerge from this difference between aspect and subject marking.

The first concerns lexical expression: we expect to find lexical expression of aspect as a common phenomenon, but lexical expression of subject agreement by person much more rarely. This prediction seems to be correct. English has lexical pairs that differ only by inchoative aspect, such as *know* vs. *realize*, and also pairs that differ by completive aspect, such as *do* vs. *complete*. Latin had aspectual distinctions expressed by derivational morphology, such as the inchoative in *amō* 'I love' vs. *amascō* 'I begin to love', *caleō* 'I am warm' vs. *calescō* 'I get warm' and *dormiō* 'I sleep' vs. *obdormiscō* 'I fall asleep'. Examples of lexical aspect are so common that Lyons (1977:705) asserts that there are few languages that do not have aspect. Lexical (or derivational) expression of person agreement, however, is extremely rare. English has a single example: in the verb *to be*, 1st and 3rd singular are distinct in *am* and *is*. In this case, however, the lexical distinction is the residue of an older inflectional distinction. Examples of the lexical or derivational expression of person agreement on the verb independent of a diachronic source in inflection do not seem to occur.

The second prediction concerns inflectional expression: we expect to find aspect expressed as an inflectional category for verbs more often than subject agreement for person. Greenberg (1963) has tested a similar hypothesis, and found that the presence of person/number inflection on verbs in a language implies the presence of tense, aspect or mode inflection. This supports our general hypothesis, since tense and mode are also more relevant to the verb stem than person agreement is.[1]

The prediction our hypothesis makes, then, is that semantic elements that are highly relevant to one another are likely to be packaged together

and expressed lexically, or will be the most common inflectional or derivational categories. Less mutually relevant semantic elements will be expressed
less frequently in morphology, and mutually irrelevant semantic elements
will come together only syntactically. Relevance, which is a semantic criterion, makes predictions concerning the *degree of fusion* of formal elements.
Particular correlates of the degree of fusion of stem and affix will be discussed
in sections 6 and 7 of this chapter.

Another consequence of relevance, which we discussed above in connection with lexical expression, is the fact that concepts formed by the combination of other mutually relevant concepts are highly distinguishable from one
another. This applies to the relevance of inflectional categories as well. The
application of a highly relevant inflection to a stem produces a greater semantic change than the application of an inflection with lesser relevance. For
instance, the following Spanish sentences differ only in the aspect of the verb:

Anoche Juan leyó una novela. (perfective) "Last night John read a
novel."

Anoche Juan leía una novela... (imperfective) "Last night John was
reading a novel..."

In these two sentences, however, the verbs describe different events, in that
in the first, the event described is the reading of a *complete* novel, while in
the second, the event is the process of reading some part of a novel. Consider
in contrast two sentences that differ only in the person of the verb:

Anoche leí una novela. "Last night I read a novel."
Anoche leyó una novela. "Last night s/he read a novel".

In this case, the events described are at least potentially the same, only the
participants have changed.

The degree of semantic differentiation, then, is another consequence of
relevance, and it has as a formal correlate *degree of relatedness* in a morpho-
phonological sense. We will not discuss the degree of relatedness in any
detail in this chapter, but will take it up again in Chapter 3, where we will
see the consequences it has for the structure of verbal paradigms, and again
in Chapter 4, where we will see how the degree of relatedness conditions
the likelihood of inflectional and lexical splits.

2.2. *Generality*

The second factor that needs to be taken into consideration in determining what can be an inflectional category is *lexical generality*. By definition,

an inflectional category must be applicable to all stems of the appropriate semantic and syntactic category and must obligatorily occur in the appropriate syntactic context. In order for a morphological process to be so general, it must have only minimal semantic content. If a semantic element has high content, i.e. is very specific, it simply will not be applicable to a large number of stems. Consider the notions of *path* or *direction* that are sometimes expressed lexically in motion verbs. Many languages also have morphological means of indicating direction with motion verbs. For instance, Latin prefixes indicate direction: *eō* 'I go', *exeō* 'I go out', *transeō* 'I go across'; *ducō* 'I lead', *producō* 'I lead forth', *traducō* 'I lead across', *reducō* 'I lead back'. But each of these prefixes has a limited lexical applicability, for they are only appropriately added to verbs indicating motion of some sort. Their semantic content prevents them from meeting one of the criteria for inflectional status.

The diachronic counterpart to this is the semantic generalization that takes place in the evolution of inflection. In the passage of a word to a clitic and eventually to an inflection, both its phonological shape and its semantic content must be reduced. In order for the form to occur commonly enough to be reduced and become bound, it must have a meaning that is widely applicable — that is, general enough to be appropriately combinable with any stem of the syntactic category. In addition, it must have a meaning that is communicatively useful enough to ensure a high frequency of occurrence.

Most potential categories that are highly relevant to verbs are not general enough to attain inflectional status. The reason for this is that high relevance tends to *detract* from generality. Because relevant categories produce derived words that are more distinct in meaning from their bases than the ones produced by less relevant categories, the combinations of relevant notions tend to be lexicalized. There are two ways that lexicalization detracts from generality. On the one hand, if the combination of meanings that would be expressed morphologically is already expressed lexically, the morphological process does not usually apply. For instance, since English has a lexical reversative for *freeze*, which is *thaw*, the formation *unfreeze* is unnecessary, and indeed, not possible. On the other hand, a morphological category may have a generally applicable semantic content, but still make a rather substantial semantic change in the stem when the two are combined. If this occurs, then the resulting words will tend to become lexicalized. These lexicalizations detract from the generality of the category.

Causatives may serve as an example here. The causative meaning is highly relevant to verbs, since it affects quite directly the event or state being described by the verb stem. However, a causative meaning combined with a verb stem describes quite a different action than the verb stem alone does.[2] For example, dying and causing to die (killing) are two quite different activities. Further, the causative notion itself describes quite different activities according to the verb stem it occurs with. This can easily lead to a situation in which the products of a morphological causative process could become unpredictable semantically and therefore lexicalized. When many of the words resulting from a morphological process become lexicalized, it becomes more and more difficult for speakers to learn to apply the process productively, and the process might eventually lose its productivity.

Consider as an example Causatives in Luganda, a Bantu language. One of the causative formations of Luganda is quite general, and widely applicable, due to the fact that it is used to express the occurrence of either an agent, instrument, reason or purpose in the sentence (Ashton et al. 1954). For many verbs the meaning of a verb stem plus causative is predictable, although some causative verbs are ambiguous between an agent or instrument interpretation. For example, *kùsalà* means 'to cut', and *kùsazà* means 'to cut with'; *kùleèta* means 'to bring' and *kùleèsa* means 'to make to bring, or bring by means of' and *kùgoberera* means 'to follow' and *kùgobereza* means 'to cause to follow'. Even though the addition of the causative suffix to the verb always produces a predictable meaning, there are many verb plus causative combinations that now have in addition an idiosyncratic meaning. For example, the causative of *kùbala* which means 'to count or calculate' is *kùbaza* and means 'to multiply'. The causative of intransitive *kùkyûka* which means 'to turn around, change or be converted' is transitive *kùkyûsa* meaning 'to turn, change or convert (transitive)' or 'to retrace steps' or 'to translate'.

Because the semantic element *causative* makes a considerable semantic change in the event or state being described by the verb, and because the resulting meaning varies considerably according to the verb stem it is combined with, a morphological causative may be very general, but it is prone to lexicalization. In some languages it is totally lexical (and syntactic) as in English, and in others, such as Luganda, it is morphological with many cases of lexicalization.

Now compare the *causative* notion with *tense*. Tense combines quite acceptably with the notions expressed by verbs, in that the verb describes a situation and the tense fixes it in time with respect to the moment of speech. Tense does not, however, alter the situation described by the verb at all. It is the same event no matter when it happens. Thus, while we expect the expression of tense as a verbal inflection, we also expect that tense distinctions would rarely lead to lexical distinctions. In English we have a fair number of verbs with unpredictable phonological expression in the Past Tense, but there are few tense distinctions that lead to unpredictable semantic representations. An example of the lexicalization of a former tense distinction that is in progress in American English is in the verb *get, got. Get* means 'acquire'. *Got* means 'acquired', but because it is past, implies possession in the present: 'I got it, now I have it.' For a substantial group of American children I have observed, *got* can be used in the present tense: *I got; you got; he, she, it gots; we got; I don't got; he doesn't got; do you got? does he got?* are all frequently heard. It is not yet used after modals, **I'll got it; *I can got it,* but its use in the Present Tense shows lexicalization. Note, however, that once this change occurs, the difference between *get* and *got* is not one of tense, but rather of stativity. I know of no examples of the true lexicalization of tense.

The reason that causative is often lexicalized and tense never is, is that the combination of the causative meaning with a verb stem has a radical effect on the meaning of the resulting verb, while the combination of tense with a verb stem does not affect the inherent meaning of the verb. The consequence of this is that even productive morphological causative processes will produce many verbs that will be lexicalized, and it will be difficult for such a process to remain productive. Since tense does not change meaning, and does not give rise to lexicalizations, there is no problem with tense inflections remaining productive.

To summarize the hypothesis: there are two factors that determine the likelihood that a semantic notion will be encoded as an inflectional category. First, the semantic notion must be highly relevant to the meaning of the stem to which it attaches. Second, it must be a very generally applicable semantic notion, or it simply will not apply to enough different items to be inflectional. The interaction of these factors is such that the semantic notions with the highest relevance tend not to be generally applicable, for the reasons outlined above. Thus if morphological categories are graded in terms of relevance, we will find that the most common categories to be inflectional are those that appear in the center of the scale, where relevance is sufficient, but not so high that the meaning changes produced by the process tend toward lexicalization.

3. *Inflectional categories*

The remainder of this chapter concentrates on elaborating and testing the hypothesis that the relevance of one semantic concept to another in part determines the type of expression the concepts will take. The present section discusses some inflectional categories commonly occurring with verbs, and specifies how the hypothesis presented in the preceding section applies to these categories. Deriving from the discussion are certain predictions concerning the relative frequency with which these categories occur as inflectional categories of verbs. These predictions are tested in section 5, where the results of an extensive cross-linguistic survey are reported. Furthermore, this section lays out certain predictions concerning which categories may have lexical expression. No systematic test of these predictions has been carried out, but the reader is invited to apply his or her knowledge of the languages of the world to test these predictions. The categories to be discussed here are valence, voice, aspect, tense, mood and agreement.

Valence-changing categories such as transitive, intransitive and causative are highly relevant to the situation described in the verb stem, since the situation expressed by the verb stem changes according to the number and role of the participants in the situation.[3] The change is sometimes dramatic, as in the case of the causatives discussed above, predicting a tendency toward lexical expression of valence categories, such as English *lay*, *lie*; *sit*, *set*; *go*, *send*, etc. But in other languages the transitive/intransitive distinction figures as an important morphological distinction, even if it does not always qualify as an inflectional one. For example, the following intransitive/transitive pairs represent a widespread distinction in Hebrew (Berman 1978): *avad* 'work' vs. *ibed* 'cultivate'; *yaca* 'go out' vs. *yice* 'export'; and *paxat* 'lessen' vs. *pixet* 'devaluate'.

Voice distinctions, according to a description by Barber 1975, change the relation that the surface subject has to the verb. In the active, the subject is the doer of the action; in the passive, the subject is affected by the action; in the reflexive, reciprocal and middle, the subject both performs the action and is affected by the action. Voice, then, is relevant both to the verb and to its arguments. In signalling a "deviant function" of the subject, it changes the roles of the NPs in the sentence, as well as the perspective from which the situation described by the verb is viewed. It is not surprising, then, that voice may be morphologically coded on the NPs of the sentence, on the verb, or on both. Distinctions in *perspective* that resemble voice distinctions also occur lexically, for instance English verbs *buy* and *sell*, *give* and *receive*. Some reflexive verbs in Romance languages, such as Spanish, have taken on unpredictable meanings, and have become lexicalized: *acordar* 'to agree, to decide upon' vs. *acordarse (a)* 'to remember', *echar* 'to throw' vs. *echarse (a)* 'to begin to', *volver* 'to turn, to return' vs. *volverse* 'to become'. These examples show that the meaning expressed by voice categories is relevant enough to the verb to be combinable in lexical expression, and further that the amount of semantic change is sufficient to lead to lexicalization, at least in some cases.

As we mentioned earlier, distinctions in *aspect* include different ways of viewing "the internal temporal constituency of a situation" (Comrie 1976, taken from Holt 1943). The perfective aspects (inceptive, punctual and completive) view the situation as a bounded entity, and often put an emphasis on its beginning or end. The imperfective aspects in contrast do not view the situation as bounded, but rather as ongoing in either a durative, continuative or habitual sense. Aspect, then, refers exclusively to the action or state described by the verb. It does not affect the participants, nor does it refer to them.[4] Thus, it might be said that aspect is the category that is most directly and exclusively relevant to the verb.

Many languages have aspectual distinctions expressed lexically (*Aktionsart*), such as English *do* vs. *complete*, and *know* vs. *realize*. It is also common to find aspectual distinctions expressed in derivational morphology, as in the Latin example given in section 2.1 of this chapter. These usually express more specific meanings, such as inchoative, as in the Latin example, or completive as in Russian *užinat'* 'have supper', which contrasts with *otužinat'*, which means 'finish supper'.

When *aspect* is an inflectional category, the meaning change effected by it tends, as predicted, to be small. Hopper (1977) has argued that inflectional aspect serves to indicate how the action or state described by the verb should be viewed in the context of the whole discourse. Background information is expressed by imperfective verb forms, and the foregrounded information of the main narrative line appears in perfective verb form. This discourse use of aspect leaves the basic meaning of the verb unaffected, and only changes its relation to the discourse unit.

Tense is a deictic category that places a situation in time with respect to the moment of speech, or occasionally with respect to some other pre-established point in time. It is a category that has the whole proposition within its scope, and yet it seems to be always marked on the verb, if at all. This is so in part because it is the verb that binds the proposition together, and makes it refer to a situation that can be placed in time. But another reason that tense is marked on the verb rather than on, for example, the nominal arguments, is that, as Givón 1979 has observed, nouns usually refer to time-stable entities, while verbs refer to situations that are not time-stable. Thus it is the verb that needs to be placed in time if the event or situation is to be placed in time, since the entities involved in the situation usually exist both prior to and after the referred to situation. Since tense is not exclusively relevant to the verb as aspect is, it is less relevant to the verb than aspect. On the other hand, tense is somewhat more than mood and agreement categories.

A *tense* distinction does not affect the meaning of the verb, since the situation referred to by the verb remains the same whether it is said to occur in the present or the past. Consequently, it is rare to find examples of a tense distinction expressed lexically. To illustrate what a real case would be like, consider English *go* and *went*. They are lexicalized in form, since there is no way to predict the form of one from the other, but they do not constitute a real example of lexical expression, since they must be viewed as a suppletive expression of a general inflectional category of English. A similar pair in a language with no inflectional tense categories would be a genuine example. Consider also the case of *get* and *got* discussed above. Here a tense distinction is becoming lexicalized, but note that when *got* is lexicalized it differs from *get* in stativity, not in tense.

Mood distinctions express what the speaker wants to do with the proposition in the particular discourse. This will include expression of assertion (indicative), non-assertion (subjunctive), command (imperative), and warning (admonitive). It also includes other expressions of the speaker's attitude about the truth of the proposition, such as indications about the source of the information (evidentials). Even when mood is expressed as a verbal inflection, it is clear that it has the whole proposition in its scope, and does not only modify the verb. Furthermore, since it expresses the speaker's attitude, it does not have a direct effect on the situation described by the verb. Both of these properties make mood less relevant to the verb than either aspect and tense are. Thus we might expect mood to occur less frequently as an inflectional category of verbs than aspect and tense. Since mood does not affect the meaning of a verb, examples of lexical expression of mood-like distinctions are rare or non-existent.[5]

Agreement categories in verbal inflection refer not to the situation described by the verb, but rather to the participants in the situation, as we mentioned before. Thus we expect subject and object agreement categories to be less frequent than categories that more directly affect the verb. Agreement categories commonly include distinct markers for *person* (usually 1st, 2nd and 3rd), *number* (singular, dual and plural) and less frequently agreement by *gender* or *classifier*. Not all of these agreement categories have the same status with regard to our hypothesis, however. While *person* and *gender* categories seem to have little effect on the meaning of a verb, and are, as mentioned above, rarely lexicalized, *number* is somewhat different. The number of participants in a situation, whether agents or recipients of an action, can affect the situation profoundly. Thus lexicalized distinctions based at least in part the number of participants do exist, e.g. English *run* vs. *stampede, murder* vs. *massacre*. Ainu, which has no inflectional agreement categories, nonetheless has a number of irregular and suppletive verb stem pairs that are distinguished semantically solely on the basis of the number (singular vs. plural) of the object (Batchelor 1938). We will return to a discussion of examples such as these in Chapter 4.

To summarize this section, a diagram is presented below with the inflectional categories we have discussed arranged in approximate order of degree of relevance to a verb. The categories on the higher end allow lexical as well as inflectional expression, while those on the lower end allow only inflectional. The diagram, then, represents only a gross overall pattern of tendencies to be tested in the next section.

This scale alone does not predict which categories are the most likely to be expressed as inflectional categories. To arrive at that prediction, we must take this linear scale and bend it into a bell-shaped curve. The categories in the middle will be the highest points on the curve, that is, the most likely to be inflectional categories for verbs. The likelihood of inflectional expression drops off on either end, but for different reasons. On one end it drops off because the categories become less relevant to the verb. On this end of the scale lie the agreement categories. On the other end the scale drops off because the categories involved make larger and less predictable semantic changes, and are thus more likely to be lexicalized. Such a curve, then, emphasizes nicely the position of inflectional morphology as lying between syntactic and lexical expression.

The relevance, generality and semantic change criteria have yielded a testable hypothesis concerning the relative frequency of certain verbal categories. In addition, two other testable predictions emerge. The first concerns the order in which affixes appear in relation to the stem of the verb. If linguistic expression is iconic, then we would predict that the categories that are more relevant to the verb will occur closer to the stem than those that are less relevant. The second prediction is related. It is that the categories that are more relevant will have a greater morpho-phonemic effect on the stem than the less relevant categories. Thus the greater semantic cohesion of concepts is reflected in a higher degree of fusion in their corresponding expression units. These predictions concerning the frequency of inflectional categories in the languages of the world, their order with respect to the stem, and their degree of fusion with the stem were tested on a stratified probability sample of 50 languages of the world. The next section describes the methodology employed in carrying out these tests, and the following sections present the results.

Expression type

Category	inflectional	lexical
valence	x	x
voice	x	x
aspect	x	x
tense	x	
mood	x	
number agreement	x	(x)
person agreement	x	
gender agreement	x	

4.   Cross-linguistic survey

Most previous work in cross-linguistic typology and univerals research has paid very little attention to the problem of selecting an appropriate sample for the testing of hypotheses. Often, hypotheses are formulated and "tested" taking too few languages into consideration. Even when a large number of languages is used, little attention is given to the problem of making the sample representative of the languages of the world. Instead, samples are chosen for convenience — the main criterion used is the availability of information about the language (Bell 1978). This is understandable, but it introduces a bias into the data, because languages in certain parts of the world are better described than languages in other parts. Thus a sample chosen for convenience may have in it too many languages that are genetically related, or too many languages that are in areal contact. Convenience may also weight a sample heavily in favor of languages that are written and standardized, which may also introduce an unwanted bias (Perkins 1980).[6]

The only way to make a fair test of a hypothesis about the languages of the world is to use a sample of languages that is truly representative. The sample must attempt to be representative of *all* the languages of the world and at the same time be as free as possible of genetic or areal bias. The sample used in the present study has these properties. It is a sample of 50 languages chosen by Revere Perkins (1980) in such a way that no two languages are from the same phylum (according to Voegelin and Voegelin 1966) and no two are from the same cultural or geographic area. The division of the world into geographic and cultural areas that was used in the sampling procedure was made by Kenny (1974) based on the listing of cultures in Murdock (1967). The full procedure is outlined in Perkins 1980.

This method ensures a representative sample free of known biases. There are, however, a few problems associated with the sampling procedure. One problem is that some language phyla will not be represented in the sample at all. The reason is that some phyla occur only in the same cultural area as another language phylum, and only one of these can be included in the sample. The difficulty presented by this problem is small in a sample of 50 languages. Bell 1978 has calculated that in a sample of 50 languages, a type that occurs in only 10% of the world's languages will have 999 chances out of 1000 of occurring in the sample. This means that only a rather rare type of language would be totally absent from the sample.

A second problem is associated with choosing languages at the level of the *phyla* as established by Voegelin and Voegelin, because language isolates (individual languages with no known genetic affiliations) are treated as phyla. This means that there are probably too many language isolates in the sample, and that some areas, such as North American are over-represented because more language isolates occur there than elsewhere. Once this source of bias is recognized, it is easily controlled, by checking whether frequent phenomena are concentrated in one area or have broad distribution.

A third problem with this sampling procedure is inconvenience. Perkins selected the languages from each cultural group randomly (by using a table of random numbers), and then attempted to find information about the language. In some cases, no adequate documentation exists, and Perkins then randomly chose another language. Inevitably, in some cases the information about some languages in the sample is better than the information about others. In four cases, I found the information Perkins had used about a language inadequate for my needs, and was forced to substitute another closely related language. Perkins' original sample contained Haisla, a Wakashan language, for which I substituted Kwakiutl; Ingassana, a Nilo-Saharan language, for which I substituted Logbara; Ket, for which I substituted Gilyak; and Yuki, for which I substituted Wappo. (The languages used in the survey are listed in the Appendix.)

The advantages of using the Perkins sample far outweigh the disadvantages. This sample was drawn up independently of the hypotheses to be tested, so there is no chance of bias introduced by the investigator consciously or unconsciously choosing languages that are known in advance to fit the hypothesis. Since it is a representative sample, it allows the possibility of quantifiable results that are not only valid within the sample, but extendable to the universe from which the sample was drawn. That is, if 52% of the languages in the sample have inflectional aspect, then we can predict that inflectional aspect occurs in approximately 52% of the languages of the world. A consequence of using this type of sample is that there are languages included that do not have any inflectional morphology at all. In many respects these languages are irrelevant to the hypotheses to be tested. It is necessary to include these languages in the investigation, at least at first, to ensure that the hypothesis is tested on the full range of morphological types. Moreover, the inclusion of non-inflectional languages allows inferences about the relative frequency of inflection in the languages of the world, and the possibility of attempting correlations of inflection with basic word order type (see section 9 of this chapter).

In order to test the current hypotheses, the information about each of the 50 languages was examined and certain facts about the inflectional morphology of verbs was extracted. A list was made of the morphological categories that appear inflectionally marked on verbs in each language. For each language and for each category a sublist of the meanings distinguished in the categories was made. And for each meaning, the associated mode of expression (suffix, prefix, zero marker, stem change, etc.) was recorded. In addition, information about the order of morphemes, the conditioning of allomorphy, irregular and suppletive verbs, and basic word order were recorded. The criteria applied in coding each type of information will be discussed in connection with the particular hypothesis being tested, throughout this chapter and following chapters. In this section, the criteria for coding a morphological category as inflectional are discussed.

Inflectional expression must be distinguished from *syntactic* expression on the one hand and *derivational* on the other. *Boundedness* is the primary criterion for distinguishing inflectional from syntactic expression. If a morpheme is inseparable from the stem, and/or occurs in a fixed order contiguous to the stem, or with only closed class items intervening between it and the stem, it is considered bound. If in the language descriptions this information is not given explicitly, then the author's decision to write the morphemes as separate or bound is taken as an adequate indication of their status. Of course certain unclear cases were encountered and decisions had to be made that might be controversial. In some cases, the second major criterion had to be relied upon.

The second major criterion distinguishes inflectional from derivational morphology, and in some cases, inflectional from syntactic expression. This criterion is *obligatoriness*. An inflectional category is obligatorily marked every time a stem category to which it applies appears in a finite clause.[7] The consequences of this are that there must be some means of expression for the category with every stem. A statement in a grammar to the effect that a certain arbitrary set of stems does not appear in the Causative, for example, would mean that the Causative is derivational, not inflectional.

A third criterion associated with the previous one is *predictability of meaning*. The meaning of the category must be predictable with every verb. If the grammar lists the meanings of the combinations with different stems, then the category is not inflectional.

Further, in inflectional expression, the lack of a marker must be interpreted as meaningful (as zero expression) rather than as the absence of the category. Thus in Tiwi verbs are marked for time of day. There is a prefix for morning and one for evening. However, the author notes that the absence of a mark for time of day does not mean "mid-day", but rather that time of day is not indicated in the sentence (Osborne 1974). Thus time of day is not an obligatory category.

In general, in examining the grammars it was possible to follow the author's division of categories into derivational and inflectional, even if explicit criteria were not given. It was assumed that most linguists' intuitive understanding of the inflectional/derivational distinction coincides with the criteria made explicit here, and that the author, who is the expert on the language, should be given the last word.

For certain categories, more specific criteria could be used. For instance, person and number categories are not obligatory unless they are required in clauses where the subject (or object) with which they agree also appears.

Morphological categories were assigned *labels* based on a list of definitions drawn up before the coding began. With few exceptions, which will be mentioned below, the categories found fit these definitions. When determining how to label the inflectional categories for a language, the labels used by the authors were not relied upon as heavily as the description the author gave of the *function* of the morphemes. For instance, if a grammar characterizes a "Present Tense" as used in the present and past for incomplete action, and a "Past Tense" as used for completed action in the past, these "Tenses" are coded as *aspect*. The following is the list of definitions of the categories used in coding the data:

Valence refers to differences in the number or role of argument that the verb stem can take.

Voice indicates the perspective from which the situation described by the verb stem is viewed.

Aspect refers to the way the internal temporal constituency of the situation is viewed.

Tense places the situation in time with respect to an established point in time, either the moment of speech, or some other point in time.

Mood refers to the way the speaker presents the truth of the proposition in the discourse and real-world context. Included here are expressions of probability, possibility and certainty. *Evidentials* indicate the source of the information expressed by the proposition and were included under mood.

Number agreement is concord with one or more of the arguments of the verb. Subject, object and indirect object agreement are distinguished.

Person agreement is concord by person with one or more of the arguments of the verb. Subject, object and indirect object agreement are distinguished.

Gender agreement is concord with one or more arguments of the verb according to their assignment to lexical classes either arbitrarily or based on inherent qualities of the entity referred to.

While there is a rich enough variety of meanings distinguished under these categories, it was found that by and large these categories and definitions were adequate to cover the inflectional categories described for the languages. The category *mood* contains the widest variety of meanings, and occasionally its boundaries fade off into other categories, as for instance, in one case where it is difficult to distinguish an intentional mood from a future tense. Only two new categories had to be created during the examination of data. One was *purposive*, to use the terminology of Andrews 1975 in his description of Classical Nahuatl. This category usually distinguishes two meanings, one is "going to" and the other is "coming to". This category was found to occur in three languages. In Zapotec, its meaning is close to that of an intentional and even a future. The other was *status* which refers to markers of the relative social standing of the speech act participants. This was found as a verbal inflection only in Korean.

Once the information from each language was extracted from the grammars, it was entered on a computer so that various correlations could be attempted. The most basic of these was the determination of the relative frequency of these inflectional categories for verbs. We turn now to an examination of these data.

5.   The distribution of verbal categories

Figures 1 and 2 show the frequency of morphological categories for verbs in the 50-language sample. Figure 1 shows those categories that were considered to be inflectional (obligatory and bound), and Figure 2 shows the occurrence of the same categories counting both inflectional and derivational affixes.[8] Note that an exhaustive survey of derivational morphology was not undertaken — there are many more possible derivational categories than the ones mentioned here. Rather, the presence or absence of derivational morphology with meanings related to those expressed by inflectional categories was noted. The direct test of the *relevance* principle is in Figure 2, where both types of morphological categories are considered. Figure 1 is the test of the relevance principle in conjunction with the effects of *generality*, which predicts fewer inflections among the most highly relevant categories. In general, both sets of results conform to the predictions made by the hypothesis, although neither conform perfectly. This indicates, of course, the need to investigate additional factors that might determine morphological status. Let us discuss briefly the specific findings of the survey.

Perhaps the most striking finding in this survey is the near universality of the morphological expression of *valence*. In 90% of the grammars consulted there was mention of an affix or stem change which could be applied to a verb to change the number of arguments required by the verb. The most frequently mentioned morpheme of this sort was a causative morpheme. The

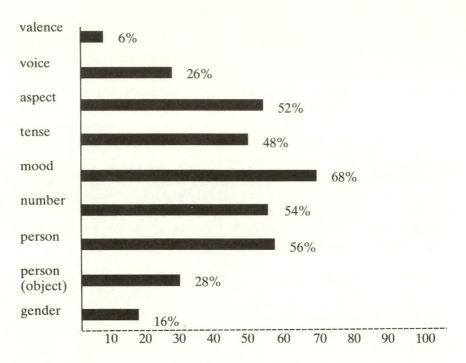

Figure 1: Inflectional categories for verbs

languages for which I found no mention of valence-changing morphology are Haitian, Karankawa, Navaho, Serbo-Croatian and Vietnamese. All of these languages do have other morphology, so it is possible that valence-changing morphology was just not mentioned in the sources.[9]

As might be expected from the high frequency of valence morphology, there are languages which have no other verbal morphology at all, and yet have affixes which change the valence of the verb. Such is the case, for example, in Ainu, Khasi, !Kung and Palaung. The basicness of valence morphology is also seen in developing creoles, such as Tok Pisin, where the first verbal morphology to develop, after the general predicate marker *i-*, is the causative suffix *-im*. Tok Pisin also shows the development of aspect and number markers, but these are not bound to the verb (Mülhäusler 1980).

Figure 1 indicates a very low frequency of valence-changing morphology as inflection. The reason for this is that it is rare to find a case where valence could be considered obligatory in the sense that every finite clause contains a morphological indicator of the number and role of the arguments. All

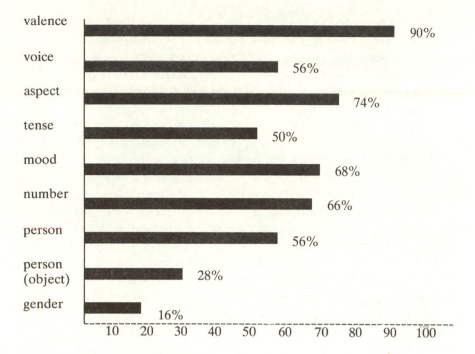

Figure 2: Derivational and inflectional categories marked on verbs

languages seem to have verbs that are inherently transitive and verbs that are inherently intransitive. On the other hand, languages that have object agreement marked on the verb have an obligatory expression of valence, but its markers are not uniquely valence markers, since they signal number, person and sometimes gender as well. Thus object agreement was not counted as an obligatory expression of *valence*. There were, however, three languages in the sample that could possibly be considered to obligatorily express valence. Consider first Kutenai and Maasai: both have object agreement markers, and both have instrumental and benefactive markers on verbs. Presumably these markers occur obligatorily in clauses that have an instrument or a benefactor present, and their absence signals the absence of these arguments. There might still be verbs that do not need these markers, but inherently take instruments or benefactors, in which case the inflectional status of valence would be questionable. Furthermore, in Maasai if object agreement is not present on a transitive verb, the verb is still interpreted as transitive with a 3rd person object. If an intransitive reading is desired, then a suffix must be added to the verb: *arany* "I sing it or them", *áranyıshɔ* "I sing", and *adɔl* "I see it or them", *adɔ lɪshɔ* "I see" (Tucker and Mpaayei 1955). The third example of possible obligatory valence is in Gilyak, where a stem initial consonant alternation coincides with the transitivity of the verb. All transitive verbs have consonants from one series, while intransitive verbs have consonants from another series (Jakobson 1957).

The lower frequency of *voice* categories (as compared to *aspect*) is due to the fact that there are other ways of signalling changes in the perspective of the sentence: sometimes the marking occurs on the noun phrases, and sometimes changes in perspective are accomplished solely by changes in word order. However, *voice* can produce a substantial meaning change in the verb, as evidenced by the occurrence of voice as a derivational category. *Voice* morphemes were considered derivational in cases such as Diegueño, where two suffixes were described as having passive-like meaning (be in a state resulting from an action), but were described under the heading of "stem-formation". These suffixes appear to be restricted to certain verbs, and further, Langdon points out that in some cases it is not clear whether a form should be analyzed as containing one of these suffixes or not, because the meaning is not transparent enough to be a sufficient clue (Langdon 1970: 97).

Morphological aspectual categories followed valence as the most frequently described verbal categories. The meanings most often recorded in the sources were *perfective, imperfective, habitual, continuous, iterative* and *inceptive*. Again it is at times difficult to distinguish obligatory from non-obligatory aspect. This issue is discussed in detail in Chapter 4, and again in Chapter 6. A rough guess is that a little more than half the languages of the world have inflectional aspect.

Fewer languages have *tense* as an obligatory category, and only one language (Kwakiutl) was found to have *tense* as a derivational category. The lower frequency of *tense* as compared to *mood* is due almost entirely to the near ubiquity of an *indicative/imperative* distinction in languages that have any verbal inflection at all. Here we must invoke some notion of communicative importance, for the distinction between a command and an assertion is a very basic distinction in natural language. Details of the distinctions expressed in the *mood* category, as well as a critical examination of the coherence of this category are found in Chapters 8 and 9.

Person and *number* as inflectional categories tend to co-occur. Diegueño is the only example in the sample of a language with inflectional person agreement that lacks inflectional number agreement. However, Diegueño has a derivational category of number. In fact, several language in the sample have derivational expression of "number" in the verb, and some even have lexical expression of "number". This phenomenon is discussed in Chapter 4.5.2.

The differences between the frequency of inflectional *aspect, tense, mood* and *subject agreement* categories is probably not highly significant. However, if *aspect, tense* and *mood* are grouped together and compared to *subject agreement*, then a greater difference emerges: 72% of the languages of the sample have *aspect, tense* or *mood* inflections, while only 56% have subject agreement. Further, in accordance with Greenberg's 1964 finding, no language in this sample has subject agreement that does not also have either aspect, tense or mood.

It appears, further, that the presence of inflectional *aspect* or *tense* in a language implies the presence of inflectional *mood*. The only exception in the sample is the case of Susu, where the unmarked form of the verb may serve as both an Aorist and an Imperative, so that there is no inflectional marking of mood. On the other hand, *mood* inflections occur in languages which do not have inflectional aspect or tense, according to the descriptions consulted. The four languages with this arrangement, Keresan (Acoma), Quileute, Kwakiutl, and Yupik, are all North American languages, and all four of them have considerable derivational morphology, which includes derivational *aspect* in the case of Keresan, Quileute and Kwakiutl. Sufficient data on Yupik are not available to determine the existence of derivational aspect. It appears, then, that a typical inflectional system for verbs will express *mood*, but almost always accompanied by the morphological (usually inflectional) expression of *aspect* or *tense* or both.

Finally, it should be mentioned that derivational expression of *agreement* categories other than *number* was not encountered.

6.   *The order of morphemes*

It is often observed that derivational morphemes occur closer to the root to which they attach than inflectional morphemes do. If there is a correspondence between what can be derivational or lexical and its relevance to the root meaning, then we might also expect the degree of relevance in general to predict the order of occurrence of morphemes with respect to a root or stem. More specifically, among the inflectional categories that we have surveyed, we would expect the most relevant to occur closest to the verb stem, and the least relevant to occur at the greatest distance from the verb stem. This type of ordering relation appears to hold for nouns. Greenberg 1963 reports that when both number and case are present on the same side of the noun base, "the expression of number almost always comes between the noun base and the expression of case" (Greenberg 1963:112). We would interpret this as having a principled basis: namely that the expression of number occurs closer to the noun base because it is more relevant to the meaning of the noun. Number has a direct effect on the entity or entities referred to by the noun. Case, on the other hand, has no effect on what entity is being referred to, but rather only changes the relation of that same entity to the other elements in the clause.

The prediction concerning the ordering of verbal inflections was tested on the most frequent of the inflectional categories — aspect, tense, mood, and person — in the 50 languages surveyed, and it was found to be a valid prediction with very few exceptions.

Before presenting these results, it is necessary to mention several factors that complicated the test of the ordering hypothesis. First, there are many cases in which it is impossible to discern the relative order of two morphemes because they are fused together in *portmanteau* expression. This was especially true of aspect and tense morphemes, and of mood and person morphemes. These cases had no bearing on the test of the hypothesis. Second, in some cases, the two morphemes in question occurred on different sides of the verb stem. These cases were also irrelevant, unless one morpheme occurred adjacent to the stem while the other occurred at least one morpheme removed from it. Then, in these cases, the former was counted as being closer to the stem than the latter. A third situation which rendered a case irrelevant was a situation in which the morphemes in question were mutually exclusive and occurred in the same position. Finally, there were cases in which one morpheme was an affix, but the other was expressed through a modification of the stem, i.e. by reduplication or a vowel change. In these cases, the morpheme expressed by stem modification was counted as occurring closer to the stem than the morpheme expressed by affixation.

The morphemes were examined in pairs to determine their relative order. The results are as follows:

Aspect markers were found to be closer to the stem than *tense* markers in 8 languages, while the opposite order did not occur in the sample. There were a total of 18 languages that have both aspect and tense, but in 10 cases their ordering was not relevant to the hypothesis.

Aspect markers were found to be closer to the stem than *mood* markers in 10 languages, out of a total of 23 that have both aspect and mood. There were no languages in the sample in which the mood marker occurred closer to the stem than the aspect marker.

Aspect markers were found to be closer to the stem than *person* markers in 12 out of 21 languages. In one language, Navaho, the person markers occur closer to the stem than the aspect marker.[10]

Tense markers occur closer to the stem than *mood* markers in 8 languages out of 20 that have both tense and mood. In one language, Ojibwa, the mood marker occurs closer to the stem than the tense marker.

Tense markers occur closer to the stem than *person* markers in 8 languages out of the 17 that have both tense and mood. In one language, Navaho, the person markers occur closer to the stem than the tense markers.

Mood markers occur closer to the stem than *person* markers in 13 languages out of 26. In 5 languages the opposite order occurs.

The position of *number* markers was not tested because in a large majority of languages these markers occur in portmanteau expression with person markers and an ordering of elements is impossible to determine. Thus for the most part, where "person" occurs above, one may read "person and number". This fusion of person and number markers is no doubt due to their diachronic origins as subject (or object) pronouns. We will have more to say below about the diachronic source of the order of morphemes in a verb form.

The results of this survey give striking confirmation of the hierarchical ordering of aspect, tense, mood and person. The strongest differences are found between aspect and the other categories, and between tense and the other categories, where there are almost no counter-examples to the predicted ordering. The ordering of mood and person is somewhat freer. These results would correspond to the higher relevance of aspect and tense to the verb, and lesser relevance of mood, which has the whole proposition in its scope, and person, which refers to the participants. These results suggest a "diagrammatic" relation between the meanings and their expression, such that the "closer" (more relevant) the meaning of the inflectional morpheme is to the meaning of the verb, the closer its expression unit will occur to the verb stem. This type of diagrammatic relation is also evident in the degree of fusion between the expression of the verb stem and the inflectional morphemes, a topic to which we now turn.

7. *Degree of fusion with the stem*

If the meaning of an inflectional morpheme is highly relevant to the verb, then it will often be the case that their surface expression units will be tightly fused, while the less relevant morphemes will have a looser association with the verb stem. This hypothesis can be tested by examining both the effect that the inflectional category has on the surface expression of the stem, and the effect that the stem has on the surface expression of the inflectional category. We are interested here in morpho-phonemic effects that have gone beyond the point of being phonologically-conditioned, and are morphologically- or lexically-conditioned. Examples of cases where the inflectional category has an effect on the verb stem are languages in which a change in the verb stem is the main signal for an inflectional category, or regularly co-occurs with another overt signal of an inflectional category.

Aspect conditions changes in the verb stem more frequently than any other inflectional category. In Burushaski and Touareg, vowel and consonant changes in the stem are the primary signals of aspect. In Temiar, reduplication of the stem is the only signal of aspect. In Sierra Miwok and Wappo, stem changes (especially of stress and length in the former language) regularly accompany aspectual suffixes. In Serbo-Croatian, a system of highly fused prefixes and suffixes, accompanied at times by internal stem changes, are the signals of verbal aspect. In Nahuatl, Pawnee, Ojibwa and Zapotec there are internal sandhi processes that accompany the affixation of aspectual morphemes. This internal sandhi is often specific to these morphemes, and involves fusion of the affix to the stem by means of consonant and vowel loss or modification.

Stem changes are much less frequent with other categories, but they do occur. Sierra Miwok and Wappo have stem change processes for *tense* that are similar to those for aspect. Nahuatl has stem changes associated with tense in some irregular verbs. As for *mood*, Sierra Miwok has stem changes associated with the Volitional, while Pawnee and Ojibwa have internal sandhi associated with the affixation of various mood morphemes. There seem to be no examples in the sample of languages in which the only method of signalling tense or mood is by internal changes in the verb stem.

There are no cases in which simple *number* agreement conditions stem changes as a regular process, but in Acoma and Pawnee there are some verb stems that change in the plural forms. In cases such as Diegueño, where number distinctions by stem change permeate the whole system, number is not so much an agreement category as it is an aspectual one. See the discussion in Chapter 4.5.2.

Stem changes with *person* categories are even rarer (Hooper 1979a). Acoma has stem changes with non-third person objects in a handful of verbs, and Navaho and Zapotec have limited internal sandhi with some stems when certain of the person markers are contiguous. Only Maasai has something slightly more spectacular: reduplication of the stem in second person plural of the habitual, and reduplication of the suffix in the same person of the continuous. Further, in second singular and plural, and in first plural, some verbs take an extra nasal after the stem prefix.

There are some languages in the sample that undoubtedly have stem modifications that were not mentioned in the descriptions because the descriptions were brief, e.g. Yukaghir. For that reason, the data presented here are not complete, and are not reliably quantifiable. However, they most likely indicate what would be found in a more complete survey — that stem modifications associated with aspect are about twice as frequent as those associated with other categories.

The effect of the verb stem on the affix, when it is not a purely phonological effect (and perhaps also when it is), may be taken as an additional measure of the degree of fusion of the two elements. Under this heading are cases in which the particular verb stem determines the choice of the allomorph of the inflectional morpheme. For example, in Spanish, the entire verb conjugation system is based on three lexical classes of verb stem — the three conjugation classes. These lexical classes determine the choice of the allomorphs of certain aspects, such as the Imperfect, but have no effect on the person or number morphemes. This dependency of the Imperfect allomorphy on the verb stem is taken to be an indication of greater fusion.

In the sample, we find lexically-determined allomorphy for *valence* in Ainu, Georgian, Malayalam and Quileute, for *voice* in Nahuatl, Georgian and Quileute, for *aspect* in Serbo-Croatian, Nahuatl and Pawnee, for *tense* only in Malayalam, and for *mood* in Burushaski, Iatmul and Yupik. There are no cases of lexically-determined allomorphy for number or person.

The data, then, support the relevance hypothesis and the hypothesis that the semantic fusion of elements is paralleled in the fusion of expression units. In the case of the effect of the inflectional category on the stem, *aspect* stands out as the category most frequently affecting the stem. In the case of the effect of the stem on the inflectional allomorphy, *number* and *person* stand out as the categories most rarely affected by the lexical choice of the verb stem.

8.   *Explaining the correlations*

We have now examined data on the frequency of occurrence of inflectional categories in the languages of the world, the relative order of occurrence of the expression units of these categories within an inflected verb, and the degree of fusion of these expression units with the verb stem. We have found, as predicted earlier in this chapter, that some categories occur more frequently in the languages of the world, and these same categories tend to occur closer to the verb stem, and exhibit a greater degree of fusion to the stem. These correlations are undeniably strong, but their proposed explanation — that some categories are semantically more relevant to verbs than others — is viable only to the extent that mechanisms can be proposed which suggest how relevance may influence the evolution of inflectional categories. Here we will propose such mechanisms. Since much less is known about the evolution of languages than is known about their synchronic states, this section must of necessity be speculative.

First, it is assumed that inflectional morphemes have their origins in full words that develop a high frequency of use. These frequent items are gradually reduced both phonologically and semantically, and are simultaneously gradually fused, again both phonologically and semantically, with lexical matter contiguous in the syntactic string. The relevance hypothesis predicts that morphemes expressing meanings highly relevant to verbs will be more likely to fuse with verbs than morphemes whose meanings are less relevant. I would claim that there are two reasons for this: first, material that is highly relevant to the verb tends to occur close to the verb in the syntactic string, even before fusion takes place, and second, the psychological restructuring of two words into one depends on the relatedness of the semantic elements being joined, and their ability to form a coherent semantic whole. These two points will be discussed separately.

It seems to be generally true that the order of morphemes within a word reflects an earlier ordering of words within a sentence (Givón 1971, Vennemann 1973). Thus the high frequency of, for example, aspectual inflections, and their proximity to the verb stem, could be traceable solely to the occurrence in earlier times of words expressing aspectual notions in positions contiguous to the main verb. This undoubtedly accounts for most morpheme order, but it defers the questions rather than answering it, for we must still explain why words expressing aspectual notions occur close to the main verb. Here we find a wider domain for the *relevance* principle. It has often been observed that words that function together in the sentence tend to occur together in the sentence. Vennemann cites the "principle of natural constituent structure" proposed by Bartsch, which he describes as follows:

> This principle says that elements belonging together in the hierarchy of semantic representation tend to be lexicalized and serialized in the surface representation in such a way that hierarchical dependencies are directly reflected in categorial operator-operand relationships and the closeness of constituents to each other in the surface string. (Vennemann 1973:41)

Vennemann illustrates this principle with examples from the ordering of modals and auxiliaries, and the order of elements in a noun phrase. A similar analysis is proposed by Foley and Van Valin 1981 who argue that the ordering of elements in the English auxiliary reflects the increasingly wider scope of the operators. The operator whose scope is primarily the verb (aspect) appears closer to the verb, while the operator whose scope may include the whole proposition (tense) occurs furthest from the verb.[11] If there is a diagrammatic relation between the function of two semantic units and the proximity of their expression units in the clause, then the morphological universals we have discussed here may follow directly from these syntactic principles.

While it is true that a great deal about morphology may be explained by applying the relevance criterion on the level of syntax, we cannot assume that morphology is only fossilized syntax and stop at that. There is a great deal of evidence that speakers actively reanalyze and sometimes restructure their morphological systems, especially during language acquisition. For instance, in Bybee and Brewer 1980 we discuss the restructuring of the preterite in Provençal. In Old Provençal, the segmentation of the preterite forms into clear markers for aspect vs. person and number had become difficult. The only consistent mark of the Preterite was the stressed vowel following the verbal root:

canta	'to sing'	*venre*	'to sell'
cantéi	cantém	vendéi	vendém
cantést	cantétz	vendést	vendétz
cantét	cantéren	vendét	vendéron

Many Provençal dialects restructured these forms by taking a consonant, often the /t/ of the Third Singular, to be the Preterite marker, and adding person/number markers to it (Ronjat 1937:193):

cantéte	cantétem
cantétes	cantétetz
canté	cantéton

In this particular dialect, the Third Singular form eventually lost its final /t/ due to a regular sound change. However, we can still observe the clear pattern of restructuring, in which /-ét-/ functions as the Preterite marker with the person/number markers added after it. It is interesting to note that among all the variations on this restructuring pattern in the many dialects of Provençal, not one added the Preterite marker after the person/number markers.

Another interesting example of restructuring that more directly involves the order of morphemes within the verb occurs in Pengo, a Dravidian language (Burrow and Bhattacharya 1970). In Pengo, the Past Tense has the following conjugation.

Past Tense   'to see'

	Singular		*Plural*	
1	huṛtaŋ	ex.	huṛtap incl.	huṛtas
2	huṛtay		huṛtader	
3m	huṛtan		huṛtar	
3f,n	huṛtat	f.	huṛtik n.	huṛtiŋ

The Perfect was apparently originally formed by the addition of the auxiliary /na/ to the forms of the Past Tense. In fact, this pattern is still observable occasionally, in forms such as *vātaŋna* 'I have come', *kuccikna* 'they (fem. pl.) have sat down' and *ravtiŋna* '(the rats) have excavated'. However, the more usual conjugation shows forms in the First Singular, and in the Third Feminine and Neuter Plural in which a person/number marker is added after the Perfect marker, with phonological changes in the Perfect marker in the Third Feminine and Neuter Plural.

Perfect

huṛtaŋnaŋ	huṛtapna huṛtahna
huṛtayna	huṛtaderna
huṛtanna	huṛtarna
huṛtatna	huṛtiknik huṛtiŋniŋ

In addition, sometimes the other forms are heard with the person/number suffix added after /na/: *tustannan* '3s has put on', *kuccatanat* 'Fem. or Neuter Sg. has sat down', *temal pantatnat* 'hair has grown long' and *vātapnap* 'we have come'. In a less common paradigm the person/number suffixes occur only once *after* the Perfect marker:

huṛtanaŋ	huṛtanap hurtanas
huṛtanay	huṛtanader
huṛtanan	huṛtanar
huṛtanat	huṛtanik huṛtiniŋ

These example show that the order of morphemes need not necessarily reflect an earlier order of words, nor the chronological order in which inflectional morphemes develop. Cases of reordering of morphemes are not very common, so it will often be the case that morpheme order reflects an earlier order of words, but it is important to recognize that morphology is not immovable fossilized syntax. Speakers will sometimes rework parts of their morphology. Thus the facts that have emerged from the cross-linguistic survey may be interpreted as indicating the existence of universal synchronic principles of linguistic organization. The implementation of these principles, however, must be understood partly in diachronic terms. Thus I have claimed that the order of morphemes is in large part a result of the order of words in the verb phrase, and that the frequency of occurrence of certain categories as verbal inflections is a reflex of their frequent occurrence contiguous to the main verb. I have claimed that the order of words in the verb phrase is at least partly determined by the relevance principle. And this same principle may continue to apply in the active restructuring of morphology that goes on in every generation of language users.

Now we return to the question of whether the frequency of occurrence of categories such as aspect in the languages of the world is merely a reflex of the fact that words expressing aspectual notions often occur contiguous to the main verb. I will claim that the creation of an inflectional category by fusion is not entirely a mechanical operation that takes place automatically when one word is reduced in the company of another. Rather, the process depends upon the relatedness or relevance of the semantic notions in question, and their ability to form a coherent semantic structure. A reducing morpheme cannot fuse with just any adjacent lexical matter. Its fusion is both phonological and semantic, and the conditions must be right in both domains.

An interesting case that is relevant here is the case of the English auxiliaries, which undergo extreme phonological reduction, attaching themselves to the subject noun or pronoun: *I'll, I've, I'd, I'm, he's,* etc. These forms are highly fused phonologically, and yet when children acquire them, they carefully split pronoun from auxiliary, and go through a long stage in which the auxiliaries are produced primarily in their emphatic, whole word forms (Bellugi 1967, Slobin 1973). The fusion of these elements is delayed, or perhaps prevented entirely, by the incompatibility of modifying pronominal meanings with aspectual notions. On the other hand, the reduced form of *have* that follows the modals *should, would, could*, and *might* has largely lost its identity as the separate aspectual marker *have* for many speakers of English, who spell *should've* as *should of*, and *would've* as *would of*, etc. Here the *'ve* has come to signal a tense difference, and is well on the way to becoming fused to the modal it follows. The combinability of the tense notion with the modality notions accounts for the possibility of total fusion in this case.

The total fusion of two morphemes into one word, whether it be a lexical and inflectional morpheme or some other combination, depends entirely upon the ability of a generation of language learners to analyze the sequence of morphemes as belonging together in a single word. This means that the sequence must have a meaning that is learnable as a whole. Interestingly enough, the child language literature is full of observations about the very early interpretation of verbs as expressing aspectual notions (Antinucci and Miller 1976, Stephany 1981, Simões and Stoel-Gammon 1979, Bloom et al. 1980), even in languages where aspect is not a part of the inflectional morphology (i.e., in Turkish (Aksu, personal communication), and in Hebrew (Berman, personal communication)). In languages that inflect verbs for aspect as well as person and number, for instance, children mark the aspectual distinctions on verbs long before they mark person/number agreement. It is not that person and number are difficult concepts, because they are mastered in the pronominal system long before they occur on verbs. It is simply the combination of the notions referring to person/number agreement with verbal notions that is more difficult to master. It seems that children exhibit a natural tendency to treat certain notions together. This is a clear manifestation of the relevance principle, and it has an effect on the formation of inflectional morphology.

Consider now the developments in Romance languages, especially Spanish. There is a series of direct and indirect object pronouns which have become clitics and occur in a fixed position right before the finite verb. These pronouns are considered clitics because they are unstressed and do not occur unless the verb is present. They are not considered inflections, however, because they are not obligatory. If full noun phrases for direct or indirect object occur in the sentence, the clitic pronouns need not occur. In other words, the transitive verb is complete without the object pronoun clitics. In another development in Spanish and other Romance languages, the Latin auxiliary verb *habere* in its Present and Imperfect forms developed into a suffix that marks Future tense and Conditional mood. These suffixes are bound to the infinitive, and are an obligatory part of the verb conjugation. If a verb refers to a future activity it must be in the Future Tense, even if the tense is clear from the context. Incidentally, object pronoun clitics formerly occurred between the infinitive and the form of *habere*. Since the forms of *habere* have become attached the clitic pronouns no longer occur in this position. The clitic pronouns and *habere* are juxtaposed here to suggest that there may be semantic reasons why the formation of inflection has gone to completion where tense and mood concepts are concerned but is delayed where person/number agreement with objects is concerned. Since we have no absolute timetable for the formation of inflection, this case can only be used to illustrate my suggestion, and not as evidence in favor of it.

My conclusion, then, with respect to the frequency of occurrence of inflectional morphemes, as well as their order with respect to the verb stem, is that the relevance principle governs the formation of inflection at every stage. It sets up the syntactic conditions necessary, and in addition governs the likelihood that an actual fusion will eventually take place.

The application of the relevance principle to the degree of fusion of the inflectional morpheme with the verb stem will be treated in detail in the next chapter. To a large extent the degree of fusion is determined rather mechanically by how long and in what order the inflectional morphemes have been attached to the stem. But this is not entirely the case with stem changes that co-occur with inflectional categories, because these can be affected by morpho-phonemic changes. These changes are also governed by the relevance principle, and will be treated along with other matters relating to the organization of verbal paradigms.

9.   *Morphology and word order*

In the survey of 50 languages, information about the basic word order typology was recorded along with the information about verbal inflection. While correlations with word order do not bear on the central hypothesis of this chapter, it is interesting to consider briefly the frequency of occurrence of inflectional languages among the different word order types. It is also interesting to compare Greenberg's (1963) findings on the frequency of the different word order types with the present survey. There are some significant differences, which are probably due to differences in sampling techniques. We take up this matter first.

Greenberg used 30 languages from a wide range of families and areas, but the languages were largely selected for convenience, as Greenberg notes (1963:75). The distribution of the three main types of word order in his sample is shown in Figure 3, followed by the distribution in the Perkins sample, which was used here. For Perkins' sample, the total is only 40 languages because there was one VOS language (the Car dialect of Nicoborese), one langauge, Logbara, with the contrastive use of SOV and SVO order for imperfective vs. perfective sentences, five languages with reportedly free or variable word order (Nahuatl, Navaho, Sierra-Miwok, Tarascan, and Ojibwa, all North American Indian languages), and three in which information about word order was not available (Karankawa, Timucua and Yupik).

The interesting point to note is that in Greenberg's sample there are slightly more SVO languages than SOV, while in Perkins' sample there are nearly twice as many SOV languages as SVO. This is a rather striking difference, and an interesting indication of the importance of sampling techniques. Greenberg's sample is rather heavily weighted in favor of languages in certain areas — there are 7 European languages, 5 of them Indo-European, 7 African languages, and no languages from Australian or North America. I estimate that about one-third of the languages in his sample are closely related genetically to another language in the sample. This leads us to suspect that the distribution of word order types in his sample is not representative of the languages of the world.

Another point of discrepancy between the results from the two samples is that Greenberg found that 10 out of 11 SOV languages were exclusively suffixing (1963:92), while in the Perkins sample only 6 of the 21 SOV languages are exclusively suffixing, while 11 have both suffixes and prefixes.

With the Perkins sample we can also determine the frequency of the different morphological types among the languages of the world, and correlate this typology with the basic word order typology. The basis of morphological typology, as established originally in the nineteen century, and further developed in our own, most notably by Sapir, is the extent of fusion of morphemes. An *analytic* language does not have fusion of morphemes, rather each morpheme is a separate word, while a *synthetic* language does have fusion of morphemes, and consequently morphologically-complex words. This typology suggests that there is no necessity that a language have morphological expression. Clearly all languages have the possibility of syntactic expression, but not all languages use morphological expression. But just how common are purely analytic languages? In the Perkins sample 28% of the languages have no *inflectional* morphology on verbs. But some of these languages, for example the Car dialect of Nicoborese, have extensive *derivational* or non-obligatory morphology. Others, e.g. Vietnamese, make extensive use of compounding and reduplication. In fact, languages with absolutely no morphologically-complex words do not occur in this sample. The closest case is Palaung, which, according to the description by Milne 1921, has only two prefixes, both of which attach to verbs to give a causative meaning. In addition, Khasi and !Kung have very little affixation, but both of these languages allow the formation of compounds.

Another distinction made in morphological typology distinguishes degrees of fusion in synthetic languages. In *agglutinative* languages, morphological boundaries coincide with phonological boundaries (especially syllable boundaries) to an extent that makes segmentation of morphemes transparent. In *fusional* languages, there is greater fusion of morphemes characterized by sandhi at boundaries, allomorphy, and simultaneous expression, all of which make morphological segmentation more opaque. This can be illustrated with the following two extreme examples:

Agglutinative: Garo
/sok + ba + ku + ja + ma/ = /sokbakujama/
arrive + toward + yet + neg + int
"has he not yet arrived?"

Fusional: Hebrew   (the verb "to write")
Past 3s masc: katav
Present, 3s masc: kotev
Future, 3s masc: yixtov
Imperative, masc. sg: ktov

In the case of Garo, the morphemes occur sequentially, one per syllable, but in the case of Hebrew, the consonants of the stem interdigitate with the vowels that signal the inflectional categories, so that no clear segmentation is possible. Further, there are alternations in the consonants of the stem in the case of Hebrew, illustrated here by the /k/ and /x/ alternation, while Garo has virtually no allomorphy.

These are extreme cases. Most languages utilize a combination of agglutination and fusion, so that a clear classification of synthetic languages into the two types would be difficult. An impressionistic classification of the languages of Perkins' sample into agglutinating and fusional, however, shows that pure agglutinating languages are much rarer than languages with greater fusion. The mechanism behind this distinction may be phonological. Most languages have reductive phonological processes that obscure the boundaries between morphemes and create allomorphy. Phonological processes in agglutinating languages apparently do not have this effect, or alternatively, have not had this effect yet, assuming that agglutinating languages can become more fusional. If the mechanism is primarily phonological, however, it is difficult to explain the observation, first advanced by Lehmann 1973, and confirmed impressionistically in the current sample, that agglutinating languages tend to have SOV as their basic word order.

Another parameter that might yield a morphological typology is the number of categories expressed inflectionally: some languages have no inflections, some have a few, and some have a great many. In section 5 it was pointed out that some languages have only *aspect, tense* or *mood* inflections, while others have one or more of these in addition to inflections to mark agreement in *person* and *number* with the subject. If the languages are divided according to whether they have no inflection (I), *aspect, tense* or *mood* (II), and one of the preceding plus *person* and *number* (III), then the correlations shown in Figure 4 result. The figure shows that SOV languages may be of any inflectional type, but VO languages are evenly divided between those with no inflection and those with the full array of inflections. There are no VO languages with *aspect, tense* or *mood* that do not also have *person* and *number* agreement. Furthermore, while SVO languages are divided between the no-inflection and full-inflection types, VSO languages tend to have full inflection in this sample. At the present moment I do no know the significance of these correlations between inflection and word order.

	SOV	SVO	VSO
Greenberg's sample	37% (11)	43% (13)	20% (6)
Perkins' sample	42% (21)	22% (11)	16% (8)

Figure 3. Comparison of the distribution of basic word order types in two samples.

	I	II	III
SOV	19% (4)	33% (7)	48% (10)
SVO	64% (7)	0	36% (4)
VSO	12% (1)	0	88% (7)
VOS	100% (1)	0	0
all VO	45% (9)	0	55% (11)
all languages	32% (13)	17% (7)	51% (21)

Figure 4. Distribution of inflection in languages with different basic word order.

NOTES

1. Greenberg does not explain how the term "mode" is defined in his study.

2. Haiman 1983 points out that the difference in meaning between a periphrastic and a lexical causative is reflected in the expression type. For a lexical causative in which cause and result are expressed in the same stem, the cause and result are at the same time and the same place. This is not necessarily the case for a periphrastic causative.

3. The following conventions are followed throughout the book: the names of categories and members of categories that are defined here and intended as universal labels are printed in italics with lower case letters. The names given categories and their members by authors of language-specific grammars are printed with initial capital letters.

4. An interesting exception is the Finnish genitive vs. partitive distinction. An object marked in the partitive gives an imperfective reading to the sentence, while a genitive gives a perfective reading. Interestingly enough, young children acquiring Finnish do not learn this as an aspectual distinction at first, but rather as a distinction applying to the noun (Melissa Bowerman, personal communication).

5. Lexical items such as *think, know, believe,* or *doubt* do not represent the lexical expression of mood, but rather periphrastic or syntactic expression. Lexical expression would involve a basic verb meaning, such as "go" appearing in two contrasting lexical items where the only difference between them is a mood difference. Two examples in English that come close to meeting the criterion are the verbs *scram* and *scat,* which are only used in the imperative. What English lacks is a true complement to these verbs: a verb for "go away" that is never used in the imperative.

6. The difference in results obtainable using different sampling techniques is demonstrated in section 9, where the distribution of word order types in Greenberg's 1963 sample is compared with the distribution in the sample used here.

7. Non-finite forms were excluded from the study.

8. Categories that occurred in four or fewer languages were not included in Figure 1. Missing from the table are (1) evidentials, which are included under mood, since all the languages that have evidentials also have mood, (2) purposives and (3) status markers. Status markers code the

social status of the speech act participants and are even less relevant to the verb than agreement markers that refer to participant in the situation.

9. These figures differ slightly from those reported in Bybee 1984 since they are based on a re-examination of a portion of the data.

10. In Georgian the marker for 1st person occurs as a prefix following the aspectual preverb. Other indicators of person and number are suffixes.

11. Certain disagreements with the ordering of morphemes proposed here and those proposed in Foley and Van Valin 1984 will be discussed in Chapter 9.2.

CHAPTER 3: THE ORGANIZATION OF PARADIGMS

A paradigm is a group of inflectionally related words with a common lexical stem. Such a group of words is not comparable to an unstructured list, in which each word bears an equal relation to every other word. Rather, a paradigm has internal structure: there are relations among words that are not symmetrical, and some relations are stronger than others. Descriptive morphology, whether Item and Arrangement, Item and Process, or Word and Paradigm, has not concerned itself with these relations directly, but has rather concentrated on describing the internal structure of each individual word of a paradigm. This chapter will not be concerned so much with descriptions of how to combine morphemes into words, but will concentrate on discovering, through the use of various kinds of evidence, what types of relations obtain among the words of a paradigm.

In all models of morphological description it is recognized to some extent that not all forms of a paradigm have the same status. In Item and Arrangement grammar the fact that some allomorphs have a wider distribution than others is highlighted. In Item and Process grammar there is an underlying form for each paradigm, which does not necessarily correspond directly to any form that actually occurs on the surface. Relations among surface forms are not described, rather all surface forms bear a similar relation to the underlying form, in that they are derived by rule from it. The only difference among these relations is that it might take more rules to derive one surface form than it takes to derive another.

The only descriptive framework that confronts directly the relations among surface forms of a paradigm is traditional grammar, where paradigms are described by structured lists that group forms together according to how closely related they are to one another. While this chapter is not concerned with advocating one descriptive model over another, we will see that the structure implicit in the traditional representation of paradigms is often supported by data from child language, experimentation, historical change and universals.

In this chapter it is proposed that paradigms consist of clusters of closely related surface forms, one of which is basic and the others are derived from it. It is claimed that the structure on the expression level parallels or diagrams the structure on the semantic level. Many aspects of this structure can be understood by referring to the two diagrams that will be defined in this chapter, the *basic-derived relation*, and the *degree of relatedness* among forms.

1. The basic-derived relation

In inflectional paradigms, it often happens that a form can be described by taking another form as a base, and adding a marker to it. Thus Nahuatl (Andrews 1975) 3s Present Indicative of 'to eat' *tlacua* can be made into the 3p Present Indicative by adding *h* (glottal stop) *tlacuah*. With a lengthened final vowel, the same form can be made into the 3s of the Customary Present by adding *ni*, *tlacuāni*, or into the 3s Imperfect by adding *ya*, *tlacuāya*, or into the Future by adding *z*, *tlacuāz*, and so on. Spanish 3s Present Indicative *canta* can be made into 2s by adding *s*, *cantas*, or into 1p by adding *mos*, *cantamos*, into 2p by adding *is*, *cantáis*, or into 3p by adding *n*, *cantan*. The interesting point is that the form that can be used as the starting point for deriving the others is identifiable in morphological terms. Furthermore, there is a great deal of cross-linguistic agreement about which form it is: most often the 3s of the present indicative.

Moreover, the same sort of relation seems to obtain in less obvious cases, for example, where a change in the stem is concerned. Consider English forms such as *weep*, *wept*, *sleep*, *slept*, and so on. The Past Tense of these verbs differs from the Present in that the Past has a suffix *t* and a different vowel. The analysis of the suffixation is obvious, but the vowel alternation may be described in two ways — we may say that the basic vowel is /iy/ which is changed to /ɛ/ in the Past, or that the basic vowel is /ɛ/ which is changed to /iy/ in the Present. It is not descriptive economy that makes the former the correct choice, but rather the fact that only the former description makes the correct predictions for child language and historical change.

A child begins the task of acquiring an inflectional paradigm by first using just one form of the paradigm, and substituting it for all the other forms of the paradigm. The one form chosen is almost always the basic form from which the others may be derived, usually a singular form of the present indicative. So a child acquiring Spanish will use the form *canta* for all persons and tenses, and a child acquiring English will use the form *sleep* for all tenses, in the earliest stages. Then when the child begins to acquire the functions that go with the other forms, he or she builds the other forms using the first one as a base. This is evident from the errors that the child makes. For example, an English-speaking child will often make the error *sleeped*, but never err in the opposite direction, i.e. by using a form *slep* for a Present form. Similarly, Simões and Stoel-Gammon 1979 observed children acquiring Brazilian Portuguese who used the vowel of the 3s present of certain verbs with vowel alternations in the 1s: adult forms: 1s /bebo/, 3s /bɛbe/, from *beber* 'to drink', and 1s /durmo/, 3s /dɔrme/, from *dormir* 'to sleep'. The children's early forms were: 1s /bɛbo/, 3s /bɛbe/, 1s /dɔrmo/, 3s /dɔrme/. In this case, the 3s form is acquired first, and used as a base for the formation of the 1s form. In the acquisition of the irregular Preterite of the verb *fazer*, whose Preterite 3s form is *fez* and 1s is *fiz*, one child made errors which indicated that she was trying to form the Preterite from the stem of the Present, i.e. she produced *fazei* and *fazi* for 1s (using the regular suffixes for 1s). No errors were observed, nor are any likely to be observed, in which the child uses the stem of the Preterite in forming the Present tense.[1] The reason for this assymmetry in error patterns is that the child imposes a basic-derived relation on these forms, such that the Present is basic and the Preterite is derived.

The parallel with historical changes in morphology or morpho-phonemics are striking (Hooper 1979a).[2] For instance, the changes in English verbs always involve a substitution of the Present base for the Past base. Thus *dreamed* is replacing *dreamt* and *leaped* is replacing *leapt*. */drɛm/ does not replace *dream*, and */lɛp/ does not replace *leap*. In fact, morpho-phonemic changes in favor of certain morphologically-identifiable forms are so common that Mańczak 1980 has formulated principles that predict that certain forms of paradigms will retain their conservative or archaic form while others are prone to change, and that these same forms will more often cause re-formation of the other forms than vice versa. Mańczak argues that it is the forms that are more frequent in discourse which remain unchanged and trigger re-formations in other forms. As more frequent, he identifies the singular (vs. other numbers), the present (vs. other tenses), the indicative (vs. other moods), the third person (vs. other persons), inferior numerals (vs. superior numerals), and cardinal numerals (vs. ordinal numerals) (Mań-czak 1980: 284-285). We will see immediately below that these are precisely the forms of paradigms that tend to play the role of "basic" in the basic-derived relation.[3]

The evidence from child language and historical change suggests that the basic-derived relation is a very strong relation among forms of a paradigm. (See also Bybee and Brewer 1980). In the next three sections, we will examine this relation in more detail. In section 1.1. we examine the cross-linguistic distribution of "zero expression", as an indicator of the basic member of a category. In section 1.2 we discuss the diachronic sources of zero expression as further evidence of the basic-derived relation. In section 1.4 we discuss the factors that contribute to the choice of a basic form.

1.1. A phenomenon closely related to the existence of basic forms is the existence of "zero expression" by which one member of a category contrasts with other members by having no overt marker. A good example is the singular of nouns in English. The sentence *Sally picked up the book* bears no representation for singular in the direct object, yet the meaning of the sentence is that Sally picked up *one* book. Number is not left unspecified. The lack of a marker for number on *the book* has a definite meaning. Nevertheless, since it has a simple form, it can be taken as the base for the formation of the plural, *books*, which is accomplished by the addition of a suffix. So if we study the distribution of zero morphs in the languages of the world, we will be studying the distribution of forms that would make good base forms.

Jakobson observed in 1939 that there was a significance to the occurrence of zeroes. They tend to occur in the unmarked members of categories. Jakobson's main criterion for the unmarked member of an opposition is a semantic one: while the marked member of a category signals the presence of a property, the unmarked member is ambiguous — it may be used to indicate the absence of that property, or it may be used in a neutral way in which nothing at all is indicated about that property (Jakobson 1957b). So the term *poet* is opposed to *poetess* by the absence of the property "female", but *poet* may be used to refer to either a male or a female. If it is generally true that zero expression occurs in unmarked members of categories, then there should be some cross-linguistic agreement about the distribution of zero expression.

This hypothesis is easily tested on the language sample described in the preceding chapter, since *mode of expression* was recorded for all members of all categories. If we study the distribution of zero expression, we find some very clear assymetries. The most overwhelming is the occurrence of zero expression in singular vs. plural verb forms. Of the 27 languages that mark *number*, 21, or 78% mark the singular with zero, while zero occurs as an alternate means of expression in the plural in only two languages. As a parallel to Greenberg's findings concerning noun inflections, zeroes never occur as the only means of expression for the plurals of verbs. In the cases where singular has a non-zero expression it is usually a portmanteau expression of both person and singular. An overt mark exclusively for singular is very rare. Continuing in *agreement* categories, among the 28 languages that mark person agreement with the subject, 15, or 54% use a zero for 3rd person, and 4 or 14% use a zero with 1st person. Georgian is the only examples of a language that has a zero with the 2nd person in the indicative. Of the 14 languages with object agreement for person, 8, or 57% use a zero for agreement with 3rd person, and only one (Ojibwa) has a zero allomorph, along with other allomorphs, for 1st and 2nd person object.

Among *mood* categories, there were 25 languages that have expression of the indicative, and 15 or 60% of these express the indicative with zero. Of 25 languages with the imperative, 8 or 32% use zero expression. Only one language has a zero-marked subjunctive. Members of the category *tense* included present, past, future and anterior or perfect. All 19 of the languages that had present also had past. In 12 or 63% of them zero expression occurs in the present tense. There are two languages (Gilyak and Iatmul) in which the past has zero expression, and one (Kiwai) in which the anterior is marked with zero. Of the 22 languages with the future, none uses zero expression for the future.

The distribution of zero expression for *aspect* is the least clear. Of the 20 languages that have imperfective aspect, only 3 or 15% mark the imperfective with zero. Of the 22 languages with perfective aspect, 9 or 41% use zero expression for the perfective. In addition, 8 languages distinguish a habitual from other imperfectives, and only one of these marks the habitual with zero. Ten languages distinguish a continuous aspect, and 6 mark an inceptive aspect, but neither of these occur with zero expression.

These findings are summarized in the following table.

ZERO EXPRESSION IN MORPHOLOGICAL CATEGORIES

Category	More frequently zero		Less frequently zero	
aspect	perfective	41%	imperfective	15%
			habitual	12.5%
			continuous	0%
			inceptive	0%
tense	present	63%	past	11%
			anterior	9%
			future	0%
mood	indicative	60%	imperative	32%
			subjunctive	12.5%
			other moods	0%
number	singular	78%	plural	7%
			dual, trial	0%
person	third	54%	first	14%
			second	7%
person-O	third	57%	first	7%
			second	7%

The high frequency of zero expression in general, however, means that in a large number of cases in virtually every language that has inflection, it is possible to identify basic-derived relations among forms. In order to demonstrate that these facts have a real bearing on the organization of verbal paradigms, we must consider briefly the diachronic source of zero expression.

1.2. From a diachronic perspective, it seems obvious that the reason zeroes exist is because markers arise for one member of a category, creating an opposition with the other member, for which no marker arises. So if an interrogative marker arises and becomes a verbal inflection, it will occur only in questions, and the corresponding declarative will bear no mark. Or a morpheme meaning "imperfective" may develop and attach itself to a verb that was previously free of aspectual marking. The meaning of the uninflected verb will then be automatically restricted to perfective meaning. Similarly, the occurrence of inflectional zeroes in 3rd person is traceable to the tendency for languages not to have real pronominal forms for the 3s. Thus it might appear that the distribution of zeroes in morphology is just a consequence of their distribution in syntactic expression. There is positive evidence, also diachronic in nature, that demonstrates that this is not entirely so. There is evidence that speakers actively create zeroes in the positions predicted by the universals, as they restructure their morphological systems.

Watkins 1962 presents several examples from the development of Celtic languages that show a restructuring of whole paradigms based on an analysis of the third singular form as having a zero mark for person and number. The examples are similar to the following example discussed in Bybee and Brewer 1980 (and presented for other purposes in Chapter 2): In Old Provençal the Present and Preterite paradigms appeared as follows:

Present   *Preterite*

           ama 'to love'

ámo	amám	améi	amém
ámas	amátz	amést	amétz
ámat	áman	amét	améren

As we pointed out in Chapter 2, a clear segmentation into aspect marker plus person/number marker is not possible here. Even the stress was not a consistent mark of the Preterite, since there was some variation in 1p and 2p between final and penultimate stress, and there were many verbs with irregular stress patterns. One type of restructuring that occurred subsequently is illustrated by the following two Preterite paradigms from different Modern Provençal dialects:

Charente (Meyer-Lübke 1923: 352)   *Clermont-Ferrand* (Ronjat 1937: 193)

cantí	cantétem	cantéte	cantétem
cantétei	cantétei	cantétes	cantétetz
cantét	cantéten	canté	cantéton

In these dialects *t* or possibly *et* has become the marker of Preterite, with one exception in each dialect: in Charente, the 1s form resisted the restructuring (a point to which we will return below), and in Clermont-Ferrand, the final *t* in the 3s was eroded by regular phonological change. What is the source of the new Preterite marker, *t* ? Its source is the old 3s marker *t* inherited from Latin and evident in the Old Provençal paradigms above. The forms above can be segmented so that it is evident that the restructuring that occurred involved taking the 3s form *cantét* as the basis for the Preterite and adding person/number markers to this form: Clermont-Ferrand 1s, *cantét* + *e* , 2s *cantét* + *es*, 1p *cantét* + *em*, 2p *cantét* + *etz*, 3p *cantet* + *on*. The important point here is that in order for this restructuring to take place, the form *cantet* had to be analyzed as consisting of base plus Preterite marker, rather than as base plus Preterite plus 3s marker. In other words, this form had to be analyzed as having a zero for a person/number marker. It is significant that it was the 3s form that was reanalyzed as having a zero mark in this case and in all the cases that Watkins cites as well. It is also significant that it is the person/number marker that is taken to have zero expression, while the more relevant tense/aspect category emerges with a clear segmental marker. This phenomenon demonstrates that the occurrence of zeroes in paradigms is not just an accident of the diachronic developments in the syntax, but is a viable synchronic principle that reflects the psychological structuring of verbal paradigms.

The phenomenon of creating zeroes where there were full morphemes previously must have its origin in the language acquisition process where a frequent, first-learned form is given a wider application than in adult language. While other forms with specific marks are acquired for specific functions, and this restricts the domain of the first form, the fact that it bears a specific marker of its more restricted function may never be recognized. In the present example, *cantét* would be the first Preterite form acquired, and it would be used for all the person/numbers of the Preterite. (Cf. the discussion below on the acquisition of the Preterite in Brazilian Portuguese, where the 3s Preterite form precedes the 1s form.) As the other forms are acquired, or, during the restructuring process, re-created, the fact that the *t* meant 3s rather than Preterite may never be recognized. Thus zeroes or unmarked forms develop naturally because of the order in which forms of a paradigm are acquired.[3]

A similar process is at least partially complete in the creolization of Tok Pisin (Mosel 1980). What was originally a 3s marker *i-*, which derived from the English 3s pronoun *he* or the 3s marker *i* in the substratum languages is becoming a general predicate marker. It is obligatorily prefixed to all predicates, except those that have *yu* or *mi* as subjects. Thus it occurs not only with 3s subjects, but also with 3p subjects, as in *ol man i wok* 'The men are working', and with the dual and plural of the second and third person, i.e. *yutupela i laik kisim wanem*? 'What do you (two) want to get?, *mitupela i laik kisim kaikai* 'We want to get food'. There is also an example from Mosel (1980:123) showing the use of *i-* after a 1s subject separated from the verb by the future marker: *mi bai i go long taun* 'I will go to town'. Just as in the Provençal example discussed above, a verb with an overt mark for the "unmarked" subject is taken as having no mark, and the *i-* is analyzed as having the function of signalling predicates in general.

1.3. Let us turn now to a discussion of the factors that determine the choice of a base form from the forms of a paradigm. In Bybee and Brewer 1980 we argued that the semantic criterion proposed by Jakobson was correct, but not always sufficient to determine the basic form in a group of forms. For one thing, one paradigm in a language might have only one basic form, while another paradigm may have two or three or more, as in cases of extreme irregularity or suppletion. We suggested using the notion of *autonomy* proposed by David Zager. The degree of autonomy of a word determines the likelihood that the word has a separate lexical representation. We identified three criteria that affect this likelihood. One is the semantic categories represented by the word. A semantically basic or unmarked word is likely to have a separate lexical entry, while a word that is semantically derived or restricted in function is less likely to have a lexical entry of its own. But semantic predictability does not necessarily entail autonomous status, since there are two other factors that must be considered.

A second factor is the frequency of the word. In order for a word to have its own lexical entry or to be basic, it must be learned and stored independently. In order for this to happen, it must be frequent enough to be rote-learned. This means, also, however, that a word that is semantically derived or marked, if it is frequent enough, can nevertheless be autonomous. Of course, it happens that for the most part the same forms that are identified as being unmarked or basic are also the most frequent, so that the first and second criteria usually converge (Greenberg 1966). What the second criterion allows for, however, is the possibility that in a very frequent paradigm there may be many autonomous forms. Frequency also detemines the ability of a form to resist morpho-phonemic change. Consider for example the forms displayed above from the Charente dialect. Note that the 1s form did not undergo restructuring, but retained its old shape. This is not surprising, since 1s forms are almost as frequent as 3s forms (see section 4, below). The resistance of forms to change is a consequence of their autonomy. Those forms that are learned and stored as independent items do not as easily fall victim to restructuring. One main reason, then, for defining a notion of 'autonomy' that is independent of the notion 'basic', is that the same forms that may serve as basic also resist change, even when they are not serving as base forms. Mańczak's statement to this effect is cited above, and we will see more examples of this phenomenon below.

A third factor that influences autonomy is morpho-phonemic irregularity. If a word is so irregular that it cannot be derived from any other related words, even if it is semantically marked, it will have to be autonomous. An extreme case is found in suppletive paradigms — *went* must be autonomous because it cannot be derived morpho-phonemically from *go*. Note however, that only very frequent paradigms can tolerate high degrees of morpho-phonemic irregularity, which demonstrates the importance of the second criterion (see Chapter 5).

These criteria determine autonomy. The basic-derived relation arises be veen two forms if one is autonomous and the other is less so, and if the two are closely related morphologically, that is, in both content and form. In the next section we investigate what it means for two forms to be closely related morphologically.

2.   *Degree of relatedness*

A paradigm may have only one basic form from which all others are derived, or it may consist of several clusters of closely related forms, each of which has a basic form and a set of derived forms. These clusters of forms, which are the domains in which the basic-derived relationships apply, are determined by shared membership in morphological categories. However, the morphological categories do not all function equally in determining how closely forms are related, and how a paradigm will be divided. Rather the morphological categories function according to the hierarchy proposed in Chapter 2. The higher the category is on the relevance scale, and the more it affects and changes the meaning of the verb stem, the less closely related the forms are that have different values for this category. *Valence* makes the largest meaning change, and as we have already pointed out, transitive / intransitive pairs have such different meanings that often the relation between them is derivational and not inflectional. What this means is that both members of a transitive /intransitive pair are lexicalized or autonomous and each has its own paradigm. *Aspect* also makes a large meaning change in the verb, compared to other categories, so forms in different aspects will not be as closely related as forms in different tenses or moods. *Agreement* markers have less of an effect on the meaning of the verb stem, and so forms in different persons or numbers, if they are in the same aspect or tense or mood, will be very closely related. The basic-derived relation, then, applies within major category lines, and across minor category lines.

To illustrate this with a very simple example, we will turn again to Brazilian Portuguese to examine the way this organization is manifested in child language acquisition. Consider the acquisition of the Singular forms of the Present and the Preterite. There are only two Singular forms in each aspect, a 1st person and a single form used for the 2nd and 3rd person.

infinitive:	1st conjugation falar 'to speak'	2nd conjugation bater 'to hit'	3rd conjugation abrir 'to open'
Present			
1s	falo	bato	abro
2s/3s	fala	bate	abre
Preterite			
1s	falei	bati	abri
2s/3s	falou	bateu	abriu

As we mentioned earlier, the child uses the 3rd Singular Present form for all functions at first, and then acquires the 3s Preterite form, which assumes the function of all the persons of the Preterite. So the first major distinction in the inflectional system is an aspectual one of Present vs. Preterite. It appears, furthermore, that the Preterite forms are learned at least somewhat autonomously at first, because there is remarkable accuracy in assigning them to conjugation classes, some of which are not predictable from the 3s form of the Present (Simões and Stoel-Gammon 1979).[5] The next step is the development of the 1s of the Present. We discussed above the evidence that this form is built directly off of the 3s of the Present. Similarly the 1s of the Preterite, which is acquired next, is built off of the stem of the 3s of the Preterite. Thus the major distinction, the aspectual distinction, is made first, and the minor categories, the agreement categories are elaborated within the major category distinctions. The same type of development holds for the Imperfect forms as well (Simões and Stoel-Gammon 1979 and Hooper 1979a).

Present		*Preterite*		*Imperfect*	
1s	□	1s	□	1s	□
	↑		↑		↑
3s	□	3s	□	3s	□

These data show that the scale described in Chapter 2 is not just a linear ranking, but represents, at least for some categories, a real hierarchy in which some categories are subordinate to others.

Now this simple model can be applied to a fully elaborated adult system. Consider first a very regular case, a 1st conjugation verb, *cantar*, in Spanish, as shown in Table 1. The basic, or least marked form of this paradigm is the 3s of the Present Indicative, *canta*, which happens also to be the 2s Familiar Imperative. The vast majority of forms in this paradigm can be built off of *canta* by the simple concantenation of suffixes: the person/number suffixes, *s, mos, is, n* are added in the Present Indicative, the Imperfect adds *ba* plus the agreement suffixes, the Imperfect Subjunctive adds *ra* plus the agreement suffixes, Future and Conditional add *r* and agreement suffixes, the infinitive adds *r*, the Participles add *ndo* and *do*. These forms require no other changes except for a change in stress placement. Interestingly enough, the forms with the highest autonomy, the 1s of the Present Indicative, and the 1s and 3s forms of the highly frequent Preterite require changes in the final vowel, as does the less frequent Present Subjunctive. These forms may be derived from the basic *canta* by changing the final vowel, or they may be autonomous forms themselves. For instance, the entire Present Subjunctive could be derived from the 3s form *cante* by suffixation. The Preterite forms could be derived from an autonomous 1s or 3s form, a proposition for which there is positive evidence in some dialects (Bybee and Brewer 1980). Thus we already see that the hypothesis has made correct predictions. The Spanish verbal paradigm is arranged in such a way that the semantically basic and most frequent form, the 3s of the Present Indicative, can serve as a basis for the derivation of all other forms. Other forms of high frequency and semantic basicness are less easily derivable, and could also be considered autonomous, or even basic for subparts of the paradigm. A look at less regular Spanish paradigms will bring us back to this issue in section 4.

PRESENT

Indicative		Subjunctive	
cánto	cantámos	cánte	cantémos
cántas	cantáis	cántes	cantéis
cánta	cántan	cánte	cánten

PAST

Preterite

canté	cantámos
cantáste	cantásteis
cantó	cantáron

Imperfect

cantába	cantábamos
cantábas	cantábais
cantába	cantában

Past subjunctive

cantára	cantáramos
cantáras	cantárais
cantára	cantáran

SUBSEQUENT

Future		Conditional	
cantaré	cantarémos	cantaría	cantaríamos
cantarás	cantaréis	cantarías	cantaríais
cantará	cantarán	cantaría	cantarían

Infinitive: cantár

Present participle: cantándo

Imperative:
    familiar: cánta cantád

    formal: cánte cánten

Past participle: cantádo

Table 1: Spanish *cantar* 'to sing'

PRESENT

Indicative		Subjunctive	
caedō	caedimus	caedam	caedāmus
caedis	caeditis	caedās	caedātis
caedit	caedunt	caedat	caedant

IMPERFECT

caedēbam	caedēbāmus	caederem	caederēmus
caedēbās	caedēbātis	caederēs	caederētis
caedēbat	caedēbant	caederet	caederent

FUTURE

caedam	caedēmus
caedēs	caedētis
caedet	caedent

PERFECT

cecīdī	cecīdimus	cecīderim	cecīderimus
cecīdistī	cecīdistis	cecīderis	cecīderitis
cecīdit	cecīdērunt	cecīderit	cecīderint

PLUPERFECT

cecīderam	cecīderāmus	cecīdissem	cecīdissēmus
cecīderās	cecīderātis	cecīdissēs	cecīdissētis
cecīderat	cecīderant	cecīdisset	cecīdissent

FUTURE PERFECT

cecīderō	cecīderimus
cecīderis	cecīderitis
cecīderit	cecīderint

Imperative: caede   caedite   *Infinitive*: Present: caedere

Participle: Present: caedēns   Perfect: cecīdisse

Passive: caesus   Future: caesūrus

Future: caesūrus

Gerund: caedendī

Table 2: Latin *caedō* 'to cut, kill'

To take a somewhat more complex case, consider the Latin paradigm for *caedō* in Table 2. For a first conjugation Latin verb such as *amāre*, the Singular Imperative *amā* can serve as base form with derivations that are as straightforward as the Spanish conjugation just discussed. For this 3rd conjugation paradigm, however, the choice of almost any form will involve numerous vowel changes. What is interesting here is not the high degree of fusion, for this will cause descriptive problems in any theory, but rather the fact that *one* base form is not sufficient to handle this paradigm. The entire perfective aspect is built on a different stem than the imperfective. The particular example happens to be a reduplicated stem, but there were several types of stem changes that affected Latin verbs and characteristically divided the paradigm into perfective and imperfective forms. The examples below illustrate the *s*-Perfect, vowel changes, reduplicated Perfects, and suppletive Perfects:

1s Present	*1s Perfect*	*gloss*
mittō	mīsī	to send
ponō	posuī	to put or place
adimō	adēmī	to take away, deprive
agō	ēgī	to do, to drive
tangō	tetigī	to touch
dō	dedī	to give
ferō	tulī	to bear, bring or carry

The stem changes that correspond to the aspect distinction cut across all other categories. The aspect distinction is the major distinction in the verbal paradigm, and all other distinctions are subordinate to it. There are three tenses and two moods distinguished in each aspect. All the tenses and moods are built on the stem of the aspect they belong to. There is even an infinitive for each aspect, each one built on the characteristic stem for the aspect. Each aspect can be thought of as being derived from a different base form: for the imperfective it is either the Imperative or the 1st or 3rd Singular Present Indicative, and for the perfective it is the 1s of the Perfect.

The forms of each aspect are more closely related to one another than they are to forms in the other aspect. Thus the Future Perfect is more closely related to the Perfect than it is to the Future, the Present is more closely related to the Imperfect than it is to the Perfect. These relations hold on the semantic level, as well, where aspect creates the major distinction because it affects the meaning of the verb to a greater degree, and they hold on the expression level, since aspect changes the outward form of the stem more than any other category. It is in this sense, then, that we can say that the degree of relatedness of forms on the semantic level is diagrammed by their degree of relatedness on the morpho-phonemic level.

Since relations among the morphological categories are very similar cross-linguistically, we would expect that in many languages stem changes in verbal paradigms would correspond to distinctions in categories that produce greater meaning changes. This is indeed the result reported in Chapter 2.7: aspect conditions stem changes much more frequently than tense, mood or agreement categories. The question we need to explore now is whether aspect conditions stem changes only because aspectual morphemes tend to occur closer to the stem than other morphemes, or if there is another source for morpho-phonemic diagrams of degree of relatedness.

Since most stem alternations arise originally as phonetic processes conditioned by the phonetic shape of affixes attached to the stem, and since it is possible for any verbal markers to be contiguous with the stem (because, for example, person markers might occur on the opposite side of the stem from aspects markers), then it is logically possible for any verbal inflection to condition a stem change. But when stem alternations are morphologized they undergo further changes. These further morpho-phonemic changes serve to align the stem alternations with the semantic relations that hold within a paradigm. That is, morpho-phonemic changes tend to be of a very specific type: they tend to eliminate alternations among closely related forms. Thus the more closely related two forms are, the more likely that an alternation between them will be eliminated. This is illustrated nicely for ongoing changes in Hebrew by Bolozky 1980. It can also be illustrated with a morpho-phonemic change that occurred between Old English and Middle English. Consider the forms of the verb "to do" as they are reported in Moore and Marckwardt 1968:

		Old English	Middle English
Pres. Ind. Sg.	1	dō	do
	2	dēst	dost
	3	dēth	doth
Plural		dōth	do
Pret. Ind. Sg.	1	dyde	dide, dude [dydə]
	2	dydest	didest, dudest
	3	dyde	dide, dude
Plur.		dydon	dide(n), dud(n)
Past Participle		dōn	don

The major non-phonetic change that has occurred in this paradigm is the change of the stem vowel of the 2s and 3s of the Present. There is also a stem change between the Present and the Preterite in Old English, but this stem change remains. Indeed, it is still present in Modern English. The example illustrates our hypothesis in the following way: since the person/number forms of a tense are more closely related to one another than they are to forms in other tenses, it is predicted that the loss of a stem alternation will be more likely among the person/number forms of a single tense, than among forms that span more than one tense. Thus the loss of the alternation between *dō* and *dēst* is more likely than the loss of the alternation between *dō* and *dyde*.

Another logically possible morpho-phonemic change in the Old English paradigm would be the extension of the vowel alternations in the Present to the Preterite. For instance, the 1s of the Preterite might be re-formed on the basis of the 1s of the Present, giving *dōde*, and the 2s of the Preterite might be re-formed on the basis of the 2s of the Present, giving *dēdest*. Our hypothesis concerning the organization of paradigms predicts that such a change *cannot* occur. The basic-derived relation holds among clusters of closely related forms. Morpho-phonemic changes occur *across* minor category lines, *within* major category lines, and not vice versa.

Again, child language demonstrates precisely how the leveling that aligns stem alternations with major morphological categories takes place. As we saw earlier in the Brazilian Portuguese example, the child first uses one verb form for all functions, and then distinguishes one form (usually the 3s) for each aspectual function. Later the different person/number forms for each aspect are built off of the base or 3s form for that aspect. The stem of the most autonomous form is substituted at first for the stems of the less autonomous forms. If this should result in a leveling, that is, if the alternation in the less autonomous stem is not acquired, then the leveling would always replace the stem of the more autonomous form for the stem of the less autonomous form, *in the same tense or aspect*. There is simply no opportunity for the stem of a 1s Present form to substitute for the stem of a 1s Imperfect or Preterite form. This is not to say that alternations between forms in different aspects cannot also be leveled. Any alternation among productively related forms can be leveled. The point at present is only that leveling among very closely related forms is more likely, and it produces a situation in which stem alternations diagram major category distinctions in paradigms, such that similarity on the semantic level is reflected in similarity on the expression level.

3. *Experimental evidence*

The hypothesis that a hierarchy of morphological categories determines the domain of basic-derived relations can be tested experimentally. Such an experiment, reported in Bybee and Pardo 1981, was a nonce-probe task using 20 Spanish speaking adults from outside the United States. The subjects heard nonce verbs with Spanish-like stem alternations used in sentences, accompanied by pictures, and were asked to complete sentences begun by the investigators, using the nonce verb in some form other than the one originally given by the investigator. Since the experiment used adults subjects, it also serves to demonstrate that the adult's approach to the organization of a paradigm is based on the same principles as the child's.

Quite a number of Spanish verbs undergo an alternation in the stem between a mid vowel and a diphthong. The diphthong appears when the stem syllable is stressed, and the mid vowel appears when it is unstressed. This is illustrated for the Present Indicative and the Preterite in Table 3. There are verbs in Spanish with non-alternating mid vowels, but no non-derived verbs with non-alternating diphthongs. Thus a diphthong in a stressed form is an almost certain indication of a mid vowel in an unstressed form. In an earlier experiment, Kernan and Blount 1966 gave subjects nonce forms such as 3s Present Indicative *suécha* and asked the subjects to use a 3s Preterite or an Infinitive, both forms in which the stem is unstressed. While Kernan and Blount apparently expected to hear *sochó* for the Preterite and *sochár* for the infinitive, their subjects uniformly supplied *suechó* and *suechár*. We

comenzár 'to begin'   contár 'to tell, count'

Present Indicative

comiénzo	comenzámos	cuénto	contámos
comiénzas	comenzáis	cuéntas	contáis
comiénza	comiénzan	cuénta	cuéntan

Preterite

comenzé	comenzámos	conté	contámos
comenzáste	comenzásteis	contáste	contásteis
comenzó	comenzáron	contó	contáron

Table 3: Spanish dipthong / mid vowel alternations

also found that our subjects tended, although not uniformly, to use the diphthong despite the fact that the stem syllable was unstressed. They treated the verb as though it was non-alternating. However, we also used test items in which the subject heard the verb in two stem forms, one with a diphthong (with a stressed stem), and one with a mid vowel (with an unstressed stem). In these cases, it should have been quite clear that the nonce verb had a stem alternation. Indeed, presentation of the two allomorphs affected the results: when the subjects were asked to use a form requiring an unstressed stem, they supplied a form with a mid vowel about 75% of the time.

We hypothesized that the percentage of responses with a mid vowel would vary according to the morphological category of the form presented with a mid vowel and its degree of relatedness to the form required in the response. Under one condition, the subject heard a 3s Present Indicative form, *puénza*, and the Infinitive form *ponzár*, and was asked to form a 3s Preterite.[6] The expected responses were either *ponzó* or *puenzó*. In the other condition, the subject heard a 3s Present Indicative form *puénza*, as above, but this time the form with the mid vowel was the 3s Preterite, *ponzó*, and the subject was asked to complete a sentence requiring the 1s Preterite, with the expected responses of either *ponzé* or *puenzé*. In this condition, the model with the mid vowel is the closely related 3s Preterite form, a form of the same aspect as the required response form. We predicted that the subjects would supply more forms with a mid vowel in this condition in which the form with the mid vowel is more closely related to the response form, than in the first condition, in which the model with the mid vowel is the Infinitive, a form, which, despite the fact that it is used as the citation form in all Spanish grammars, is only remotely related to the finite forms.

These predictions proved to be correct, as shown in Table 4. Table 4 reports on a total of 80 responses. Each of the 20 subjects was given four nonce verbs, two with front vowel/diphthong alternations, *megar* and *nelar*, and two with back vowel/diphthong alternations, *ponzar* and *monar*. In different versions of the test, the alternates occurred in different orders, and each nonce verb was used in a different condition. The results show that the subjects are more likely to use a mid vowel in the Preterite if they have already heard a mid vowel in the Preterite than if they have only heard the mid vowel in the Infinitive. This is support, then, for the hypothesis that there are different degrees of relatedness among forms, and that semantic relatedness determines the formal structure of members of a paradigm.

I. Infinitive, 3s Pres. → 3s Preterite			II. 3s Pres., 3s Pret. → 1s Preterite		
	e/ie	o/ue		e/ie	o/ue
Diphthong	32%	23%	Diphthong	18%	14%
Mid Vowel	64%	73%	Mid Vowel	82%	82%

Overall:	Diphthong 27%	Diphthong 16%
	Mid Vowel 68%	Mid Vowel 82%

$$x^2 = 3.07$$

(significant at the .05 level)

Table 4: Percentage of diphthong and mid vowel responses according to the form in which the mid vowel was presented (from Bybee and Pardo 1981).

4. *Velar subjunctives*

In this section and the next, some very specific characteristics of the Spanish verb conjugation are examined in their current state, and with reference to their historical development and dialectal variation, to show how the two diagrams we have been discussing here apply to these cases. In both cases we will see that morpho-phonemic alternations, which arise primarily through sound change, and are originally morphologically arbitrary, can be preserved if they coincide or can be made to coincide with the morphological relations among forms. It is no accident that certain alternations have had a long and stable history.

This section treats the alternation in certain Spanish verbs that is characterized by the appearance of a velar stop in the 1s of the Present Indicative and all forms of the Present Subjunctive, illustrated by the following two verbs:

crecer 'to grow'		*salir* 'to leave'	
Present Indicative			
crezco	crecemos	salgo	salimos
creces	creceis	sales	salís
crece	crecen	sale	salen
Present Subjunctive			
crezca	crezcamos	salga	salgamos
crezcas	crezcais	salgas	salgais
crezca	crezcan	salga	salgan

(Forms are given in traditional orthography: *c* represents [k] when it occurs before a back vowel; *c* before a front vowel and *z* represent [s] or [θ] depending on the dialect.)

These alternations have received considerable attention in the Romance literature, for instance in Kuryłowicz 1968, Malkiel 1974, Baxter 1975, Hooper 1979b, and Klausenburger 1981. It is generally agreed that this alternation arose through a regular sound change that palatalized velars before front vowels. The Latin verb *crēscō* had a velar in all forms of the Present Indicative, but the velar palatalized before *e* and *i* giving [s] or [θ], and [k] remained only before the vowels *a* and *o*. There were quite a number of verbs with the *-sc-* sequence, since this was a part of the inchoative suffix that enjoyed productivity for a time in early Romance, but a similar alternation arose in verbs such as *fingō* 'I knead or shape', and *tangō* 'I touch', where after the sound change, a nasal-velar sequence alternated with a palatal nasal.

It is often the case that such alternations persist for a time in the positions where they arose for phonetic reasons, and then are gradually lost as the alternating forms are replaced by the basic form of the stem. In this case, however, the alternation was not leveled, but rather was extended to other verbs. Verbs that previously had no alternation or had a different alternation, now have the velar consonant appearing in the 1s of the Present Indicative and in the Present Subjunctive. Thus Modern Spanish has *tener* 'to have', 1s *tengo*; *venir* 'to come', 1s *vengo*; *poner* 'to put', 1s *pongo*; *valer* 'to be worth', 1s *valgo*; *caer* 'to fall', 1s *caigo*; *traer* 'to bring', 1s *traigo*; *oir* 'to hear', 1s *oigo*; *decir* 'to say', 1s *digo*; *hacer* 'to make', 1s *hago*. It is worth noting that these verbs are among the most frequent in the language, and many of them have alternations in other parts of their paradigms as well. The existence of the alternation in these verbs, where it could not have arisen through sound change, demonstrates that at some period in the pre-history of Spanish, this alternation was productive to a significant extent. Furthermore, this period of productivity has been followed by a long period of stability: these alternations show no signs of weakness. Most of the modern dialects still maintain them.[7] More importantly, they show no signs of changing their distribution. That is, there are no Spanish dialects in which the 1s Present Indicative has lost the velar, while the Present Subjunctive maintains it, although that would be the prediction of the notion of degree of relatedness presented above.[8] Nor has the opposite occurred. There are no reports of dialects in which the Present Subjunctive has lost the velar, while the highly autonomous 1s Present Indicative has clung to its conservative form, although that would be predicted by the notion of autonomy. Indeed, the stability of the alternation may be due to a kind of stand-off between these two factors. Let us consider the possibility that this alternation is diagrammatic.

First, it should be established that the alternation is morphologically conditioned, and not phonologically conditioned. Even in the modern language it is possible to predict the occurrence of the velar by reference to the backness of the following vowel. The question of whether speakers use phonological or morphological conditioning for this alternation has been answered experimentally. In the nonce-probe task described above some nonce verbs were included that had the same alternations as the real verbs listed above, for example *palir, palgo; roner, rongo; lecer, lezco; faer, faigo*. The subjects heard these verbs in the 1s and 3s of the Present Indicative, and were asked to use a Present Subjunctive form. We were interested in seeing whether or not they would use the velar in the Subjunctive. In other test items, the subject heard an Infinitive and a 1s Present Indicative form, and were asked to use the 3s Present Indicative in a sentence. Here we were interested to see if they would use the velar in the Indicative. The results were mixed. With some of the nonce verbs (particularly those with -*sc*- and those ending in a vowel (similar to *caer*), the subjects followed the patterns of the real Spanish verbs. In other cases their responses were way off the pattern, e.g., a common response for the 3s Present Indicative was to use the velar, but to make the verb 1st conjugation, giving *ronga* where the expected form was *rone*. It is possible to determine whether the distribution of the velar is primarily phonologically conditioned by comparing the number of times the velar occurred before a back vowel. Since a number of responses involved the verb in the 1st conjugation, the occurrence of back vowels is not necessarily influenced by the Subjunctive in these data. The results showed no phonological conditioning: in all the responses where the velar occurred, it was before a front vowel in 52% of the cases and before a back vowel in 48% of the cases (Bybee and Pardo 1981). There was other evidence that the velar element is associated with the Subjunctive mood. In some nonce items that required responses in the Subjunctive there were no velar stops in either of the allomorphs of the stem. Yet some subjects formed Subjunctives with velars. The verbs in question were purposely constructed with non-Spanish alternations. They were 1s *lastro*, 3s *lase*, and 1s *seto*, 3s *sade*. For the first verb, there were two Subjunctive responses *lazca*, and one *laga*. For the other verb there was one *sezca* and two *saga*.

The evidence suggests, then, that there is morphological conditioning to the alternation, and that the velar stop might be part of the signal for Present Subjunctive. The question that presents itself now is whether there is any significance to this particular combination of morphological categories, Present Subjucntive *and* 1s of the Present Indicative. The only feature that they all share is that of present tense. They do not form a coherent semantic set. It is possible, however, that they do form a coherent morphological set, in the following sense. The forms of the Present Subjunctive are set off by tense and mood lines from other forms, and should be similar on the expression level. The Present Subjunctive is the more marked member of the mood category compared to the Present Indicative. Thus the forms of the Present Subjunctive could be in a basic-derived relationship with some form of the Present Indicative. This would be a highly autonomous form such as the 3s or the 1s. In this case, of course, it appears to be the 1s.

It was mentioned earlier that 1s forms are almost as frequent as 3s forms. Figures from two frequency counts of Spanish, one from written sources (Juilland and Chang-Rodríguez 1964), and the other from the spoken language of school-age children (Rodríguez Bou 1952), show the relative frequency of 3s, 1s, and the other person/number forms:

Written sources:

Present Indicative (N=3570)		*Preterite* (N=405)	
1s 23%	1p 7%	1s 31%	1p 4%
2s 16%	2p 1%	2s 7%	2p 0%
3s 44%	3p 9%	3s 47%	3p 10%

Spoken sources:

Present Indicative (N=14,332)		*Preterite* (N=10,414)	
1s 24%	1p 4%	1s 22%	1p 4%
2s 11%	2p --	2s 4%	2p --
3s 41%	3p 20%	3s 51%	3p 19%

Note that in every case, the 1s is second in frequency following the 3s. The relative "basicness" of 1s can also be noted in the distribution of zero expression in the Spanish verbal paradigm. In the Present Subjunctive, the Imperfect, the Past Subjunctive and the Conditional, the 1s like the 3s has no marker for person. In these parts of the paradigm, the 3s and 1s are equally unmarked, at least on level of expression.

The frequency of 1s makes it resistant to change, as mentioned earlier in connection with the Provençal Preterite re-formation, where, in some dialects the 1s form resists change, and keeps its conservative shape. In Bybee and Brewer 1980, we discuss this case, and also the case of the Preterite in some dialects of northern Spain, where the 1s demonstrates its autonomony by serving as the basis of change for the 1p, 2s, and 2p Preterite forms. (See section 5 for a brief outline of the data.)

The suggestion, then, for the case under discussion is that there are two autonomous forms for the Present Tense in these alternating verbs. The 3s Present Indicative serves as the base for all of the Present Indicative, except 1s, and the 1s form serves as the base for all of the Present Subjunctive. This analysis would account for the stability of the alternation in this particular combination of forms, without appealing to phonological conditioning, which is unsupported by experimental data, and without appealing to some common morphological property shared by the forms in question.[9] Interestingly enough, there is further evidence from another alternation in one dialect area of Spanish that demonstrates the viability of this combination of morphological forms.

The alternation in question is the mid vowel/diphthong alternation illustrated in Table 3. Originally, and in most dialects, the mid vowel occurs in unstressed stem syllables, and the diphthong occurs in stressed syllables. This means that in both the Present Indicative and Subjunctive, the diphthong occurs in all the singular forms, and in the 3p form. There are two verbs that have a different pattern to the diphthongization. These are both verbs that also have the velar subjunctive. *Tener* 'to have', and *venir* 'to come' both have diphthongs in 2s and 3s and in 3p, but have 1s *tengo, vengo*, and Subjunctive forms based on these, e.g. *tenga, venga*, etc. Thus the mid vowel occurs in the 1s of the Present Indicative and in all of the Present Subjunctive. In a dialect of western Asturias, described by Menéndez García 1963, there are some 35 verbs that have the diphthongs and mid vowels distributed as in *tener* and *venir* rather than on the basis of stress. That is, the stressed vowels of the 1s Present Indicative, and also the Present Subjunctive are all mid vowels. Consider the following paradigm, bearing two points in mind. One is that in this dialect, an unstressed [o] has become [u]. The other point is that in this dialect, as in many others, in the 2nd and 3rd conjugation, the stress in the subjunctive has retracted in the 1p and 2p forms, so that the stress is uniformly on the last stem vowel. This, by the way, is a change predicted by the degree of relatedness, since it makes the stress uniform with respect to the stem in all of the Present Subjunctive, as it is in all other tenses and moods, except the Present Indicative (Hooper 1976a).

    murder 'to bite'   ferber 'to boil'

Present Indicative

mórdo	murdémos	férbo	ferbémos
muérdes	murdéis	fiérbes	ferbéis
muérde	muérden	fiérbe	fiérben

Present Subjunctive

mórda	mórdamos	férba	férbamos
mórdas	mórdais	férbas	férbais
mórda	mórdan	férba	férban

It should be added that many of the verbs with this diphthong/mid vowel alternation would not etymologically have had diphthongs at all. Thus *cumer* (Castilian *comer*) 'to eat', *currer* (*correr*) 'to run', *beber* 'to drink', for example, are all non-alternating in Castilian, and other dialects of Spanish, but alternate as *murder* and *ferber* do in this dialect.

What this dialect shows, then, is the massive extension of an alternation type occurring in only two verbs, *tener* and *venir*, an alternation pattern that sets apart the 1s of the Present Indicative and all of the Present Subjunctive, from other Present forms. Since there is no question here of phonological conditioning by front or back vowels, this examples is further evidence for the viability of this particular set of morphological forms.

The hypothesis that the 1s of the Present Indicative serves as a base form for the Present Subjunctive was also tested in the nonce-probe experiment discussed earlier. To test this hypothesis independently of the class of verbs that takes the velar element, two nonce verbs were constructed that had different stem allomorphs for the 1s and the 3s Present Indicative, but neither allomorph contained a velar consonant. One of these was based directly on an occurring Spanish verb that has a stem allomorph that distinguishes the 1s Present Indicative and the Present Subjunctive from all other forms. This verb is *caber*, which has 1s *quepo*, Subjunctive *quepa*, etc., but 3s *cabe*. The nonce verb differed from this verb only in consonants. It was *sader*, with 3s *sade*, and 1s *seto*. The subjects were given the 1s and 3s Present Indicative forms and asked to use the verb in the Present Subjunctive. The other nonce verb was phonotactically well-formed, but had an alternation that was totally unlike any alternations occurring in Spanish. This verb had 3s Present Indicative *lase*, and 1s *lastro*.[10] The goal in using these items was to determine whether the subjects would use the stem of the 1s or the 3s in forming the Subjunctive. If they used the stem of the 1s, it would suggest that they had formed a generalization about the relation of 1s Present Indicative to Present Subjunctive that was independent of any particular lexical items or possible rules, such as velar-insertion. The results indeed showed this very clearly. Of all the responses that used one stem allomorph or the other (rather than something entirely different, such as a combination, as in *sate*), there were 25 responses with 1s stem *lastr-*, and 7 with 3s *las-*, a ratio of 78% to 22%, and 18 responses with 1s stem *set-* compared to 6 with 3s *sad-*, a ratio of 75% to 25%.

All the data suggest that one possible configuration for a group of tense forms spanning the indicative and subjunctive is for one relatively frequent form of the indicative to serve as the base for the subjunctive. This configuration appears to differ from the more usual one in which the base form is a member of all the same aspect, tense and mood categories as the derived forms. The difference is minimal, however, since the mood distinction is subordinate to the tense distinction. That is, the entire Present Tense (both Indicative and Subjunctive) forms a cluster of closely related forms. Within this cluster, there are two basic forms: the 3s of the Indicative cuts across person and number lines to serve as the base for the other Indicative forms (excluding 1s), and the 1s Indicative cuts across person, number and mood lines to serve as the base for the Subjunctive forms. The difference is that the 1s is not as closely related to the forms for which it serves as the base as the 3s form is. On the other hand, it is separated from its derived forms only by the relatively minor category distinction of mood. A model for the formal representation of these morphological relations in outlined in Chapter 5.

5.   *Local markedness*

In a recent paper, Tiersma (1982) examines cases where what would ordinarily be a marked or derived form in a paradigm serves as the basis for reformation of other forms. He cites the following examples from Frisian, where falling and rising diphthongs alternate in singular and plural noun forms. Where the alternation is being leveled, the result is usually as given below, with the diphthong originally belonging in the singular appearing in the plural:

Conservative alternation	Innovative forms
hoer / hworren 'whore'	hoer / hoeren
koal / kwallen 'coal'	koal / koalen
miel / mjillen 'meal, milking'	miel / mielen
poel / pwollen 'pool'	poel / poelen

A smaller number of words are leveling in the opposite direction, with the diphthong of the plural appearing in the singular: (These forms are mainly dialectal and not accepted in Standard Frisian.)

Conservative alternation	Innovative forms
earm / jermen 'arm'	jerm / jermen
goes / gwozzen 'goose'	gwos / gwozzen
hoarn / hwarnen '(animal) horn'	hwarne / hwarnen
hoas / vjazzen 'stocking'	vjazze / vjazzen
kies / kjizzen 'tooth'	kjizze / kjizzen
spoen / spwonnen 'shaving, splinter'	spwon / spwonnen
toarn / twarnen 'thorn'	twarne / twarnen
trien / trjinnen 'tear'	trjin / trjinnen

Tiersma points out that the nouns in this second group are nouns that are frequently used to refer to objects in pairs or in groups, and he cites frequency counts that show that indeed for these nouns the plural is more frequent than the singular. It is normally the case, as Greenberg 1966 has shown, that the singular of a noun is much more frequent than the plural. Tiersma proposes that in cases such as these where the plural is more frequent, that the plural is unmarked. He proposes to refer to instances of this type, "where due to semantic or (perhaps better) real-world considerations a certain well-defined set of lexical items constitutes an exception to the general markedness conventions" as *local markedness*" (Tiersma 1982: 834-5).

Tiersma's data suggest that these highly autonomous plural forms may actually serve as the basis of the paradigm, and form a basic-derived relation with singular forms. Thus these paradigms will have a very different organization from the more usual and more numerous paradigms in which the singular serves as the base.

Further evidence for the autonomy of the plural form in cases such as these, are "double plurals" in which a plural morpheme is added to an already plural noun. Thus the following West Frisian plurals have two plural markers, *-en* and *-s* suffixed to them:

Singular	Double plural	Gloss
boei	boeijens	handcuff
lears	learzens	boot
reed	redens	skate
trep	treppens	stair
weach	weagens	wave
wolk	wolkens	cloud

Note again that these nouns all designate objects that are usually referred to in pairs or groups. As Tiersma points out, the fact that a plural -*s* may be added, for example, to the already plural *boeijen*, is evidence for the under-analysis of this plural form. That is, the form is learned and stored as a monomorphemic, autonomous item. It is not analyzed as containing the plural morpheme, or else another plural morpheme could not be added to it. Evidence that the plural in these cases can actually serve as the basis of paradigms are cases in which the singular consists of a form containing the plural morpheme. Thus Afrikaans *eier* 'egg' contains an old plural morpheme -*er*, as does *hoender* 'hen'. Similarly, some Frisian dialects have the singular *wolken* 'cloud' and *treppen* 'stair'.

In some cases, morpho-phonemic determinates of autonomy converge with semantic determinates. Thus the few irregular plurals in the English noun system belong to a semantic group in which the plurals are highly frequent, as Tiersma points out: compare *men, women, children, feet, oxen, geese, lice, mice,* and *teeth*. Their high frequency protects them from regularization on the basis of the singular form. These highly autonomous plurals may even split away from their singulars, as *dice* and *lice* have done. *Dice* is so frequent in the plural that the singular *die* is hardly used in colloquial speech. *Lice* in its most used sense refers to an affliction, while its singular, *louse*, is most used to refer to an unpleasant sort of human being. A pair or group of the latter would not be referred to with the word *lice*. Paradigmatic splits such as these will be discussed more thoroughly in the next chapter.

These examples illustrate for nouns the possibility of paradigms with different organizations in the same language. Can the same sort of evidence be found for differing organizations of verbal paradigms? Split paradigms (such as *go / went*) are more common among verbs than among nouns. They indicate strong autonomy of non-basic forms of a paradigm, and will be discussed in more detail in the next chapter. Local markedness as measured in terms of frequency is evident in verbal paradigms, and clearly associated with the inherent semantics of the verb stem. Tiersma points out that the 1s is the most frequent Present Tense form for some verbs of emotion and perception in Spanish, while the 3s is usually the most frequent. Inherent aspectual meaning determines the frequency with which different lexical stems are paired with different aspectual inflections. This is evident in early child language, where perfective inflection is first used on telic, punctual verbs, while progressive or imperfective inflection is first used only on activity verbs (Bloom et al. 1980). This skewing is also reflected in frequency counts of adult language. Finally, further evidence of local markedness is found in imperative paradigms where other persons exist. In such cases, the 2s is basic (rather than the 3s). Thus for some irregular verbs of Irish the 2s of the Imperative has zero expression, while 1st and 3rd person are marked.[11]

All these facts lead us to the conclusion that different verbal paradigms may well have different organizations due to the semantic relations among the forms of the paradigm. In verbs, as in nouns, these differences among paradigms may account for apparent counter-examples to the generalization that leveling of alternations is restructuring on the basis of the unmarked form.

6. *Summary*

Paradigms have been discussed here as groups of related surface forms. Various kinds of data supply evidence about the kinds of relations that hold among these forms. In particular, some forms can be said to be more closely related to one another than they are to other forms. This degree of relatedness is based on common membership in the more relevant verbal categories, i.e., those that have more of an effect on the meaning of the verb stem. Therefore, the more closely related two forms are semantically, the more closely related they will be in the form of their expression. But there are both weak and strong relations among the forms of a paradigm, and the effect of competing relations has not been explored in this chapter. The directionality of these relations *has* been explored here. It is proposed that paradigms are organized around a series of basic-derived relations, again based on the semantics of the verbal categories, and that many properties of the form taken by members of a paradigm can be traced to this type of expression.

What has not been discussed here at all is the issue of the representation of paradigms in the speaker-hearer's grammar. The relations among forms that have been discussed here are compatible with a Word and Paradigm model in which all the forms of a paradigm are listed in the lexicon. These proposals are also compatible with a model that represents a paradigm by listing one or more words from that paradigm, and specifies in addition how all the other words are to be derived from those basic ones. It is also possible that a model that lists verb stems might be made compatible with the proposals made here for paradigm organization. These proposals will be taken up again in Chapter 5, where it is suggested that different languages might require slightly differing modes of representation.

NOTES

1. Further, children learning English never use the stem of the Past in forming the Progressive, as in *tooking* (Cazden 1968).

2. The term "morpho-phonemic change" is used here instead of the traditional term "analogical change", following Andersen 1969 and 1980. Morpho-phonemic change refers to changes in the relations among the expression units of morphemes.

3. The relation between frequency and basicness will also be discussed below.

4. Greenberg 1969 discusses a case in Slavic where a marked category developed a zero allomorph due to a phonetically conditioned deletion. Subsequent developments show the spread of the non-zero allomorphs in the marked categories. Conversely, in an unmarked category with both zero and non-zero allomorphs, the zero allomorph spead to replace the non-zero.

5. The independence of the Preterite from the Present in very early Brazilian Portuguese is quite clear in the contexts of use. The two aspects are used in entirely different types of discourse, and in the earliest uses, with different verbs. (I am grateful to Claudia de Lemos for making available to me transcripts of early child language in Brazilian Portuguese.)

6. An example test item would read as follows: "Osito *muena* sopa todos los días. Le gusta mucho *monar* sopa. Ayer en la tarde se ---------- un plato grande." "Little Bear (nonce verb) soup every day. He likes to (nonce verb) soup a lot. Yesterday afternoon he ---------- a big bowl of it."

7. Some dialects of León, Asturias and Portugal have leveled the alternation in the verbs that had the inchoative -sc-. Some of these dialects never acquired the alternation in many other verbs, while some have acquired it and retained it, in all but the inchoative.

8. Provençal dialects have the velar in the Subjunctive but not in 1s Present Indicative. To my knowledge no Spanish dialect has this distribution.

9. Klausenburger 1981 proposes that the velar occurs as a signal of a marked category. The problem with this proposal is that the 1s form can hardly be considered the most marked of Present Indicative forms.

10. The subjects had rather negative reactions to these two verbs. They felt that the alternations, even the one between *sade* and *seto* were very difficult to deal with.

11. One well-known example of double marking in verbs is group of verbs in Germanic referred to as the Preterite-Present verbs. This small set of very common verbs in Old English had old strong Preterite forms used as the Present tense, and had newer Preterites formed by adding the weak suffix to the old Preterite form. Unfortunately, these developments occurred long before the Germanic languages were written, and it is impossible to reconstruct the semantic changes that would lead to the creation of a "double preterite".

CHAPTER 4:

THE LEXICAL / DERIVATIONAL / INFLECTIONAL CONTINUUM

1. *Distinguishing derivation from inflection*

One of the most persistent undefinables in morphology is the distinction between derivational and inflectional morphology. While linguists seem to have an intuitive understanding of the distinction, the objective criteria behind this intuition have proved difficult to find. The most successful criterion is *obligatoriness*, applied to the definition of derivation and inflection by Greenberg 1954. Obligatory categories force certain choices upon the speaker. In English every noun phrase must be either Definite or Indefinte, every finite clause either Past or Present. Derivational morphemes are not obligatory in this sense. Derivational morphemes are, according to Greenberg:

> morphemes which, when in construction with a root morpheme, establish a sequence which may always be substituted for some particular class of single morpheme in all instances without producing a change in the construction. (p. 191)

Greenberg goes on to say that the noun *duckling* may be substituted for monomorphemic nouns such as *turkey* or *goose* or even *duck* , without changing the construction. That is, no construction requires the *-ling* suffix. An inflectional morpheme, then, is a bound nonroot morpheme whose appearance in a particular position is compulsory. Thus English progressive *-ing* appears obligatorily in a sentence such as *The duckling was swimming*. There is no monomorphemic word that can be substituted for *swimming* without changing the construction entirely.

Matthews' (1974: 48) definition and S. Anderson's (1982) proposal are similar to Greenberg's in that they both suggest that inflectional morphemes are those which are required by the syntax of the sentence. But there are also quite different approaches to the distinction. Kuryłowicz 1964 proposes that derivational processes create new lexical items, while inflectional processes do not. This, unfortunately, is a theory-internal definition, since it is an open question what constitutes a separate lexical item. Bloomfield 1933 observes that inflection is characterized by a "rigid parallelism of underlying and resultant forms" (p. 223). He means by this that inflectional paradigms are highly structured sets of words with regular patterns. So, for example, nearly all English nouns underly a derived plural. Bloomfield, Nida 1946 and many others have observed that derivational morphemes occur closer to the root than inflectional morphemes. It is also a common observation (Nida 1946, for example) that a language has more derivational morphemes than inflectional ones, and this is backed by Greenberg's 1963 finding that the existence of inflection in a language implies the existence of derivation. Some authors attempt to define inflection by the meanings represented by inflectional morphemes. Nida points out that expressions of grammatical relations, if morphological, are inflectional, and Cowgill 1963 supplies a list of the categories expressed inflectionally in Indo-European as his characterization of inflection. Finally, a frequently-cited criterion is that derivational morphemes may change the syntactic category of the resulting word, while inflectional morphemes never do.

None of these criteria, except perhaps the obligatoriness criterion, actually provides a discrete division between derivational and inflectional processes. Nonetheless, they all point to some interesting differences among non-root morphemes. In Chapter 2 I introduced principles that determine what can be expressed lexically and inflectionally. Using these same principles, it can be shown that derivational morphology is transitional between lexical and inflectional expression, and that the differences that can be observed between inflectional and derivational expression are just more prominent instances of the differences identifiable among inflectional categories.

1.1. *Relevance and two types of derivational morphology*

In order to apply the relevance criterion to derivation, we must first recognize two types of derivational morpheme: those that change the syntactic category of the word to which they apply, and those that do not. Let us consider the latter type first, for here we can apply the relevance criterion in much the way we have been applying it to inflectional categories, by considering the extent to which the meaning of the affix alters or affects the meaning of the stem. In the case of verbs, this means the extent to which the meaning of the morpheme affects the description of the situation, and for nouns, the extent to which the meaning of the morpheme changes the referent of the noun.

Large meaning changes are characteristic of derivational processes which do not change syntactic categories. In Chapter 2 it was pointed out that valence-changing categories produce large meaning changes in verbs, since an event can be changed substantially if the number of participants and the nature of their roles change. Thus *kill* differs from *die*, and *send* differs from *go* in the events being described. So it is not surprising that in the cross-linguistic survey, valence was found to be frequently mentioned as a *derivational* category for verbs. Large meaning changes are also evident in other derivational categories. The event described by *un-* plus a verb in English, e.g. *untie, unhook, unzip*, is a closely related but distinct event from that described by the verb alone. Similarly with nouns, a derivational process affecting a noun produces a noun with an entirely different referent, e.g. *garden, gardener; auction, auctioneer*; or Spanish *higo* 'fig', *higuera* 'fig tree'; *durazno* 'peach', *duraznero* 'peach tree' (Malkiel 1978).

Applying the relevance criterion to derivational morphemes that change the syntactic category of the stem they modify is somewhat different. Here we must consider the result of the derivational process and apply the notion of semantic differentiation that I argued in Chapter 2 was a consequence of relevance. The questions then become: does the derived word differ substantially in meaning from the basic one, and does the derived word represent a coherent concept? Two general points suggest affirmative answers to these questions. First, the syntactic category of a word is an inherent part of its semantic representation, so an indicator of syntactic category will always be highly relevant to the word as a whole. Second, a point which applies to all types of derivational morphology is that the results of derivational processes usually have a few lexical counterparts, that is, lexical items in which the same combinations of meanings are expressed monomorphemically. For example, *sad* for *unhappy*, *pilot* for *flyer*, *size* for *largeness*.[1] This indicates that words derived by derivational morphology do represent conceptually coherent units — units that could as well be expressed by single morphemes.

Derivations that change the syntactic category of a word make varying amounts of semantic change, depending on how much semantic content they contribute along with the category change. Some morphemes that make category changes add little further meaning, and thus border on inflection. For instance, English gerundial nominalizations in *-ing* allow a verb to appear in a noun position in a clause, but do not change the situation the verb describes. Thus in *Bill reads in bed* and *Reading in bed is fun* there is little difference between the interpretation of the nominal and verbal forms of *read in bed*. The suffix *-ly* that is added to adjectives to produce adverbs does not change the quality described by the adjective, although it does add the sense that the word desribes the *manner* in which the event took place. Cf. *Sara is intelligent* vs. *Sara answered intelligently*. The agentive suffix *-er* that is added to verbs, as in *rider, baker, player*, etc., does more than change the verb to a noun, since it specifies that the noun is the agent of the activity named by the verb.

Thus while the amount of meaning change produced by a morpheme is an important difference between derivational and inflectional morphology, it does not produce any discrete division between the two because there are also wide differences among derivational morphemes in the amount of semantic change they effect.

1.2. *Lexical generality*

Derivational processes are more likely than inflectional processes to have lexical restrictions on their applicability. Of course, non-productive processes will have arbitrary lexical restrictions, but even productive derivational processes may be applicable only in a very restricted semantic, syntactic or phonological domain. For example, the verbal prefix *un-* applies only to verbs that are inherently reversible, even though it is productive in this domain (Thompson 1975). The suffix *-ize* applies productively only to words of more than one syllable, e.g., *idolize, magnetize, fossilize, traumatize*. On the other hand, inflectional categories *must* have full lexical generality: if a category is *required* by the syntactic structure, then there must be an exponent of that category for any lexical item that fits that slot in the syntactic structure. This does not mean that all expressions of an inflectional category must be regular or productive — it does not matter if an English verb forms its Past Tense by suffixation or vowel change — it just means that there must be some way to form the Past Tense of every English verb.

The more general a morphological process, the more it will resemble an inflectional process. For instance, the *-ly* suffix in English that produces an adverb from an adjective has full lexical generality in the sense that any member of the category *adjective* can take this suffix. The few exceptions resemble the exceptions to inflectional processes: *good* and *well* may be thought of as suppletive forms, and *fast* may be thought of as having a zero allomorph. It could even be argued in this case that the morpheme *-ly* is required by the syntax, since whenever an adjective appears in certain syntactic positions, it is obligatorily modified by *-ly*. For instance, an adjective is required in the sentence *Sara gave a thoughtful answer* but an adverb is required in *Sara answered thoughtfully*. In fact, it is possible that the principle that morphology that changes the syntactic category of a word is always derivational is a false principle, and that *-ly*, gerundial *-ing* and comparable morphemes in other languages should be considered inflectional.

The criterion of generality does not absolutely distinguish derivational and inflectional morphology, since inflectional processes are not always totally general either.[2] For example, Beard 1981 points out that in English for the category of number in nouns, which is ordinarily thought of as an inflectional category, there are a number of defective paradigms. These include plurals that do not have singulars (*pluralis tantum*), such as *pants, oats, measles*, and *pliers*, and singulars that do not have plurals (*singularis tantum*), such as *air, fleece, peace, contemplation, cleanliness*, and so on. While Beard argues from these and other facts that Indo-European nominal number is a derivational category, in the present framework these facts can be interpreted as supporting the proposal that all morphological categories belong on a continuum that ranges from lexical to inflectional. Noun number lies closer to the lexical end of this continuum than case (with which Beard compares number), or definiteness. This follows from the fact that a change in number produces a change in the entity or entities being referred to, while case signals the relation of the noun to other constituents in the sentence, and definiteness shows the place of the noun in the discourse. Case and definiteness have no effect on the inherent qualities of the entity or entities being referred to, while number does.

Other examples of inflection that is not totally general are frequently encountered. For example, in Acoma, negation and other moods are indicated by the obligatory choice of one of a set pronominal prefixes for the verb. In the case of negation, however, there is a distinct pronoun only in the 1st person. The other persons use an unmarked pronominal prefix and a negative adverb to indicate negation (Miller 1965). In Serbo-Croatian, there is a very general distinction between the perfective and imperfective aspects, but only some verbs further distinguish the iterative and durative in the imperfective (Partridge 1964).

Even where inflection is not totally general, it must nonetheless have at least one type of formation that is productive, but this is not a requirement in the case of derivation. If inflections are defined as obligatory categories, then there must be some means of applying the inflection to new lexical items. English plural formation with the /-z/ suffix is productive, even though the defective paradigms we discussed above do exist, and even though other means of plural formation, such as vowel change, do exist, because new nouns automatically take this inflection. Productivity is not necessarily affected by lapses in generality, by irregularity, nor by the derivational - inflectional continuum, since derivational processes may or may not be productive.

1.3. *Causes of lack of lexical generality*

There are several reasons why a morphological process may lack lexical generality. A brief consideration of these reasons will help us understand the difference between derivation and inflection.

First, consider the fact that because of their high relevance, derivational processes often create meaning combinations that are already represented lexically. I have already mentioned examples such as the agentive formation *flyer* for *pilot*, and the negative adjective formation of *unhappy* for *sad*. These cases are unusual because both a derived and a nonderived form exist. As Clark and Clark 1979 have observed, it is usual for the derived form to be rejected if the semantic combination is already represented lexically. Thus *unpretty* is rejected because of *ugly*, *cutter* cannot be used to mean *scissors*, and so on. Valence-changing processes are very good examples of this phenomenon, because they are very frequently represented morphologically in the languages of the world, yet they are often not general, because valence is an inherent part of the meaning of a verb, and differences in valence are so often represented lexically. Even though, for example, transitivizing morphology occurs in a large percentage of languages, there are probably not any languages in which all lexical verbs are intransitive, and all transitives are formed by affixation. The reason is that there exist in the world as we experience it certain events that are inherently transitive, and not necessarily divisible into an intransitive event plus a transitivizer. As mentioned above, because derivational meaning is highly relevant, it is often the case that lexical expression exists for meanings similar to the derivational one.

Another cause of the lack of lexical generality is the specificity of derivational meaning compared to inflectional meaning. The greater specificity in derivational meaning restricts the applicability of derivational processes. For instance, a morpheme meaning "enter into a state" will be applicable only to stative verbs. For instance, Maasai has an Inceptive suffix for verbs of state: *á-íbór* "I am white", *á-íbórr-ù* "I become white"; *á-rɔ́k* "I am black", *á-rók-ù* "I become black"; *á-nàná* "I am soft", *á-nàna-u* "I become soft", but this suffix does not apply to active verbs.[3] The specificity of its meaning can be seen best by comparing *inceptive* to a related but inflectional aspect, the *perfective*. The meaning of the perfective is more general, for example, in Spanish, where the Preterite may apply to verbs of any type. Its general meaning is "bounded event". When it applies to active verbs, it gives a punctual or completive meaning, but as we saw earlier, when it applies to stative verbs such as *saber* "to know" an inceptive reading of "found out" results. In the case of inflection, then, the lack of lexical restrictions coincides with extreme semantic generality. When derivational categories lack semantic generality, then one can expect lexical restrictions. I will return in section 5 of this chapter to a discussion of the difference between inflectional meaning and derivational meaning.

The examination of derivational and inflectional categories shows, then, that the formal differences between these two expression types are closely related to properties of the meanings of these categories. The parameters along which meanings differ, *relevance* and *generality*, are the same parameters that are applicable to differences among inflectional categories. I conclude then that there is not necessarily a discrete distinction between inflection and derivation, but that the properties of the meanings expressed by categories correlate highly with the form in which the category is expressed. The next two sections examine the causes of lexical and inflectional splits, and show that the factors affecting splits between derivationally-related words are the same as those affecting splits among inflectionally-related words, and that the differences between the two types of morphology are just a matter of degree.

Some linguists would be unhappy with the conclusion that the distinction between derivational and inflectional morphology is not discrete, but rather a gradient phenomenon. This is especially true if one espouses a formal theory in which derivation and inflection have different types of representation in the grammar. For instance, inflection, which is required by the syntax, is derived by rule, while derivation is represented or derived in the lexicon. The model that results from the theoretical principles developed in this book, however, recognizes gradient phenomena of various sorts, and is thus capable of dealing with a non-discrete division between derivation and inflection.

2. *Lexical split*

One of the properties that characterizes derivationally-related pairs of words most conspicuously is their tendency to split up, to move away from one another both in meaning and in form. For example, even where the phonological relations are quite clear, there are often semantic differences among derivationally-related words. Thus, something can be *dirty* without involving real *dirt* at all, but rather from having, for example, maple syrup spilled on it. Even zero-derivations work this way: someone can *soil* an item without being anywhere near real *soil*. Similarly, something that is *awful* does not inspire *awe* anymore, nor do you have to be *terrified* to think something is *terrific*. There are also cases where phonological distance contributes to the dissociation: *despair, desperate*; and cases where the lack of productivity of the relating process aids in the demise of the relation: *bake, batch; shade, shadow*. Lexical split may be described in terms of the theory developed in Chapter 3, as due to the increasing autonomy of the derived member of the pair. The factors that determine *autonomy* also determine the likelihood of lexical split:

(1) The more frequent a derived form is, the more likely it is to become autonomous.

(2) The greater its phonological distance from the basic form, the more likely a derived form is to be autonomous.

(3) The greater the original semantic change made between the basic and derived form, the more likely the derived form is to become autonomous.

While lexical splits are extremely common in derivational morphology, they are not unknown in inflectional morphology. As predicted by the lower autonomy of inflected forms, inflectional splits are relatively uncommon, but they do occur. Evidence for them is found in suppletive paradigms, such as that for the verbs *be* and *go* in English, and in former singular / plural pairs such as *brother / brethren*, and *cloth / clothes*. In this section and the next, it will be shown that the factors that determine autonomy can be used to predict the likelihood of lexical splits in both derivational and inflectional morphology.

Two absolute determinants of autonomy are semantic and morphophonemic unpredictability. If a word is not derivable by general semantic, morphological and phonological rules from some other word or stem, it must have its own lexical entry and be autonomous. However, even a word that is non-autonomous may gradually develop into an autonomous word. In this diachronic development several factors are important. First, there is the original degree of *semantic change* between basic and derived forms. In Chapter 3 it was argued that the degree of semantic difference between basic and derived forms determines the degree of relatedness among forms, and that the degree of relatedness among members of categories follows the relevance hierarchy established in Chapter 2. For derivational processes it is much more difficult to establish degrees of semantic relatedness among pairs of words, so this notion will remain an intuitive one in subsequent discussion. The general proposal is, however, that the greater the original semantic difference is between a basic and a derived form, the more likely there is to be a split between them. That is, the more likely there is to be a further semantic differentiation developed between them. A second catalyst for lexical split is the *phonological distance* between forms. The most important factor in the development of autonomy in derived forms, however, is the *frequency* of use of the derived form. High frequency correlates with both semantic and phonological differentiation, as can be seen from the following case study.

Pagliuca 1976 studied the 323 extant words with the prefix *pre-* listed in the Shorter Oxford English Dictionary. This prefix is listed as occurring with four different vowel qualities, represented as [iy], [i], [ɨ], and [ɛ]. For each prefix, Pagliuca recorded information about the vowel quality, the frequency of use in texts of each word with the prefix (as reported in Thorndike and Lorge 1944), and whether or not the meaning of the word with the prefix was a predictable sum of the meaning of the base plus the meaning of the prefix.[4] With the aid of a computer Pagliuca sought correlations of the vowel quality with the other variables. Of particular interest to us here is the fact that there is strong relationship between the vowel quality and the frequency of the word, and the vowel quality and the semantic predictability of the word. The following table shows that when the average frequency of words with each vowel quality is taken into account, the words with the most reduced vowels are the words with the highest frequency. When the percentage of words in each group that has a predictable meaning is taken into account, the words that are the least likely to have predictable meanings are those that are the most frequent and have the most reduced vowels.[5]

Vowel quality	Frequency	% of words with predictable meaning	Examples
[iy]	05.74	74.76	predecease
[i]	02.54	59.52	predestine
[ɨ]	49.80	03.30	prediction
[ɛ]	81.32	02.89	preface

Table 5: Correlation of vowel quality, frequency and semantic predictability in *pre-* words.

Pagliuca's interpretation of these facts is that high frequency leads to semantic differentiation of derived from basic forms. A high-frequency derived word can be learned by rote, without an analysis into constituent parts, and without relating it to other words. A high-frequency derived word may develop contexts of use that are independent of the contexts in which the related base word is used. (This is also possible for lower-frequency words, but not as likely.) Thus, to use an example cited earlier, uses of *dirty*, as in "the dirty clothes hamper" or "the pile of dirty clothes" may occur partially independently of references to actual *dirt*. Similarly, references to an *interstate highway* may occur in contexts other than those in which the notion of actually traveling between states is important. Thus the term may come to mean any four-lane highway. On the other hand, a term such as *pre-wash* is currently restricted to contexts in which the term *wash* and its associated notion also occur. This helps to maintain a transparent semantic relation between *pre-wash* and *wash*. The important point is that the higher the frequency of a derived word, the more likely it is to occur in a variety of contexts, including some in which its related base word, and the semantic notions expressed by it, do not occur.

The data on the prefix *pre-* also show a correlation between the loss of semantic transparency and the change of the vowel away from the canonical [priy]. It is not certain whether original phonological differences between derived and basic forms encourage lexical split (see the discussion of split in inflectional paradigms below), but it is certain that the semantic changes that occur in lexical splits are accompanied by phonological differentiation of derived and basic form. Phonological changes affecting the derived form as its relation to its base slackens are reductive changes such as loss of secondary stress, with concommitant vowel and consonant reductions, and greater fusion of the originally separate units of the word. Compare for example the word *highness*, as in the phrase *Your Highness*, to the word *slyness*. The former rhymes with *sinus*, having a shorter vowel in the first syllable, and no secondary stress on the second syllable, and the vowel of this second syllable is also more reduced in *sinus* than in *slyness*. Reductions of this sort are well-known from compounds in English, such as *forehead* and *breakfast*, which have highly reduced second syllables in most dialects.

3. *Inflectional split*

Splits in inflectional paradigms are conditioned by precisely the same factors as splits between derivationally-related words, i.e. frequency, semantic relatedness, and, to a lesser extent, morpho-phonemic unpredictability. Any situation in which two inflectionally-related words lose their inflectional relation can be characterized as a split, but such splits may come about in slightly different ways, and have different consequences. Consider the case of the split between the verb *work* and its former past participle, *wrought*. In this case, a new regular past participle was formed, which was in competition with *wrought* for a time. The new past participle then completely replaced *wrought* in all uses that were transparently relatable to *work*, while *wrought* remained in certain fixed phrases, such as *wrought-iron, overwrought* or *highly wrought*, and certain specialized language, such as poetic and biblical language. Thus *work* now has a regular paradigm, and *wrought* is an isolated, largely archaic word. The split between *cloth* and its former plural *clothes* is somewhat different. The plural *clothes* became specialized to refer only to garments, while the singular continues to refer to woven material in general.

Sometimes splits in inflectionally-related forms result in suppletive paradigms — inflectional paradigms that have forms built on two or more stems that are etymologically from different sources. For instance, the English verb *to go* has Present, Infinitive and Participle forms built on *go*, but a Past Tense form, *went*, which is historically the Past Tense of the verb *to wend*. Similarly, the English verb *to be* has stems from three sources: *be, being* and *been* come from one verb, *am, is* and *are* come from another, and *was* and *were* from a third source. Let us take the example of *to go* to see how suppletive paradigms develop. Prior to the 15th century, the verb *to go* already had a suppletive Past Tense (*eode*), and the verb *to wend* had the Past Tense *went*. This latter verb had a meaning that was more restricted than *to go*, including in its meaning a notion of turning or winding. The Past Tense forms of *wend* gradually dissociated themselves from the other forms of the verb. These forms must have gradually increased in frequency, coming to have the more general meaning of *go*, while the Present Tense forms retained the more restricted meaning. Thus a lexical split occurred between *wend* and *went*. At the same time the older past forms for *to go* became less and less frequent, and were eventually lost. (See Rudes 1980 for a description of an ongoing change in Rumanian similar to this.) Since suppletive paradigms result from splits in inflectional paradigms, the characteristics of suppletive paradigms provide evidence for the factors that govern inflectional splits. The interaction of semantic relatedness with frequency of usage is important here just as it is in lexical splits among derivationally-related forms. First of all, suppletive paradigms are restricted to the most highly-frequent lexical items. Second, suppletive paradigms are divided along the category lines that involve the greatest change in meaning, i.e. in verbs, along aspect and tense lines. The second principle can be overridden in cases of extremely high frequency. Each of these principles will be discussed in the following.

It is well known that suppletive paradigms for verbs in Indo-European languages always involve the most frequent verbs. Common examples are the verbs *to be* and *to go* which are suppletive in many branches of the family. This phenomenon is not restricted to Indo-European. In the sample of languages described in Chapter 2, there were nine for which suppletive verbs were listed: four had suppletive stems for a verb meaning *to be*, six had suppletive stems for a verb meaning *to go*, and six had suppletive stems for a verb meaning *to come*. Other meanings for verbs with suppletion occurring in more than one language were *to give*, *to bring*, and *to sit* or *to be located*. The phenomenon is also observable in Indo-European adjectives, where the most common ones, *good* and *bad*, have suppletive comparative and superlative stems, e.g. English *good, better, best*, and *bad, worse, worst*, and Spanish *bueno, mejor* and *malo, peor*.

The second important factor that determines where splits occur among inflectional forms is the degree of relatedness of the forms. Closely related forms are less likely to split apart, thus inflectional splits are most likely to coincide with distinctions in the more highly relevant categories, those that make the largest semantic change. Rudes 1980 surveys suppletive verbal paradigms in Tuscarora, Muskogee, Classical Greek, Albanian, English, German, Georgian, Old Church Slavonic, Old Irish, Polish, Hittite, Italian, French and Rumanian. These languages, as well as those with suppletive verbs from my own survey, indicate that the most common place for a paradigm to split is along aspectual lines. Splits also occur along tense lines, less commonly along mood lines. My survey also turned up a number of cases of suppletion governed by the number of the subject or object. These cases are discussed in detail in section 5.2 of this chapter. A much smaller number of cases show suppletion along person agreement lines, but these occur only in the special circumstances to be described below.

It is my impression that suppletion in noun paradigms is somewhat less common than suppletion in verbal paradigms. This follows in fact from the principle that the original semantic differentiation determines the likelihood of a split. For instance, we would not expect splits to occur among nouns distinguished only for case, since case does not affect the meaning of the noun stem, but only signals its relation to other constituents in a particular sentence. Nor would we expect splits to be especially common between singular and plural nouns, since ordinarily the occurrence of one versus the occurrence of many does not change the inherent qualities of the entity. Nor would we ordinarily find many cases where a plural would be used in a context that was independent of the contexts in which the singular was used. There are cases, however, where a group of entities is conceptualized as being inherently different from an individual instance of the entity, and in these cases we do often find different stems being used. But we also find the meaning difference between the stems in such cases to be distinct enough to refer to the non-singular forms as collectives rather than plurals. Thus we do not usually think of pairs such as *cow, cattle*, and *person, people* as suppletive singular / plural pairs, but rather as singulars and collectives. When suppletion between singular and plural nouns does occur, it occurs in predictable lexical items for the most part. For example, Maasai has suppletive plurals for the nouns meaning *cow, ox, tree* and somewhat less predictably, *girl*.

The second principle, which predicts that inflectional splits are less likely among the most closely-related forms, may be violated in cases of extreme high frequency. Rudes 1980 points out that suppletion that divides the person / number forms of a tense, aspect or mood occurs only in the present tense, the most frequent tense in the languages he examined. Furthermore, this type of suppletion is extremely rare, and tends to occur in the most frequent verbs, such as the German verb *sein* 'to be' which has present tense forms with 1s *bin* and 2s *bist* from one stem (PIE **bhew-*), and 3s *ist* and plural, *sind* from another stem (PIE **es-*). In a slightly different sort of example, the Irish verb *bheirim* 'I give, bring', which uses three different stems, one for the Present and Imperfect Indicative, another for the Past, Dependent and Subjunctive forms, and a third for the Dependent Future and Conditional, has a 2s Imperative that is different from all the other Imperative forms. This is explainable in terms of the extreme high frequency of the 2s of the Imperative compared to other Imperative forms. Indeed, most languages do not even have first and third person forms in the Imperative. It should also be noted that a second person imperative form would be especially frequent for a verb such as 'to give'.

The extreme high frequency and wide variety of functions for a verb such as 'to be' probably leads to the autonomy of all of its forms, and a paradigm structured somewhat differently from that of other verbs. Consider the fact that not only does the verb *to be* in English serve a number of functions, i.e., as the copula, as part of the progressive and passive constructions, as well as the possessive, the cleft and pseudo-cleft constructions, it also has a larger number of forms than any other English verb. There are two sources for these forms. The forms that differentiate person and number in the Present (*am*, *is* and *are*) and number in the Past (*was* and *were*) are forms that have survived long after all other verbs have ceased to mark these distinctions. And each of these variants has proliferated into multiple forms through contraction with nouns, pronouns and with the negative element. Many of the contracted forms are not synchronically predictable by general rule and are thus autonomous. Moreover, forms that are predictable by rule may also be autonomous, and even forms that are phonologically "identical" may have multiple lexical representations given their extreme high frequency, and their occurrence in constructions of different types (Pagliuca 1982).

The fact that a split may occur between two different uses of an identical form necessitates dual or multiple representations for *single forms*. Consider the development of the modal use of *supposed* in English. The verb *suppose* in its meaning 'to hold as opinion or belief' has been in use since the 14th century. This use continues in sentences such as "They supposed him to be qualified", "He supposed that she would be home", or "Let us suppose that...". At the same time, however, a newer use has developed from a passive construction with this verb. Thus "They supposed him to be qualified" could also be rendered "He is supposed to be qualified". This passive use of *suppose* in sentences referring to the future, as "He is supposed to come" has gradually changed its sense to denote obligation predicated of the subject, rather than belief predicated of some unnamed agent. This differentiation in meaning is accompanied by a gradual differentiation in phonological form. The modal use of *supposed* is undergoing phonological reduction at a faster rate than the more conservative and now less frequent use of *supposed*. In the modal use, the first syllable may be reduced considerably more than in the other use, and the final consonants are usually voiceless, due to the following *to*, whereas in the "belief" use of *suppose* the final consonants are never devoiced, even when a voiceless consonant follows, as in "They supposed Tom to be the culprit".

This type of diachronic development shows that a single form with a unified meaning can split into two or more forms. Since a single form with an originally unified meaning can split into two or more forms, an original semantic differentiation, which I argued is a factor in determining the likelihood of inflectional split, cannot be considered a necessary condition for split.

A final factor to be considered is phonological differentiation between the two related forms. In the cases of inflectional split discussed early in this section, *work, wrought; cloth, clothes;* and other cases such as *brother, brethren*, or *get, got*, there is a greater phonological distance between the members of the pair than is predicted by the regular inflectional rules of the language. These differences were present before the split occurred, and could have been instrumental in producing the split, especially since the morphophonemic unpredictability would lead to autonomous lexical representations for the derived forms (see Chapter 5). In fact, in the case of *wrought* and *brethren* the main impetus for the split was the creation of a new regular form that gradually replaced the irregular one. In the case of *clothes* and *got* the differentiation in meaning may well have been aided by the formal differences in the related pairs. It is questionable whether the split between *wend* and *went* could have been aided by the small phonological difference between these two forms, but it is possible that the irregularity of the Past formation could have encouraged the development of a new regular Past for *wend* which would leave *went* available for other uses.[6] There are then two separate factors having to do with the formal relation between the inflectional pairs: the phonological distance between them, and morpho-phonemic irregularity. Neither of these is a necessary condition for split in general, however, since identical forms can also undergo split, as *supposed* has, but it is likely that in cases of inflectional split these formal properties may be important.

In this section and the preceding one, I have discussed splits among derivationally-related forms and inflectionally-related forms in order to show that the same factors are involved in both, and that, indeed, there are not any real differences in quality in splits between derivational and inflectional forms. The fact that splits are much more common where derivational relations are involved is due to the fact that there is usually a larger meaning difference between derivationally-related forms than between inflectionally-related forms.

4.   Degree of fusion

It is often observed that derivational affixes occur closer to the root or base than inflectional affixes do. This observation also holds for the languages reported on in Greenberg 1966 (see Universal #28), and it was not contradicted by any of the languages in the survey reported on here. As we saw in Chapter 2, there were also some significant generalizations concerning the ordering of inflectional affixes with respect to the verb base. In particular, the more relevant the meaning of the affix to the verb, and the greater the semantic change involved in their combination, the closer to the verb base the affix will appear. It can now be seen that this principle also predicts that derivational affixes, to the extent that they are highly relevant, will occur closer to the verb base than inflectional ones. The observed ordering regularity of derivational and inflectional morphemes does not, then, yield a discrete division between derivation and inflection, but rather follows from the hypotheses that *all* morphological processes can be ordered on a scale such as the one proposed in Chapter 2 for inflectional processes.

One language-specific example demonstrates nicely the diagrammatic relation of proximity to the stem and greater semantic fusion.[7] In the dialect of Eskimo reported on in Sadock and Olsen 1976, there is a root for "person", a suffix meaning "big", and another meaning "little". These three units can be combined in two different orders. When "big" (*-rssu-*) occurs closer to the root (*ino-*) than "little" (*-angu*), as in *inorssuanguag*, the meaning is "little giant". When "little" occurs closer to the root, as in *inunguarssuag*, the meaning is "big midget". The suffix that is closer to the root affects the inherent meaning of the root, while the outer suffix functions more like an attributive adjective. Note that both of these suffixes would probably be considered derivational. This means that the proposed principle accounting for the ordering of affixes also governs the ordering among derivational affixes.

Some examples from English illustrate a similar point: I mentioned above two suffixes that change the syntactic category of the words they attach to, but otherwise produce only a small meaning change, and are very general and regular in application, adverb-forming *-ly*, and gerundial *-ing*. These suffixes are always the *last* in the word if there are other derivational suffixes. Consider the order of suffixes in the following words with averbial *-ly*: *mercifully, regretfully, assertively, grammatically*; and words with the gerundial: *systematizing, whitening* and so on.

Statements by Burling 1961 about Garo support the same point. In Garo there are a number of productive affixes that cannot be considered inflectional because they are not obligatory. Burling calls them "adverbial affixes" and describes their distribution as follows:

> Every verb may have from none to several adverbial affixes, then, and there are no formal limits on the number or the order in which these occur. However, statistically some are more likely to occur first and others last. In general the most common ones (= most general, JLB) last, occur the rarer ones first, the rarer ones being more firmly attached to the verb base, while the more common ones are more readily substitutable affixes. (Burling 1961:17)

I equate "general" with "common" in this case because Burling is referring to how commonly the suffixes occur in different combinations, i.e., their type frequency. A suffix might have a high token frequency because it occurs in one or two very frequent words, and in this case it might not be general at all. (See Chapter 5.12 for a discussion of the effect of type frequency on affixes.)

Other measures of the degree of fusion discussed in Chapter 2 also show derivational processes to fit along the same scale proposed for inflectional processes. For example, derivational processes tend to have a greater effect on the root than inflectional processes do. They condition and are sometimes signalled solely by root changes. Reduplication is more common among derivational processes than among inflectional. Indeed, in the survey described in Chapter 2, only two languages were found to have reduplication as an inflectional process for verbs, while there were numerous instances of reduplication mentioned for derivational processes. Even more striking, however, is the fact that infixation was not found to be an inflectional process in any of the languages examined, while it was mentioned occasionally as a derivational process.[8]

The other measure of fusion is the morpho-phonemic effect that the root has on the affix. This is manifested both in greater fusion in the sense of internal sandhi processes that change the affix, and in lexically-determined allomorphy where the root determines the choice of morphological process used to express the category. Examples are numerous: English *unable* but *incapable*, and *unhappy* but *discontent*, as well as deverbal nominalizations, which seem to be partially dependent on the final segments of the verb, but are not totally predictable:

prevent	prevention	*preventment
resent	resentment	*resention
present	presentation	*presention
satisfy	satisfaction	*satisfiance
comply	compliance	*complaction
apply	application	
hesitate	hesitation	
orient	orientation	
decide	decision	
abide	-------	

A variety of lexically-determined affixes and processes are characteristic of derivational morphology, and are found in inflectional morphology to a greater or lesser extent, depending upon the degree of semantic relevance of the inflectional category to the stem. This measure of the degree of fusion, like all the other criteria that distinguish derivational from inflectional morphology, also distinguishes categories within the inflectional range.

5.   *The difference between derivational and inflectional meaning*

The major proposal developed in this chapter is that the content of morphological categories determines whether they will appear in inflectional or derivational expression. Other linguists who have studied this question have not arrived at such a firm conclusion. Sapir proposes both a classification of concepts, and a classification of expression types and suggests a correlation between them. However, he eventually concludes by saying:

> We must dispense ... with a well-ordered classification of categories. What boots it to put tense and mode here and number there when the next language one handles puts tense a peg "lower down", mode and number a peg "higher up"? (Sapir 1921: 107)

From a much different point of view Kuryłowicz 1964 argued that some inflectional categories are closely related to some derivational categories. He gives the examples, among others, of *Aktionsart* as related to inflectional aspect; collectives (derivational) as related to plurals (inflectional); and gender in nouns (derivational) as related to gender in adjectives (inflectional). This would suggest that the same meanings can be expressed in different ways. Much more recently the point has been made again by S. Anderson 1982, who argues explicitly that the inflectional / derivational distinction cannot be made on the basis of meaning. Anderson points to the examples of an ordinarily derivational category, *diminutive*, which in Fula is inflectional, and the ordinarily inflectional category of *tense*, which in Kwakiutl, Anderson claims, is derivational.[9] In view of these opinions, it is worthwhile to clarify what exactly *can* be predicted about the relation of meaning to derivational or inflectional expression.

The *relevance* principle predicts that certain categories *may* have derivational expression, in particular, *valence-changing categories, voice* and *aspect* for verbs. Categories that have propositional scope, such as *tense* and *mood*, are not derivational, nor are *agreement* categories, which index the arguments of the verb. For nouns, we can predict that *gender* and *number* may have derivational expression, because they modify inherent characteristics of the referent, but *case* and *definiteness* will not, because they serve to relate the noun to other elements in the sentence or discourse.

These predictions bring us closer to our goal, but they say nothing at all about some categories, and allow others to have either derivational or inflectional expression. For these categories it must be shown that there is some difference between the meaning expressed as derivational and the meaning expressed as inflectional. Here the criterion of *generality* comes into play, for in cases where similar conceptual content is expressed in the two different ways, we will find that the inflectional expression requires a fully general meaning, while the derivational does not. The consequences of this are that inflectional meaning is always very general, indeed, often so general as to be redundant in context, and it is always transparent in the sense that its combination with a stem always produces a predictable meaning. Derivational meaning, on the other hand, has more semantic content and often produces idiosyncratic meanings in combination with different lexical stems. In the following two sections these points will be illustrated in discussions of *aspect* as a lexical, derivational and inflectional category, and the so-called "plural" of verbs as a lexical and derivational category.

5.1. *The expression of aspect*

It is particularly appropriate to begin this discussion with the set of related notions labelled as *aspect* because this set of concepts allows every type of expression from lexical to periphrastic. Consider first lexical expression: verbs tend to have inherent aspectual meaning because the activities, events and situations described by verbs tend to have inherent temporal properties. Some verbs describe events that take place in a very short period of time, such as *cough* and *blink*. These are referred to as "semelfactive" verbs. Some verbs are stative in meaning since the situations they describe are continuous and unchanging over time, for example *to know*, *to have*; in some languages, notions such as *to be tall*, *to be black* are expressed lexically as verbs. Some verbs, "atelic" verbs, describe activities that do not have inherent endpoints, such as *to eat* or *to sing*, while others, "telic" verbs, describe events with internal structure, such as a necessary beginning and / or end point: *to dive, to devour*.

Some of these lexical distinctions may also be expressed as derivational distinctions: In Quileute, the substitution of the suffix *-(a)ts* instead of the normal *-l* "indicates a more rapid or energetic action" (Andrade 1933: 227), which appears to be semelfactive: *ceq + o + l* 'to pull', and *ceq + w + ats* 'to jerk'; *k'ix + a + l* 'to lift gradually', and *k'ix + a + ts* 'to lift suddenly'; *wa:x + i + l* 'to stop', and *wa:x + a + ts* 'to stop suddenly'; *k'wadaq + a + l* 'to tear (cloth of any fabric or textile)', and *k'wadaq + a + ts* 'to tear with a jerk'. Comrie 1976 mentions the example of a set of Russian verbs, all with a sequence *-nu-*, all of which describe semelfactive events: *kašljanut'* 'to cough', *blesnut'* 'to flash'. The identification of the *-nu-* sequence as a suffix does not seem justified since the stems do not apparently occur without this sequence. Rather semelfactive in this case has a mode of expression that is half-way between lexical and derivational.

As mentioned in section 1.3 of this chapter, inceptives tend to be restricted to stative verbs, so in languages with a morphological inceptive (or inchoative) marker, this marker is derivational. A similar observation may be made about *iterative* markers. While it is common for languages to have morphological iterative markers, these are usually derivational also, because they are applicable primarily to semelfactive verbs (although they may apply to activity verbs as well) but not to stative verbs. For example, in Kiwai, there is a suffix *wado* described by Ray (1933 :38) as indicating "the repetition of an action or its frequent or regular performance". *Wado* is usually added to a stem with a final *-ai*, which indicates "action at one time", or punctual: *irimaoor-ai-wado* 'shriek many times'; *oriodor-ai-wado* 'go astern frequently'; *iaeed-ai-wado* 'pull the bowstring many times (without shooting); *idi-ai-wado* 'come up from below often'.[10]

The preceding are examples of derivational aspect markers that are restricted by their meaning to a semantic class of verbs. Another way that derivational meaning differs from inflectional is that it is not so "pure": derivational markers that may be primarily aspectual might contain other components of meaning as well. For instance, in Slavic languages, the perfectivizing prefixes often have more specific aspectual meanings, or meaning components that are not really aspectual (Forsyth 1970 for Russian). Partridge (1964 :94) gives these examples for Serbo-Croatian: *ići* 'to go', and *proći* 'to go through, go past'; *teći* 'to flow' and *proteći* 'to flow past'; or consider the various perfective derivatives of *pisati* 'to write': *potpisati* 'to write under, to sign'; *natpisati* 'to write over'; *napisati* 'to write down'; *prepisati* 'to re-write'.

Chapter 6 discusses in detail the inflectional expression of aspect in the 50-language sample. The major cross-linguistic pattern found for inflectional aspect consists of a *perfective / imperfective* distinction sometimes supplemented by a *habitual / continuous* distinction (meaning "always do it, used to do it" versus "is doing it, was doing it") in the *imperfective*. In some languages the *perfective / imperfective* distinction is clearly inflectional, for example in Spanish, where every verb has both a Preterite and an Imperfective form. In other languages, it may be a pervasive distinction, but a derivational or lexical one, as in Serbo-Croatian. On the other hand, the *habitual / continuous* distinction is never derivational or lexical, but where it occurs, it is either inflectional or marked with free grammatical morphemes (such as auxiliaries). That is to say, whether an action is habitual or not is not a distinction that is made lexically or derivationally. The reason is that *habituality* does not combine with the semantic components denoting events or activities in such as way as to produce a distinct event or activity, which is to say that habituality is not as relevant to the meaning of a verb as some of the other concepts that are classified as aspects.[11]

An examination of the different expression possibilities for aspect shows, then, that while related aspectual notions may have more than one expression type, there is by no means complete freedom of expression for aspect.

	lexical	derivational	inflectional
telic/atelic	X	X	
semelfactive	X	X	
stative/active	X	X	
inceptive	X	X	
iterative		X	
perf/imperf			X
habitual/cont			X

Table 6: Expression types for aspectual notions.

Not only do generality and predictability of meaning condition possible morphological expression types, but even within the conceptual domain of aspect, there are differences in the relevance of aspectual notions to the verb, in that there are differences in the extent to which an aspectual modification of an activity or event produces a distinct activity or event.

5.2. *Number in verbs*

As mentioned several times, agreement categories have less relevance for a verb stem than any other inflectional categories, and person-agreement categories do not have lexical or derivational expression, except in the rarest of cases. However, agreement for *number* of the subject or object appears to present quite a different case.[12] There are some languages in which number distinctions are lexicalized in verb stems. A very clear example is !Kung, a language of southern Africa, which has no inflectional agreement categories, but does have a small but central group of verbs which has one form in a sentence in which the absolutive noun phrase (the object of a transitive or subject of an intransitive) is singular and another form when that noun phrase is plural. When the verb has a plural form, the plural suffix -*si* on the noun is optional (Snyman 1970: 124, 131-132): ([!], [|], [ǂ] and [| |] are ingressive consonants)

mi gu n!ao	'I take the bow'
mi n | 'hwi n!aosi	'I take the bows'
n!eu !o'a g!heī	'The elder breaks the stick'
n!eu kx'oma g!heisi	'The elder breaks the sticks'
kx'ao | | u hema	'Kx'ao hangs up the shirt'
kx'ao g| | ao hemasi	'Kx'ao hangs up the shirts'
n | wa !ei	'The cat dies'

n|wa !ao	'The cats die'
n!eu g|i	'The elder goes out'
n!eu g!e'i	'The elders go out'
xei šu	'The loaf of bread lies flat'
xei g≠a	'The loaves of bread lie flat'

Another language with a similar phenomenon is Ainu, which, like !Kung, does not have inflectional expression of agreement on verbs, but does have lexical and derivational expression for some verbs of the number of the absolutive noun phrase. The following lexical pairs of verb forms are given in Batchelor 1938: 121-122:

singular	plural	
a	at	'to be'
a	rok	'to sit'
ani	amba	'to carry'
raige	ronnu	'to kill'
ek	araki	'to come'
arapa	paye	'to go'

The majority of plural verbs are formed, however, by the addition of the suffix -pa to the singular form:

ama	amapa	'to put or place'
aship	ashippa	'to flower'
heashi	heashpa	'to begin'
hekatu	hekatpa	'to be born'
oboso	oboshpa	'to pass through'
rai	raipa	'to die'

In Diegueño and Kwakiutl plural verbs are derivationally related to singulars by a variety of irregular reduplicative, stem-changing and affixation processes. For these languages, the analysis of meaning makes it clear how plurality of subject or object can affect the meaning of the verb stem. Boas (1947: 246) explains that in Kwakiutl there are three distinct types of plurality for verbs: "one indicating several subjects; a second indicating an action occurring at the same time in different parts of a unit; and a third, expressing repeated action."

mɛdɛ'lqwɛla	'it is boiling'
me?mɛdɛ'lqwɛla	'many are boiling'
ma?ɛ'mdɛlqwɛla	'is boiling in all of its parts'

mɛdɛ'lxumɛdɛ'lqwɛla	'it is boiling repeatedly'
tɛ'nk˙ɛla	'it is sizzling'
te'ʔtɛ'nk˙ɛla	'many are sizzling'
tɛ'ntɛnk˙ɛla	'it is sizzling in all its parts'
tɛnx˙tɛnk˙ɛla	'it is sizzling repeatedly'

These examples show that plurality in a verb may express more than the number of the subject or object. Plurality of action may involve either distribution or iteration of the action. These various plural notions may be expressed by a single morpheme, as in Pawnee, where the prefix *wa:* may signal a distributed activity or state, an iterative action, a distributive plural object, or a dual and/or plural subject (Parks 1976: 279). Consider these examples:

/wa: + wiu:s/ wa:wiua	'to defecate here and there'
/ra + wa: + hak/ rawa:hat	'to pass to (various people)'
/wa: + u/ wa:ʔu	'to give (various things)'

Freeland 1951 observes a similar phenomenon in Sierra Miwok. She says (Freeland 1951: 112):

> Ordinarily, in Miwok there is no expression of plurality in the verb apart from person. The transition between the idea of discontinuous iteration and that of plurality of subject or object, however, is very easy. Many of these iterative verbs that are transitive in meaning convey quite definitely the idea of a plural object.

Her examples show the distributive suffix + *i:* +:

poʔa:l + 'to slit open';	poʔ:al + i: + 'to slit open several'
maʔta + 'to kill';	maʔ:at + i: + 'to kill several'
haʔta + 'to toss';	haʔ:at + i: + 'to toss away repeatedly or several'

Detailed semantic information about !Kung and Ainu are not available, but the Kwakiutl, Diegueño, Pawnee and Miwok data show that number can be much more than just an agreement category when it is expressed derivationally. In fact, this type of verbal plurality is more like an aspect, in that it has an effect on the inherent meaning of the verb. It involves meaning components other than aspectual ones, however, implying as it does, particular arrangements of the absolute argument. This is another case, then, that shows clearly the difference between lexical and derivational meaning on the one hand, and inflectional meaning on the other, for when number is expressed inflectionally, it never has such an effect on the meaning of the verb.

Observe also that inflectional number agreement is often redundant even in the context of the clause, since the verbal agreement is required even when the number is given in the noun phrases. This is not so with derivational or lexical number. Snyman notes for !Kung that the pluralizing suffix for nouns, -si, is not necessary in the examples given above, since the verb indicates plurality. Boas says about Kwakiutl, that plural verbs are not used if plurality of noun phrases is indicated by a numeral or other quantifier. Unlike inflectional number, lexical and derivational plurality is not used redundantly. This indicates that the amount of meaning supplied in this way is much greater than that supplied by inflections. I conclude that even though there are cases of what seem to be the same concepts having derivational and inflectional expression, it turns out that they are not precisely the same, but only related concepts.

6.   Compounding and incorporation

Two morphological expression types related to derivation are *compounding* and *incorporation*. Morphologically-complex words created by these processes differ from those created by derivation and inflection in that such words cannot be analyzed as consisting of a stem or root plus affixes, rather they contain more than one stem or root. That is, the elements combined in these formations are not lexical plus grammatical, but rather two or more lexical elements. *Compounding* can be easily illustrated in English, where noun - noun, adjective - noun and noun - verb combinations occur. For example: *school bus, black board, babysit*. Noun - noun and adjective - noun combinations differ from regular noun phrases but resemble monomorphemic nouns in that the primary stress is on the first element of the compound, while for phrases the main stress is on the last lexical element. Noun - verb compounds differ from verb - object phrases in the position of the noun.

The term "incorporation" has been used to cover a variety of verb-formation phenomena ranging from processes very similar to compounding to processes that are much like derivational morphology (Sapir 1911, Woodbury 1975, Sadock 1980, Rudes 1984). Typically, "incorporation" refers to the fusion of the nominal patient of the verb with the verb, but often two verb stems can be fused as well. Both of these situations can be illustrated with examples from Tiwi, an Australian language (Osborne 1974: 46-48). Consider these examples:

ji + mən + taŋkina = he + me + steal 'He stole it from me'
ji + mən + alipi + aŋkina = he + me + meat + steal 'He stole my meat'

ji + məni + ŋilimpaŋə + raŋkina
he + me + sleeping + steal 'He stole it from me while I was asleep'
ji + məni + ŋilimpaŋ + alipi + aŋkina
he + me + sleeping + meat + steal 'He stole my meat while I was asleep'

Morpheme strings such as these are considered to be instances of noun-incor-
poration because of the position of the noun between the pronominal prefixes
and the verb. A non-incorporated noun object would follow the verb, and
the pronominal prefixes would be attached directly to the verb. It is typical
for an incorporated noun, like a derivational morpheme, to occur closer to
the verb than the inflectional morphemes.

Compounding is distinct from all other combinatory processes of language in that it has the characteristics of both *syntactic* and *lexical* expression.
Compounding resembles syntactic expression in that the units combined also
always exist independently as words — that is, they are complete both
phonologically and semantically. Compounding resembles lexical expression
in that the resulting unit is a *word*, and the meaning of this word is not
predictable from a summation of the meaning of its parts. Even though
compounding may be productive in the sense that new compounds are freely
created, the results of the compounding process are lexicalized, and they
tend gradually to lose their semantic and phonological transparency.

There is a diachronic relation between compounding and derivational
morphology, in that one element of a compound may become a derivational
affix if it occurs in a large number of combinations. For instance, the Modern
English adjective and adverb-forming suffix *-ly*, as found in *friendly, manly,
kingly*, and so on, developed from an earlier compound similar to the modern
compounds with *like*, such as *child-like*, *god-like* and *phantom-like*. According to the Oxford English Dictionary, its meaning generalized from that of
"having the appearance of" (the entity described by the noun-stem) to "having the qualities appropriate to" (the entity described by the noun-stem).
Compounding is not a process which all languages use. Some languages, e.g.
French and Spanish have little or no compounding, while others, e.g. German
and Dutch, make extensive use of compounding.

In some languages the incorporation of a patient noun into the verbal
complex resembles compounding, while in others it appears to be more like
a derivational process. In Iroquoian (Woodbury 1975, Rudes 1984) the noun

and verb that are fused both also exist as independent words in other constructions. In other languages, such as Quileute and Tiwi, the incorporated elements do not always have cognate free morphemes. For instance, about Tiwi,
Osborne (1974: 48) says that the "incorporated and free forms are generally
not cognate". Andrade 1933 estimates that about 60 percent of the incorporated forms in Quileute are not cognate with free forms. In such languages
there is a closed stock of stems that can appear incorporated, and many of
them cannot occur independently. In this respect, then, they resemble derivational morphemes.

In addition, there are often morpho-phonological differences between
a free and incorporated form when they are cognate. For example, Tiwi
body parts, in incorporated and free forms:

mumu-	mumuta	'back'
aŋkəli-	jiŋkala	'upper leg'
pula-	jimpula	'knee'
mələ-	məlampwara	'foot'
mərə-	murupuaka	'ankle'

The semantic domain of the incorporated noun is usually restricted. For
instance, in Pawnee, nouns referring to body parts, natural phenomena,
foods and cultural products are regularly incorporated. In fact, terms for
body parts are almost always incorporated. On the other hand, personal
names (of individuals or tribes), kinship terms, personal nouns (*man, child*,
etc.), names of animals, and names of particular species (of tree, for example)
are not usually incorporated (Parks 1976: 251-252).[13] Further, in some
languages there are restrictions on the verbs which may take certain incorporated nouns. For instance, in Tiwi, body part names can be incorporated
into only three verbs, -*ni* 'hit', -*na* 'grab', and -*kuwirani* 'burn'. Languages
with compounding do not have restrictions of this sort. In languages where
incorporation has fewer restrictions it bears a stronger resemblance to compounding. In languages where there are more restrictions, it resembles derivational morphology. Indeed, for Greenlandic, both Sapir (1911) and Sadock
(1980) liken verbs which take incorporated nouns to verbalizing suffixes.

Compounding, incorporation and derivation are on a continuum with
respect to generality of meaning. The elements that enter into a compound
do not differ in generality from the same elements when they occur free,
except that nouns in noun - verb compounds have a generic function rather
than a referential one, e.g. *baby* in *babysit* does not refer to any particular

baby. The same applies to incorporation — the incorporated noun has a generic rather than a referential function, and moreover, often implies a category of item rather than a particular item (such as *liquid* versus *maple syrup*) (Woodbury 1975). Consider as an example, the commentary by Andrade (1933: 181):

> Thus, for example, our word *hat* can be expressed by the free morpheme *tsiya.pus* or by the post-positive (=incorporated form, JLB) -*dist'c*, but the latter can also refer to a cap or to some kinds of head-dress, if no specific hat has been mentioned in the context.

Recall also Parks' (1976: 251) comment on Pawnee, that incorporated nouns denote basic-level classification. That is, a name for a particular species of tree will not be incorporated.

While compounding is free of lexical restrictions, the ability of a noun or verb to enter into an incorporated construction depends in part on the *relevance* of the meaning of the noun to that of the verb. Thus Sapir suggests that

> ...what may be called typical or characteristic activities, that is, those in which activity and object are found regularly conjoined in experience (e.g. rabbit-killing, looking for a trail, setting a net), tend to be expressed by verbs with incorporated objects, whereas "accidental" or indifferent activities (e.g. seeing a house, finding a stone) are rendered by verbs with independent, syntactically determined nouns.

(Sapir 1911:264). Thus the meaning of the noun and that of the verb combine in such a way as to describe a single discrete and culturally salient activity. As Parks (1976) describes derivational incorporation in Pawnee, the noun builds up the meaning of the verb. The result is a new verb with a different meaning.[14]

Compounding, incorporation, derivation and inflection are on a continuum, in which compounding is the freest, involves the largest (indeed an open) class of items, with the richest and most specific meanings, and inflection is the most constrained, involves the smallest classes of items with the most abstract and general of meanings. Languages differ with respect to the extent to which they make use of these different methods of combining morphemes. Languages which allow incorporation are not common, but they are of considerable theoretical interest, since they allow the fused expression of a greater variety of semantic notions than other languages. In Part II, where we examine the semantic notions that may be expressed morphologically on verbs, we will see that while certain concepts, such as *imperative* are extremely frequent as verbal morphology, other concepts, such as deontic modality, are expressed morphologically only in languages with extremely high degree of morphological fusion.

7. Conclusion

This chapter considers the derivation / inflection distinction as a continuous scale, rather than a discrete division of expression types. I have argued that there is a correlation between the type of meaning expressed by a morphological category and the form its expression takes, and that these correlations are predictable from the semantic parameters of relevance and generality. I have also argued that inflectionally- and derivationally-related forms split apart from one another under exactly the same conditions, but these conditions are met more often for derivation than for inflection. In addition, we have seen that compounding and incorporation are related to derivational morphology. The comments offered here are intended as useful ways of viewing the distinction between derivation and inflection, and also as a way of understanding differences betwen related concepts in general categories, such as *aspect*. In the next chapter I will present a model of lexical representation that can accomodate some of the observations made here.

NOTES

1. Clark and Clark 1979 point out that ordinarily a derived innovation that is precisely synonymous to an established word will be considered unacceptable and not survive. This is the reason there are not more pairs of the type *unhappy / sad*, i.e. *unpretty, ungraceful, unbright* are pre-empted by established lexical items: *ugly, clumsy, dull*.

2. Generality is probably what Bloomfield meant by "rigid parallelism" of underlying and derived form. He also recognized that even inflectional categories are not always totally general.

3. With a few verbs, 'wish', 'want', 'hate' and 'bleed', this same suffix gives a future meaning. Its use with 'bleed' is an exception to the restriction that it be used only with stative verbs.

4. Other variables coded by Pagliuca were stress placement and the length of time the word has been used in English. These variables will not be discussed here.

5. The change of [i] to [ɛ] occurred early, affecting the words that had a high frequency, and is independent of the [iy] > [i] > [ɪ] change.

6. The class of verbs characterized by the devoicing of a final /d/, i.e., *bend, bent; spend, spent; build, built* has been shrinking faster than any other English irregular verb class. In the experiments reported on in Bybee and Slobin 1982, we found that this class provoked the highest rate of regularization of any English verb class.

7. David Zager brought this example to my attention. The morpheme segmentation is only approximate because the fusional morpho-phonemics of Greenlandic are highly complex and need not concern us.

8. Of course there are languages with with inflectional infixation, for instance, the languages of the Philippines, but the fact that no examples occurred in our 50 language sample shows that inflectional infixation is very rare.

9. The diminutive category that Anderson refers to is part of a noun classification system in which almost every noun can be used with a class suffix denoting diminution (Arnott 1970). The diminutive category here does not necessarily denote the actual size of the entity, which would be an inherent characteristic of the entity, but is used also as a pejorative which indicates the speaker's attitude about the value of the entity in question.

Non-obligatory affixes expressing temporal notions, and applicable both to nouns and verbs (comparable perhaps to English terms such as "former" or "ex-") occur in Kwakiutl. As might be expected, their scope and function is quite different from that of tense inflections. Such examples seem to be infrequent cross-linguistically.

10. I am not certain whether iteration and inception are frequent as components of lexical meaning.

11. Habituality is apparently more often conceived of as an inherent characteristic of agents than of activities, since people are often referred to with terms denoting habitual activities, such as *jogger, smoker*, etc.

12. The example of number in verbs is also discussed in Bybee 1984.

13. Parks 1976 describes two kinds of incorporation for Pawnee: one in which the incorporated noun serves as the subject or object of the clause, and one (termed "derivational") in which the noun builds up the meaning of the verb, but does not really serve as an argument in the clause. Both of these types of incorporation are subject to similar semantic restrictions on the incorporated noun.

14. The meaning of verb-adjunct incorporation was not discussed in the literature I consulted.

CHAPTER 5
TWO PRINCIPLES IN A DYNAMIC MODEL
OF LEXICAL REPRESENTATION

The linguistic evidence usually adduced in debates over the nature of the lexical representation of morphologically-complex words is distributional evidence. It is argued that recurring regularities in word formation should be represented in rules, rather than in individual lexical entries. Arguments over the exact nature of these rules and representations appeal to the simplicity or elegance of the analysis, or to the notion of "capturing significant generalizations". Occasionally diachronic evidence is also brought in, especially in the work of Kiparsky and Vennemann. There exist in addition, however, other sources of evidence — synchronic, diachronic, cross-linguistic, and developmental — that bear on the issue of lexical representation but which have not been applied in discussions of this issue.[1] Some of this evidence has been introduced in previous chapters, some will be introduced here. The evidence concerns the effects of autonomy, degree of relatedness, and the basic-derived relation on the storage and processing of words. In this chapter I will propose two general principles of lexical organization that are suggested by this evidence. I will not propose a full-blown model of lexical representation or lexical processing, rather I will concentrate on two proposals, which I hope can be accommodated in a complete theory of lexical organization and access.

1. *Rote or combination?*

The basic problem in the representation of morphology is that morphology lies half-way between syntax and lexicon. We know that speakers are capable of combining semantic notions by concatenating linguistic units, for this is the basic mechanism behind syntactic expression — words are strung together to produce sentences. We also know that speakers are capable of learning by rote and storing thousands of distinct linguistic units in their mental lexicons. The question addressed by current theories of morphological representation is which method, combination or rote (to use MacWhinney's 1978 terms), is used in the production of morphologically-complex forms? There is ample evidence for both rote and combination:

That rote learning and storage is necessary in morphology is unquestionable: suppletive forms, and most probably other irregular forms must be learned by rote. The evidence for the production of inflectional forms by combinatory rules is also unquestionable: certain morphological rules are productive and regular, and are applied consistently across speakers to new or nonce forms, producing forms that could not have been learned by rote.

Given that both rote and combination are necessary for morphological representation, recent models have proposed varying relations among them:

(1) Early generative phonology (Chomsky and Halle 1968) tried to use combination for everything except the totally intractable suppletive forms.

(2) Other models (such as Hooper 1976a) proposed rote storage for all morpho-phonemically irregular formations, and production by combination for regular forms.

(3) In Vennemann's 1974 model *all* words are stored in the lexicon, even though rules for their derivation may also be available.

Considerable evidence that calls for the rejection of the first model has been amassed over the last dozen years or so. I will not review it here, but will mention one recent and particularly persuasive addition to this body of data:

In the experimental context described in Bybee and Slobin 1982, adults were asked to respond, under considerable time pressure, to the base form of an English verb by supplying the Past Tense form. Most errors were regularizations but there were also errors of incorrect vowel change in irregular verbs. If vowel-change verbs are generated by feature-changing rules, as the Chomsky and Halle model predicts, then vowel-change errors would be the result of the misapplication of feature-changing rules, and would produce nonsense words, such as *hept* for the past tense of *heap*. An examination of the actual errors shows something quite different, however. The errors may be divided into three types: (1) Twenty-six of these errors involved the use of the Past Participle (e.g. *sung*) in the class of verbs exemplified by *sing*; (2) Twelve others involved the use of [ae] or [ʌ] in verbs ending in *-nk* or *-ng*, for example, *clank* for *clinked* and *brung* for *brought*. This error pattern is further investigated in Bybee and Moder 1983; (3) Of all the remaining vowel-change errors, more than 90% resulted in occurring words of English. The only non-words were *hept, snoze* (for *snooze*), with one occurrence each (for 20 subjects), and *glew* (for the past tense of *glow*), with two occurrences.[2] All but one of these real word responses were verbs, and 80% were Past Tense forms of verbs. The most important result, however, is that 75% were the Past Tense of a verb with a *close semantic relation* to the stimulus verb, as shown in the following:

Stimulus	Response	Number of responses
seat	sat	9
set	sat	5
lend	loaned	4
rise	raise	4
search	sought	4
sight	sought	1
sight	saw	1
crawl	crept	1

These results strongly suggest that the task of generating an irregular Past Tense form in English is a lexical retrieval task, and that these errors result from retrieving the wrong word. Note that the semantic relations are very close, and the consonantal structure of the response is either totally correct, or nearly so. This suggests that the subjects arrived at the semantic domain required by the stimulus verb and selected a form marked as Past Tense which had the proper phonological structure. These results cannot be explained in a model in which English irregular verbs are generated from an underlying form by feature-changing rules.

There is, of course, other evidence for the lexical representation of irregular forms, for instance the fact that morpho-phonemic alternations tend to be highly bound to the particular lexical items they affect, and not productive (Bybee and Pardo 1981). Furthermore, the fact that irregular forms have to be highly frequent to be maintained suggests rote learning rather than rule learning.[3] Further evidence is presented below.

2. *Lexical representation of regular forms*

Leaving aside the first model then, and accepting the necessity of lexical representation for irregular forms, we must examine the evidence that bears on the issue that distinguishes the second from the third model, the issue of the lexical representation of *regular* inflected forms. This evidence does not point unequivocally to the choice of one model over the other.

First, consider the fact that children acquiring inflectional or agglutinating languages seldom make errors involving the order of morphemes within a word. In addition they seldom apply an affix to a base of the wrong category. This phenomenon has been observed in both Hungarian (MacWhinney 1974) and Turkish (Aksu and Slobin 1984), where inflected forms often involve sequences of suffixes. In both of these languages, furthermore, suffixes are relatively transparently segmentable. The low frequency of misplacement or misordering errors suggest the children store sequences of morphemes in the form of words or longer stretches of speech. Of course, children's speech also demonstrates the productive use of rules, but the fact that the affixes are rarely attached to stems of the wrong category, and rarely placed in the wrong order, suggests that the rules are constructed on the basis of previously acquired rote forms. In a comprehensive study of the segmentation of units in language acquisition, Peters 1983 concludes that both children and adults store and access multi-morphemic sequences, even after these sequences have been analyzed.

Another category of evidence is evidence that at least *some* regular forms have autonomous lexical representations. This evidence was presented in Chapter 3. Here we saw that children learning Brazilian Portuguese made no errors of conjugation class assignment for 3s Preterite forms, but always used the correct suffixes: *falou, bateu, abriu*. This suggests rote learning rather than generation by combination from the Present form. In contrast with the error-free acquisition of 3s forms, however, the 1s Preterite forms were not distinguished for conjugation class by the children, but rather were all assigned the suffix of the first conjugation: *falei, batei, abrei* (where *falei, bati* and *abri* are the adult forms, Simoes and Stoel-Gammon 1979). So these forms must be generated by combination, rather than learned by rote. This would be just an isolated fact about child language, were it not paralleled in the historical development of related languages. In Bybee and Brewer 1980 we present evidence from certain dialects of Provençal and Spanish that 3s Preterite forms, and at times the 1s as well, serve as the base form(s) from which other Preterite forms are derived. This evidence, then, suggests that *some* but not necessarily *all* regular inflected forms may have lexical representation, and that neither the second nor the third model is fully correct.

3.   *Differences between regular and irregular forms*

Evidence in favor of the point made by the second model — that there is a difference between the way regular and irregular forms are processed — is also available. Vincent (1980) discusses this point with regard to the development of the 1p suffix, -*iamo*, which is used for Present Indicative and Subjunctive in Italian. This suffix comes from a class of Latin verbs, whose 1p Present Subjunctive was -*eamus* or -*iamus*. It was generalized in Old Florentine, the dialect that is the basis for modern Italian, to the 1p Subjunctive form of verbs of all classes. Verbs which originally had this suffix had undergone certain sound changes starting in Vulgar Latin, when the *e* and *i* of the suffix became a palatal glide or "yod". The phonetic effects of this yod are widespread. For the Italian dialects, this yod had the effect of causing the preceding consonant to lengthen, and in some cases, to palatalize as well. Vincent gives the following derivations for two Latin verbs:

	"to make, do"	"to have"
Latin:	fakiamu(s)	(h)abeamu(s)
	fakjamu	abjamu
	fakkyamu	abbjamu
	fattsamu	
Ital:	facciamo	abbiamo

In the Florentine dialect, after this suffix had spread to *all* verbs regardless of conjugation class, it began to spread into the Indicative to mark the same person.[4] Vincent points out that this spread took place in two different ways. For verbs that were otherwise irregular, and for which the -*iamo* suffix in the Subjunctive entailed a stem alternation, the entire 1p Present Subjunctive word replaced the entire 1p Present Indicative word. Thus the spread of the suffix brought with it the irregular stem. So for the following verbs, the Indicative form was replaced by the Subjunctive:

Indicative	*Subjunctive*
facemo	facciamo
avemo	abbiamo
dovemo	dobbiamo
volemo	vogliamo
sapemo	sappiamo

For verbs with no alternations, it is impossible to tell if the change took place by replacing one whole word with another, or by combining the suffix

-iamo with the stem of the Present Indicative. (E.g. Ind. *difendemo* is replaced by *difendiamo*, and *dicemo* is replaced by *diciamo*.) There are some verbs, however, for which the spread of the suffix by recombination with the Indicative stem is the only account. Consider the following Old Florentine forms:

Indicative	Subjunctive
vedemo	veggiamo
ponemo	pognamo
potemo	possiamo

For these forms, the new Indicative / Subjunctive form was *vediamo, poniamo* and *potiamo* (with the latter attested but no longer used, the modern form being *possiamo*). These forms, then, had to be constructed by recombination of the suffix with the regular stem of the Indicative. The result is a perfectly regular paradigm.

Vincent argues that the existence of two mechanisms for change in paradigms is evidence for two methods of representing inflectional forms: irregular forms must be learned by rote and listed in the lexicon, and regular forms can be generated by combining a stem with affixes. When Vincent's evidence is combined with the other evidence mentioned here, a picture emerges in which some regular inflected forms are stored in the lexicon and some are not. This makes it difficult to answer the question of what is listed in the lexicon.

So far in this discussion, I followed the tradition of generative linguists, who, for more than a decade have been asking "is it in the lexicon or not?" as though there is some "yes" or "no" answer to this question. I now propose to abandon this restricted, binary way of thinking about lexical storage, and treat the problem as the complex psychological problem that it is. There are two propasals that will serve as the basis of the current treatment of the lexicon. The first is that every time a speaker / hearer processes a word, it affects the lexicon by strengthening the representation of a lexical item (Mac-Whinney 1978). Second, every item entered in the lexicon has a large number of diverse types of relations or connections to other lexical items. Thus rather than asking about a word "is it in the lexicon?", I propose that we ask at least two other questions: the first is "what is its lexical strength?" and the second is "what are its lexical connections?"

4.   *Lexical strength*

Lexical strength is a way of modeling the notion of *autonomy* discussed in Chapter 3. If we metaphorically suppose that a word can be written into the lexicon, then each time a word in processing is mapped onto its lexical representation it is as though the representation was traced over again, etching it with deeper and darker lines each time. Each time a word is heard and produced it leaves a slight trace on the lexicon, it increases in lexical strength. The notion of lexical strength allows us to account for the various effects that frequency has on the behavior of words. These effects will be reviewed in section 6.

Let us assume that the unit of lexical processing is the word and sometimes larger units — such as verbs with particles or prepositions, certain nouns with determiners.[5] In order for a successful mapping to take place, an item in processing must be matched with a stored item. This matching depends upon both phonological and semantic similarity. Of course, in perception, the goal is the discovery of the meaning of a word based on its phonological shape, but the mapping cannot be complete until it is established that the retrieved semantic representation is appropriate in the general context. So accumulated lexical strength depends on a certain degree of phonological and semantic correspondence.

An important question is what constitutes a "match". How similar do words have to be semantically and phonologically to be mapped onto the same lexical representation? There is no clear-cut answer to this question. Rather there are many possible degrees of "goodness" of match between forms. If the similarity between two words is not sufficient for a direct match, then a closely-related, but distinct lexical representation will be set up, and we will speak of forms related by *lexical connections*, as I will explain in the next section.

Given a semantic match, a phonological representation is strengthened to the extent that a matching of a portion of the phonological string is possible. Different tokens of the same word will map onto and strengthen the same representation, but series of related words, such as *play, plays, playing,* and *played* may also map onto the same representation, since they have both the semantics and phonology of their stems in common. The unshared parts of these words, the suffixes, will be treated in section 9. In addition, any one of these complex forms may also have its own (closely related) representation and its own individual strength if it is frequent enough.

Lexical strength, then, is both a gradient and a dynamic notion. Unlike a structuralist (including generative) lexicon, which is built on the metaphor of a dictionary, set down once and for all, unchanging, the lexicon I am describing here changes with use. Not only do words gain in strength, but they can also decline in strength with disuse.

5. *Lexical connection*

Lexical connection is also both a gradient and a dynamic notion, intended to account for multiple and diverse relationships among words. Primary among these are connections based on meaning. Words can be related because of shared semantic features: *table* and *chair* are both members of the supercategory *furniture*; *mouse* and *rat* are both rodents; *deep* and *shallow* are opposite ends of a single dimension. Words are connected if they refer to entities or situations belonging to the same scene: *doctor, nurse, hospital, operate*. Phonological connections can also be drawn where semantic connections exist, and if two words are related by both semantic and phonological connections, then a *morphological relation* exists between them. The semantic connections are the strongest and the most important in determining the closeness of the relations among words. This can be seen by comparing forms that have a strong semantic connection but no phonological one, such as *go* and *went*, to forms which are phonologically identical, but have no semantic connections, such as the two sense of *crane*. The psychological relation between suppletive forms is quite strong, as demonstrated by innovations such as *goed* for *went*, but the relation between forms that are homophonous usually goes unnoticed, and lexical ambiguity is hardly ever a problem in context.

The strongest sort of relation between forms is this *morphological relation*, which consists of parallel semantic and phonological connections. Morphological relations can be closer or more distant, depending upon three factors: (1) The degree of semantic relatedness, which is determined by the *number* of shared features, and the *nature* of the shared features. (2) The extent of phonological similarity between the items (e.g. *sing* and *sang* are more closely related than *bring* and *brought*). (3) Word frequency: high-frequency words form more distant lexical connections than low-frequency words. In the case of morphologically complex words, this means that high-frequency words undergo less analysis, and are less dependent on their related base words than low-frequency words. These are, of course, the same three factors that were shown in the last chapter to determine the likelihood of lexical and inflectional split. This is intentional, since lexical and inflectional splits constitute important evidence about the structure of the lexicon.

6.   *Evidence for varying lexical strength*

The primary motivation for developing a notion of lexical strength is to account for the various morphological phenomena in which high token frequency plays a role. In this section we will discuss five phenomena associated with high frequency and explain how this model proposes to describe these phenomena. The emphasis here is on the cross-linguistic and historical facts associated with word frequency, but it should also be noted that numerous experiments have demonstrated the effect of word frequency on lexical access. In particular, high-frequency words are accessed faster than lower-frequency words in word recognition experiments. Furthermore, subjects are able to judge rather accurately the relative frequency of words of their language.

First, the notion of lexical strength models rote-learning, which accounts for the maintenance of irregularity and suppletion in high-frequency forms. Conversely, the proposal that infrequently-used forms fade accounts for the tendency to regularize infrequent irregular forms, for an irregular form that is not sufficiently reinforced will be replaced by a regular formation. The correlation of irregularity with high frequency can be documented in almost any language, but the historical mechanism behind the correlation can also be demonstrated by comparing two stages of the same language. Consider the Strong Verbs of English. During the Old English period there were many more Strong Verbs than there are now. The verbs that have regularized are those with lower token frequencies. The following table shows the modern descendants of the verbs listed in Strong Verb classes I, II and VII in Sweet's *Anglo Saxon Primer*.[6] In the left-hand column are Strong Verbs that have stayed Strong, listed with their frequency according to Francis and Kučera 1982, and in the right-hand column are verbs from the same classes that have regularized or become Weak. The frequency figures are those for all forms of the verb, followed by those for the Past Tense form only. A striking difference in frequency is apparent in the two groups.

Strong verbs				*Regularized strong verbs*			
Class I:							
drive	203	drove	58	bide	1	bided	0
rise	199	rose	60	reap	5	reaped	1
ride	126	rode	40	slit	3	slit*	1
write	561	wrote	179	sneak	11	sneaked	4
bite	26	bit	7				
Average:	223		69		5		1.5
Class II:							
choose	177	chose	37	rue	0	rued	0
fly	92	flew	27	seethe	0	seethed	0
shoot	117	shot	18	smoke	26	smoked	6
lose	274	lost	49	float	23	floated	6
flee	40	fled	22	shove	16	shoved	8
Average:	140		31		22		4
Class VII:							
fall	239	fell	87	wax	6	waxed	3
hold	509	held	125	weep	28	wept**	7
know	1473	knew	394	beat	66	beat*	12
grow	300	grew	65	hew	1	hewed	1
blow	52	blew	12	leap	33	leaped	18
				mow	1	mowed	1
				sow	6	sowed	0
				flow	40	flowed	4
				row	5	rowed	2
Average:	515		137		21		5

*Slit and beat now belong to the class of verbs that take the zero-allomorph of Past Tense.

**Weep lost its original vowel change but later acquired another one by regular sound changes.

Note that the correlation of irregularity with frequency occurs on two dimensions. The first is the lexical dimension, which we have just illustrated, where irregularity correlates with frequent lexical entries. The second is within a paradigm, where, as Greenberg 1966 observed, the greater irregularity resides in the unmarked members of categories, which are also the most frequent. Thus alternations are more likely to be found in present tense forms rather than past tense forms, in indicative rather than subjunctive forms. For example, among Spanish verbs, there are numerous irregularities in the Present and the Preterite tenses, while the Imperfect Indicative and Subjunctive are regular for all but two verbs. The Present and Preterite tenses are far more frequently used than the Imperfect Indicative and Subjunctive. (According to Gili Gaya 1970, the Present is nearly twice as frequent as the Preterite, and the Preterite is three times as frequent as the Imperfect.)

A second, very similar, phenomenon is the correlation of high synthesis or fusion with high frequency. This correlation is found both on the lexical and the paradigmatic level. Highly-fused stem and affix combinations occur among the most frequent lexical items. For instance, in Spanish, the verb "to give" has only a consonant for a stem, and so uses the same vowel for both stem vowel and suffix vowel:

Present Indicative		*Preterite*	
dóy	dámos	dí	dímos
dás	dáis	díste	dísteis
dá	dán	dió	diéron

The verb appears to be almost regular, but it differs from other verbs in that in the Singular and 3p Present the stress should fall on the stem vowel and not the suffix vowel. In this verb the same vowel must do duty for both suffix and stem.

In English, the 3s Present forms *says, has,* and *does* ([sɛz], [hæz], and [dʌz] differ from all regular forms, in which the /z/ suffix is attached to an autonomous word. In these high frequency forms the final consonant must simultaneously be the 3s marker and a stem consonant, since the form without the [z] does not contain a normal English sequence. A similar situation holds in the Past forms of these same verbs, *said, had,* and *did,* where the forms without the final [d] would not be acceptable sequences in English.

Within paradigms there is also more fusion in more frequent members.[7] If we compare the Spanish Preterite to the Imperfect, we find the Imperfect easily segmentable into a consistent Imperfect marker, *-ba-* (for 1st conjugation) and *-ia-* (for 2nd and 3rd conjugation), followed by person / number agreement:

> 3s: cant + a + ba   "sang"
> 1p: cant + a + ba + mos

3s: com + í + a
1p: com + í + a + mos

The Preterite, on the other hand, has no clear segmental markers for aspect separate from agreement markers. In *cantó* it is the final stressed *ó* that signals Preterite, Indicative and 3s. In the current model the difference between Preterites and Imperfects is that the former are lexically stronger and can be processed as whole words.

A third phenomenon that lexical strength accounts for is lexical and inflectional split. In the example discussed in Chapter 4 from Pagliuca 1976, we saw that some words derived by prefixation of *pre-* have undergone semantic and phonological changes, while some have not. This cannot be accounted for in a model in which all words with the same affix are derived in exactly the same way. It requires a model in which a particular word, despite its present or former morphological complexity, can be autonomous and develop semantic and phonological peculiarities. The same argument applies to inflectional forms. If the pair *wend, went* is processed in exactly the same way as *bend, bent* and *spend, spent*, then it is impossible to explain why *went* is no longer associated with *wend*. Rather, it appears that *went* was more autonomous than its fellow class members, *bent* and *spent*, which led to its split from *wend*. Similarly, if all instances of *supposed* are processed in the same way, then there is no way to account for the development of modal-like [spowstə]. (Again, see Chapter 4.)

A fourth phenomenon which necessitates a notion of lexical strength is local markedness (Tiersma 1982). As noted in Chapter 3.5, Tiersma observes that the relationship between apparently basic / derived pairs is not always the same. In cases where the morphological "derived" form is actually more frequent due to real-world considerations, that form will behave as though it is autonomous, and in some cases will even become the basic member of the basic / derived pair.

Finally, consider a phenomenon we have not discussed before — the development of contracted forms. Zwicky and Pullum 1983 argue that contracted negative forms in English, e.g. *don't, won't, can't, shouldn't* etc. are independent of the non-contracted combinations *do not, will not*, etc. They point to irregularities of various sorts that suggest lexical representation — gaps in the paradigms, such as the absence of contracted forms for *am not* and *may not*; phonological irregularities such as the unpredictable phonological shape of *won't* and *don't*; and semantic differences between contracted and non-contracted forms. Undoubtedly, these contractions developed gradually from non-contracted combinations, and must have had autonomous lexical representations even when the semantic and phonological differences between them and the non-contracted forms were minimal. In fact, it is possible that such frequent combinations may have their own lexical representation even when their derivation by combination is still thoroughly transparent. Otherwise, it is difficult to explain how and why contractions would develop. The changes that occur in them later must stem from the speakers' acceptance of the sequences as autonomous units.

7.   Evidence for degrees of lexical connection

The only lexical connections relevant to present concerns are those parallel phonological and semantic connections that constitute a morphological relation. I have already presented the evidence, in Chapters 3 and 4, for varying degrees of morphological relatedness based on a hierarchy of morphological features. I will only briefly review this evidence here.

First, morpho-phonemic changes tend to eliminate alternations between forms that are most closely related, e.g. person/number forms in the same aspect or tense. Second, children acquiring an inflectional language create forms that show that they are basing their new creations on a known form that is very closely related, e.g. the 3s form of the same aspect or tense. Third, experimental evidence shows that adults tend to do the same thing when they are asked to create nonce forms. This evidence is discussed in Chapter 3, sections 2 and 3. Fourth, inflectional splits that lead to suppletion do not develop freely among any members of a paradigm, but rather tend to occur among forms that are least closely related, i.e. among aspect or tense distinctions, rather than among person/number forms. This evidence is discussed in Chapter 4.

While the degree of relatedness among inflectional forms depends largely on the amount of semantic change resulting from the addition of an element expressing a grammatical category, two other factors have some effect. The first is phonological differentiation. Where irregular morpho-phonemic differences exist between forms, the degree of morphological relatedness is lessened. This is simply accounted for by the fact that connections are stronger where the number of shared features is greater.

The second factor that affects the strength of morphological relations is token frequency: low-frequency items that are morphologically complex form stronger connections that high-frequency complex items. This is the way this model represents the fact that low-frequency items are analyzed and under-stood in terms of other items, while high-frequency words, complex or not, may be autonomous, and processed unanalyzed. The evidence that frequency affects the strength of morphological relations is that very high-frequency words are candidates for inflectional splits that lead to suppletive paradigms, while low-frequency words are not.

One final word concerning morphological relations: the strongest rela-tions are relations of identity. Relations of identity lead to non-autonomous representations, the mapping of one word onto an existing representation, strengthening it. Thus non-autonomous words form the strongest relations possible — they are not represented separately at all, but form relations of identity with autonomous words.

8. *The representation of a complex paradigm*

In Chapter 3, I argued that a paradigm is a cluster of closely-related words, in which one word is basic and the others "derived". In Chapter 4 and the present chapter, I have argued that morphologically-complex words or "derived" words may also have lexical representation. The lexical rep-resentation of a paradigm, then, is a cluster of words bearing both a semantic and phonological relation to one another, in which one word (and sometimes more than one) is stronger than the others. The stronger forms are basic, the most autonomous, and the weaker forms are in a dependent relation to the basic form(s). Consider now the representation of a complex paradigm, one with many forms, and with morpho-phonemic alternations. The follow-ing is a representation of part of the paradigm for the Spanish verb *dormir* "to sleep", which has three stem allomorphs.

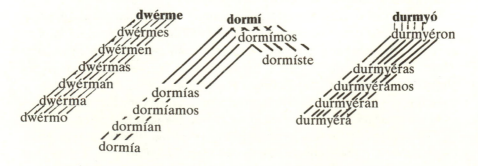

In this diagram, lines show how each word connects to a base, which is represented in bold type. The words are grouped in clusters representing close morphological relations. The least autonomous words, such as *dwermes* (2s Present), or *dwermen* (3p Present), may either have a very close relation to the base, as shown here by their position in the diagram, or they may be mapped directly onto the base. I will argue in the next section that the difference between a separate but very close relation and no separate representation is a very small difference.

In the diagram, the forms under *dwérme* are Present forms. The two forms close to *dormí*, which is 1s Preterite, are also Preterite, and the forms connected to *dormí* more distantly, Imperfect. The one form directly under *durmyó*, which is 3s Preterite, is 3p Preterite, while the more distantly spaced forms are Past Subjunctive. In this paradigm the mapping of formal similarity onto semantic similarity is not perfect. For example, the Preterite Indicative is split between two base forms, both *dormí* and *durmyó* are Preterite. Also the 1p forms of the Present Indicative and Subjunctive both diverge in base from other closely-related forms: the Indicative has *dormí* as its base and the Subjunctive has *durm* (i.e. it is *durmámos*). These forms will have phonological connections to one base and semantic connections to another. This situation is not all that unusual, given the fact that alternations arise for phonetic reasons, but it is a situation that is often corrected by morphophonemic leveling. Thus in many dialects, the 1p of the Present Subjunctive is *dwérmanos*, a form that is in line with other Present Subjunctive forms.[8]

There are three important points to note about the way this model represents a paradigm. First, all the bases are actual words, none are abstractions such as stems or roots. Furthermore, they are three of the four most frequent forms for verbs in Spanish. The four most frequent forms of this paradigm in descending order are:

3s Present Indicative / 2s Familiar Imperative: dwérme
3s Preterite Indicative: durmyó
1s Present Indicative: dwérmo
1s Preterite Indicative: dormí

Using three of these four forms, the entire inventory of overlapping sequences can be represented.

The second point concerns other strong members of the paradigm. The inflected words are listed in increasing frequency away from the bases, to show that the more autonomous words are less closely related to the base

word. Consequently, the last three words at the bottom are in themselves
fairly strong items. They are 1s Present Indicative *dwérmo*, 1s / 3s Imperfect
dormía, and 3s Past Subjunctive *durmyéra*. Note that each of these forms is
also a base form in a sense: as I argued in Chapter 3, the 1s Present Indicative
can serve as the base for the Present Subjunctive (and note that it shares a
back vowel with those forms); the 3s Imperfect can be used as a base to form
all other Imperfects, and the same can be said for the 3s Past Subjunctive.
If any of these three forms were to split from the rest of the paradigm, many
of the closely related forms (listed above them in the diagram) would follow.

The third point is that the bases strengthen each other, since they share
a number of phonological features. In particular, the sequence

    d [back vowel] rm

is the strongest sequence in the lexical entry. Occasionally this stem-like
sequence is needed to produce new combinations, such as the Italian form
vediamo, which replaced *veggiamo*, by adding the suffix *-iamo* to the regular
stem *ved-*. Furthermore, non-continuous elements can have high lexical
strength due to their frequent occurrence. The consonant structure of an
English Strong Verb, or a Semitic root, is the strongest part of the representation. The diagram above shows no relations among the bases. That diagram
can be given additional hierarchical structure as follows:

Unbroken lines indicate relations of identity, while broken lines indicate
shared features. In this case the *we* nucleus shares the backness feature with
o and *u*, and the final *e* is non-back like the *i* and *y*. The form with the highest
token frequency is listed as the strongest form, but this may not be correct.
The form *dormí* may be the stronger since it occurs in more different forms
(has a higher type frequency): it occurs in forms that were not listed above,
such as the infinitive, participle, the future and conditional forms.

While the model just presented was designed to account for the historical
and cross-linguistic regularities observed in paradigms, it accords well with
the experimental evidence on the processing of morphologically-complex

words. Stanners et al. 1979 tested the speed with which subjects could identify letter-strings as words of English. They found that the second presentation of the same word (even with several other words in between) shortened the time it takes for the word to be recognized. Furthermore, the identical effect is obtained if a regularly-inflected form of a word, such as *lifted*, is presented prior to *lift*. This suggests that the processing of *lifted* involves the processing of *lift*, and is compatible either with a model in which *lifted* is derived from *lift*, or one in which the representation of *lifted* is closely associated with *lift*. Kempley and Morton 1982 obtained the same result in auditory word recognition experiments.

A second interesting finding in the experiments by Stanners et al. is that priming with an irregular English Past Tense verb, such as *shook* or *hung*, also shortens the time it takes to recognize the base verb, *shake* or *hang*, but the effect of priming is less than with a regular verb. This supports our claim that morpho-phonemically irregular forms are more autonomous and less-closely related to the base than regular forms. Further, Stanners et al. found that it took longer to recognize (on first presentation) the Past form of an irregular verb, *hung*, than it took to recognize the base form, *hang*, even when these forms were the same length and of the same frequency. This suggests that the semantically basic form is the most autonomous, as argued in Chapter 3, and the Past form has a subordinate representation. Lukatela et al. (1980) argue for a very similar model (the "satellite-entry hypothesis") on the basis of word recognition experiments with Serbo-Croatian nouns, which show that the unmarked form, the nominative singular, is recognized faster than any other case forms.

9. *Cross-paradigmatic relations*

To this point, we have only considered paradigm-internal relations, but paradigms also relate to one another. The most obvious and general sort of relation is among the grammatical affixes of different paradigms. In the current model such relations can be treated as lexical connections, making the segmentation of complex forms into morphemes unnecessary. We must consider now whether there is evidence for or against morphological segmentation.

The fact that speakers can inflect nonce forms with regular affixes and can create new combinations of morphemes is not in itself an argument for the separate representation of affixes in the lexicon. Zager 1983 argues that the creation of words such as *workaholic*, based on nonce segmentation of *alcoholic*, demonstrates the ability of speakers to make new segmentations that would not be possible in a lexicon of morphemes where all segmentations are given.

There are many other reasons for not insisting upon the strict segmentation of words into morphemes. The common occurrence of overlapping morphemes and empty morphs show that speakers can handle words that do not yield to discrete segmentation. For instance, the velar consonant that appears in the 1s Present Indicative and throughout the Present Subjunctive of some Spanish verbs, such as *poner, ponga* and *crecer, cresca,* (see Chapter 3.4) is ambiguous in segmentation. It is in a sense part of the verb stem, restricted as it is to certain stems, but it is also part of the marker of certain inflectional categories. It would seem advantageous in such cases not to force a segmentation, but rather to use the notion of lexical connection developed in this model to associate the velar consonant to other instances of the velar in the same paradigm, as though it were part of the stem, and simultaneously to other instances of the velar in other paradigms, as though it were part of the inflectional affix. Similarly, segmentation problems surrounding "empty morphs" such as the *-ro* in Spanish 3p Preterites can be handled in this model. Thus, the *-n* of 3p *cantaron* can be associated with all other 3p markers, without leaving the problem of specifying the meaning of *-ro*.

To the extent that words have internal structure recognizable by the speaker / hearer, this structure can be represented using lexical connections which make segmentation unnecessary. For example, the internal structure of *unforgetable* can be described as a set of phonological and semantic connections to other words in which the three morphemes *un, forget,* and *able* occur. The appropriateness of this mode of representation derives from the fact that it is precisely by recognizing these morphemes in other words that one realizes that *unforgetable* has internal structure.

If we relate affixes across paradigms by means of lexical connections, then we are claiming that affixes have no existence or representation independent of the particular words to which they attach. For extremely productive affixes this claim may not be correct. The easy applicability of English plural *-s*, verb-inflecting *-ed* and *-ing*, and comparable affixes in other languages to new words suggests an independent representation. Such an independent representation does not entail, however, that there are no words stored with these affixes attached. An important point made by Peters 1983 on the basis of language acquisition data is that complex strings are not necessarily purged from the lexicon after they are analyzed by speakers into smaller parts. Thus an autonomous Past form, such as *wanted* may exist in the lexicon even though both *want* and *-ed* are also present.

Does this mean, then, that some regular verbs are derived by combination of a base and a suffix, while others can be accessed as a complex unit directly from the lexicon? It does indeed, but it should be noted that these two methods of arriving at an inflected form are not so very different from one another. Every base word identified as a verb automatically has associated with it the inflectional categories associated with verbs, so that if verbal suffixes have separate representations, they are still closely connected to verbal bases, in a sort of syntagmatic connection. If a regular verb does not have a representation for the Past Tense, it has something very close to such a representation — it has a base and an association to the verbal suffixes. If a verb does have a regular Past form represented, the stem of that verb is connected to the base representation, and the suffix is connected to the representation of the suffix. Accessing a regular Past form by either method entails accessing (at least indirectly) both the representation of the base verb and the suffix. The point I wish to make here is that from non-autonomous to fully autonomous is a continuum, with no discrete cut-off points.

10. *Morphological classes*

Morphological classes that undergo similar morpho-phonemic or morphological processes are also in the domain of lexical connections. For instance, the semi-productive Strong Verb class in English, exemplified by the verb *string, strung*, is defined by a clustering of lexical connections, termed a *schema* by Bybee and Slobin 1982. In Bybee and Slobin 1982 and Bybee and Moder 1983, we showed that the schema is a set of lexical connections among the *Past Tense* forms of these verbs, and that the schema connects the Past Tense vowels, as well as other properties of the whole word, such as the initial consonants and the final consonants. In fact, all the Past forms of this class are related by a varying number of connections to the prototypical member of this class, which appears to be *strung*. Once again, the leading connection is the semantic feature of past tense, and all the phonological connections mirror this semantic one. Consider the following diagram:

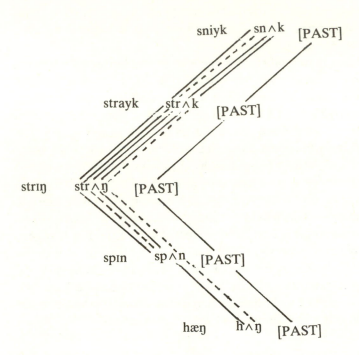

In the diagram, the base form of the verb is placed close to the Past form, and there will be connections among these forms. The connections that define classhood are among the Past forms, not among the base forms, nor among the relations between the base and Past forms. The motivation for this is discussed in Bybee and Moder 1983. There it is also shown that the most important defining feature of the class is the final consonant, suggesting that the sequence [ʌ] plus final velar and/or nasal is the marker for Past Tense in these verbs. This is precisely what the lexical connections shown in the diagram describe. Needless to say, it would be very difficult to represent such a notion in an Item and Arrangement or Item and Process grammar.

The connections illustrated by the *strung* class are quite strong — this class is still attracting new members, such as dialectal *snuck* and *brung*. In cases where morpho-phonemic alternations accompany the addition of affixes, and are only *indices* of categories rather than the actual markers for them, the connections that define classhood are considerably weaker, and in some cases not made at all. For instance, consider the stem alternations of the type illustrated by *dormir*, whose lexical representation was diagrammed above. This type of alternation occurs in other 3rd Conjugation verbs as well. There is one other, *morir* 'to die' that is like *dormir*, and a number of verbs with the same type of alternation, but among the front vowels, *e*, *i*, and *ye*.

The fact that these vowel alternants have the same distribution in several paradigms may be accounted for by lexical connections. But it is an empirical question whether speakers do or do not associate these alternations across lexical items. Many linguists assume that any regularity of distribution should be accounted for or else a "generalization" has been missed. But it is not necessarily the case that the generalizations that linguists detect are the same as the generalizations that the speakers internalize. Let us consider whether or not all regularities of distribution constitute valid generalizations.

First note that the data Tiersma presents on local markedness indicate that paradigms may not always have the same organization, despite similarities of formal structure. Second, note that, unlike the *strung* class, most morpho-phonemic alternations are *not* generalizable to new items. For instance, the extremely pervasive diphthong / mid vowel alternation of Spanish verbs is not extended to nonce items that are presented with a diphthong. The only way to get Spanish-speaking subjects to use an alternation in a nonce verb is to present the verb with two alternants (with one exception, to be mentioned below). Third, the most general rule is not always the one that speakers internalize. For instance, despite the fact that *dormir* and certain verbs with front vowels, such as *sentir*, have a completely parallel conjugation, Bybee and Pardo 1981 found that subjects would generalize with a nonce verb with a front vowel, responding to Infinitive *rentir* with 3s Preterite *rintió* (note the vowel change) 55% of the time, but produced the corresponding change in *sornir* to give *surnió* only 4% of the time. While linguists have always assumed that more general rules (in this case, covering front and back vowels) are preferable to less general (covering only front vowels), this is not necessarily true of morpho-phonemic alternations. Such alternations are heavily bound to particular lexical items, and do not necessarily involve generalization across lexical items. Further evidence for this is the fact that the leveling of alternations takes place one item at a time, and does not affect blocks of lexical items simultaneously.

In many cases, then, lexical connections among paradigms with similar alternations are not justified. Where they are justified, they can be made in the way illustrated for the *strung* class: forms with the same semantic features indicating morphological categories are associated with one another. Parallel phonological connections are also made. For instance, 3s Preterite *sintió* is connected with 3s Preterite *mintió* through the suffix vowel, as well as through the identical high front vowel of the stem.

By treating cross-paradigm morpho-phonemic similarities with lexical connections, I am claiming that connections on the level of expression are very similar in nature to connections on the semantic level. One suggestion that this is correct is the fact that morphological classes, such as the *strung* class, and others, such as the Spanish strong Preterites, have the structure of Roschian natural categories (Zager 1980, Bybee and Moder 1983). That is, they have the same structure as natural semantic categorizations.

11. *Productivity*

Wherever there are alternate processes for expressing the same categories in a language, there are differences in the degree of productivity of the processes. For example, in English Past Tense formation, suffixation of an alveolar stop is fully productive, the use of the *strung* schema is productive within a restricted domain, and most other vowel change methods are unproductive. In this section I will address the question of what determines productivity, and how productivity should be represented in the model being developed here.

As for representation, the concept of lexical strength would appear to be applicable: the most frequently-used phonological sequence associated with Past is the productive one. There is a problem, however, in making this most direct application of lexical strength to grammatical morphemes. The problem is that the irregular and non-productive methods of Past Tense formation occur among the most common verbs of the language. Indeed, in Old English, a much larger number of verbs, including the most frequent, used ablaut for Past Tense formation, and yet the suffixation rule was able to take over and become fully productive. Let us turn to some data on the acquisition of French that allows us to state the problem clearly.

Guillaume 1927 observed that the innovations in verb forms created by children acquiring French most commonly involved a regularization, in particular the use of First Conjugation suffixes with verbs of other conjugations. Of course, this is not surprising, since First Conjugation is the open-ended, productive conjugation. Guillaume further studied the rate of occurrence of verbs of each conjugation in children's speech. He observed nursery school children talking among themselves during play, and counted the number of verbs occurring in their speech. The following table shows the number of occurrences of each conjugation class, and the number of verbs used from each conjugation class:

Conjugation class	Number of uses		Number of verbs	
First (*chanter*)	1,060	36.2%	124	76.0%
Second (*finir*)	173	6.0%	10	6.1%
Third (*vendre*)	1,706	57.8%	29	17.9%

The point to focus on in this table is the fact that Third Conjugation verbs account for more than half the number of tokens or "uses" in the children's conversation. However, the number of *verbs* that actually occur in these uses differs widely: there were 124 First Conjugation verbs used, but only 29 Third Conjugation verbs. This means that First Conjugation has a high *type* frequency, although most of the individual verbs in that class have a low *token* frequency. Productivity of morphological rules must be connected to high type frequency, or as MacWhinney 1978 phrases it, high applicability.

How can the present model account for the development of productivity? Morphological markers associated with Third Conjugation have the highest token frequency, so in terms of lexical strength they would be the strongest if it were not for the fact that lexical connections among low-frequency items are stronger than those among high-frequency items. That is, high-frequency items tend to be stored as whole autonomous units, while low-frequency items are stored with strong connections to other items. Stated differently, speakers analyze low-frequency items more than high-frequency items. Thus they tend to associate First Conjugation suffixes more strongly with one another than they do Third Conjugation suffixes, and this leads to a greater lexical strength for First Conjugation suffixes.

These findings make predictions for changes in class membership. The morphological and morpho-phonemic patterns found in a few very high-frequency items will not spread to other items as readily as those patterns that are found in a larger number of medium- and low-frequency items. A case in point is the *strung* class in English. It contains fewer high-frequency and more medium-frequency verbs than all the other strong verb classes, and, as we pointed out above, is the most productive. Similarly, in the nonce-probe experiment on Spanish verbs, it was found that subjects could not extend patterns that occurred in only one or two very frequent verbs, but were more successful in extending patterns occurring in a larger number of verbs (Bybee and Pardo 1981). This further suggests that if a class contains both high-frequency and medium-frequency items, it is the medium-frequency items that contribute most to the productivity of the class, and to the establishment of the parameters that define the class.

12. *Summary of the proposed model*

Here is a summary of some of the properties of the proposed model:

1. Words are represented in the lexicon as having varying *lexical strength*. Lexical strength is increased each time a phonological and semantic match have been made between a stored word and a word in processing.

2. Morphologically-complex words that are regular and not of high frequency are mapped onto representations with the same semantic features and a shared substring of phonological features. A word with a suffix, such as *played* is mapped both onto *play* and the Past Tense suffix.

3. High frequency morphologically-complex words, and irregular morphologically-complex words have their own lexical representations, but are associated with morphologically-related words by means of *lexical connections* of both a phonological and semantic nature.

4. Lexical connections (and therefore morphological relations) vary in closeness according to the number and nature of the feature(s) consistuting the connection.

13. *Conclusion*

In this chapter I have discussed the consequences of the notions of autonomy and degree of relatedness for a model of lexical representation. This model accounts for a wider range of phenomena than most models of lexical representation in that it can account for the distribution of alternations and suppletion among morphologically-related forms. It takes into account the gradient phenomena of word frequency and degree of morphological relatedness, neither of which have a place in Item and Process, Item and Arrangement or Word and Paradigm models. This model is not intended to select *the* grammar of the ideal speaker-hearer, but rather to make testable predictions about the general properties of lexical representation. Further, the mechanisms behind the central notions of *lexical strength* and *lexical connection* are not specifically *linguistic* mechanisms. Rather they are general principles applicable to other types of human psychological processing. Lexical strength is an instance of the principle that repetition increases mental or physical facility, and lexical connection is a consequence of the fact that humans organize their environment into relations of similarity and dissimilarity.

NOTES

1. Experimental evidence is applied only sporadically to theoretical issues by some linguists. For instance, Kiparsky and Menn 1977 brush aside certain production experiments by Ohala and others, saying that their results are due to a "strangeness effect" in the experimental situation and have nothing to do with normal speech. On the other hand, they accept experimental results that were obtained with written stimuli as somehow applicable to normal speech. In the same article they exclude acquisition data when it does not suit their theory, saying that "the rules of early phonology ... are not hypotheses about data but figments of the child..." (1977:73).

2. Of course, there is a word *glue* in English, but the experimenter felt sure that that was not the word the subject had produced.

3. Vennemann 1978 present evidence from Sanskrit that the restructuring of certain sandhi processes could not occur unless inflected words (in this case, words with an alternation) have their own lexical representations.

4. The spread of a suffix from the Subjunctive to the Indicative goes against the claims made in Chapter 3 concerning the directionality of morpho-phonemic change, which should be from the basic member of the category to the derived member. The present instance is probably a case of "local markedness", discussed in Chapter 3. The 1p of Present Indicative is one of the least frequent of Present Indicative forms. It is possible that the 1p of the Present Subjunctive is more frequent due to its use in the hortative or imperative sense, of e.g. "let's ---". Note further that since *-iamo* first spread to all conjugation classes in the Subjunctive, even though it was used only in the Subjunctive, it was probably more frequent than any other 1p marker.

5. With Peters 1983 I am abandoning the idea that the items in the lexicon are all either morphemes or words, and accepting the idea that units of different sizes may be represented. Except for some very productive affixes, there is little evidence for sequences any smaller than the word, and there is evidence of various sorts that the word is a unit with psychological reality. For instance, the word is the relevant unit for lexical diffusion of sound change.

6. Other verb classes were not suitable for this comparison because too few of their members have survived into Modern English.

7. Zero marking, which tends to occur on the most frequent and less conceptually marked items, can be considered an extreme case of fusion.

8. The change in stress and stem vowel is always accompanied by a change from the 1p suffix *-mos* to *-nos* in these particular dialects.

PART II

ASPECT, TENSE AND MOOD INFLECTIONS
IN THE LANGUAGES OF THE WORLD

Introduction to Part II

Part II of this book contains the results of a survey of verbal morphology in 50 languages, with particular attention to the coherence of the categories in general and the meanings expressed within these categories. The cross-linguistic comparison of the content of morphological categories must allow for differences among languages, and it is our task as linguists to discover the systematicity in these differences. In the following chapters I continue to elaborate the principles discussed in the previous chapters, in order to arrive at a coherent way of understanding how languages differ in verbal morphology. Again we will find correspondences between the meanings of morphological units and their modes of expression.

Throughout this book I have presented inflectional morphology as a range on a scale that extends from lexical expression on one pole to syntactic or periphrastic expression on the other. In Chapter 4 the difference between derivational and inflectional expression was discussed in detail. There we saw that one of the main parameters along which inflection and derivation differ is *lexical generality*. Inflectional processes have high lexical generality, which means that they are applicable to all or nearly all lexical stems of major categories such as Noun or Verb, while derivational processes have semantic, phonological or arbitrary restrictions on their applicability to lexical stems. Of course, inflectional processes also differ with respect to their lexical sensitivity, and they are considered to be more like derivational processes if they produce stem changes, have lexically-governed allomorphy, suppletive forms or defective paradigms.

A similar comparison can be made between inflectional and syntactic expression. The parameter along which inflectional and syntactic expression differ has to do primarily with the amount of *semantic content* in a single morpheme. It is universally accepted that grammatical meaning is highly abstract and very general compared to the more concrete semantic content of ordinary nouns and verbs. In fact, much of the effort of linguists goes towards trying to characterize the abstract meaning of particular grammatical morphemes. A correlate of such abstract meaning is the very wide range of contexts in which a grammatical morpheme can be used, or is required, compared to lexical morphemes. Another correlate is the number of items in a contrast set: lexical sets of nouns and verbs are large and open to accept new members; grammatical contrast sets contain a small number of members and are open to new members only under special circumstances.

Languages documented over long periods of time show that the evolution of grammatical morphemes out of lexical ones involves the gradual erosion of lexical meaning into abstract grammatical meaning, the concommitant extension of the range of usage, the attrition of the contrast set, and the phonological reduction and fusion of form. However, we do not have to reach back into the distant past to find examples, as this process occurs continuously throughout the development of a language. For instance, English *gonna* has developed out of the phrase *going to*, which originally signalled concrete movement toward a goal. *Gonna* has lost the sense of concrete movement, and in some contexts has even lost its sense of goal-directedness, now signalling a simple *future*. Consequently, it can be used in a wider range of contexts than *go*, as for example, with subjects whose referents are inherently unable to move and incapable of pursuing goals, as in *The tree is going to lose its leaves*, or with dummy subjects, as in *It's gonna be a long wait*. The contrast set of *gonna* is not the full range of main verbs, but rather the set of modals or quasi-modals that precede main verbs.

It helps to understand the cross-linguistic data if we assume that the same type of change continues even after a morpheme qualifies as inflectional. Thus we find differences in the amount of semantic content of inflectional morphemes across languages, and these differences correlate with the degree of fusion and formal reduction. Thus not only can we predict that the amount of semantic content of a morpheme correlates with the number of members in its contrast set, but we can also predict that a morpheme with more semantic content will have a more transparent and peripheral expression with respect to the verb stem, and that it will manifest less fusion with the stem.

The following discussion, then, is based on the hypothesis that *inflection* touches on derivation on one side and syntactic expression on the other. This hypothesis makes possible a useful comparison of inflectional categories across languages. The hypothesis does not predict that the meanings expressed across languages will be the same, rather it predicts that they will vary in degree of specificity. For each morphological category, the data will be examined in search of evidence in support of the existence of viable cross-linguistic categories. The meanings and expression types in each category will be compared. The discussion includes a consideration of the related categories of *aspect, tense* and *mood*. *Valence, voice* and *agreement* are not discussed in detail, since a useful discussion of these categories necessarily involves the wider syntactic context, not just the verbal morphology.

CHAPTER 6: ASPECT

This chapter and the following ones compare the meanings or functions of particular grammatical morphemes across languages. The discussion is not meant to imply that any two morphemes in two different languages have precisely the same range of uses or functions. Indeed, the comparison is only a rough one, and depends a great deal on the quality of the analyses of the particular languages. In the survey, the general procedure was to examine the comments made by the author, as well as the examples and their translation, and if, for example, a morpheme appeared in a variety of functions that are usually associated with the *imperfective* (i.e. continuous, habitual, durative), then the morpheme was labelled an *imperfective*. If it appeared to be restricted to one of these functions, it was given a more specific label, but the particular label used by the author did not necessarily influence the categorization of the morpheme. (As throughout, the meaning labels that are intended to be universal are written in lower case, while the language-particular labels for morphemes are written with an initial capital letter.)

This chapter is organized as follows: first the more frequent inflectional distinctions — *perfective / imperfective* and *habitual / continuous* — are discussed, and then two common meanings that often have derivational expression — *inceptive* and *iterative* — are discussed. Some general remarks about the coherence of aspect as a category follow. The meaning often referred to as the "perfect" is not discussed in this section, but is discussed later (7.3) in connection with *tense*.

1. *Perfective / imperfective, habitual / continuous*

The distinction which is usually labelled *perfective / imperfective* is the most common inflectional aspectual distinction in the languages of the sample, and the distinction between *habitual* and *continuous* is the next most common. There is ample evidence that these are cross-linguistically valid parameters of grammatical meaning, and further that the two parameters are related.

The following languages were identified as having a *perfective / imperfective* distinction: Basque, Burushaski, Georgian, Iatmul, Kiwai, Logbara, Nahuatl, Pawnee, Sierra Miwok, Serbo-Croatian, Temiar, Touareg, Yanomama, and Yukaghir.[1]

Most often, the meaning behind this distinction was described as "completed" versus "not completed" activity or event. Other terms used for *perfective* are "punctual", "momentaneous", "unique" and "limited". The *imperfective* could be described by putting "non" in front of one of these terms, or by the terms "durative" or "continuous", though I attempted to ascertain whether "habitual" could also be included in *imperfective* before labelling it as that rather than as *continuous*. It is important to note that the same event can be framed as perfective or imperfective. Consider these simple examples from Spanish:

Perfective: *Llovió* ayer. "It rained yesterday."
Imperfective: *Llovía* sin parar. "It rained continuously."

The first sentence presents the event as one complete entity, while the imperfective sentence not only describes a continuing situation, but also gives the impression that it is setting the scene for some further discourse. Indeed, the function of aspect is to allow the temporal dimensions of a situation to be described from different points of view depending on how the situation is intended to fit into the discourse.

The languages in which a *habitual* contrasts with a *continuous* expressed inflectionally are: Kiwai, Maasai, Nahuatl, Pawnee, Sierra Miwok, Tarascan, and Zapotec.[2] For example, in Zapotec (Pickett 1953 :220) the following contrast exists:

Habitual: *ru* - ka?a - beé   habit + write + 3s human "he writes"
Continuous: *ku* - ka?a - beé   cont + write + 3s human "he is writing"

Note that distinctions between these two meanings that are expressed by free morphemes, such as auxiliary constructions, are common but are not included here.

Morphemes coded as *habitual* were easily identified because precisely this term or the term "customary" was used in all cases. *Continuous* might be described variously as "continuing activity", "durative" or "progressive". Comrie 1976 proposes to distinguish between "continuous" and "progressive" in that the latter term only refers to progressive meaning that is restricted to non-stative verbs. However, given the quality of the information available on these languages, I was not able to consistently apply this distinction.

In Korean, a *continuous* inflection was identified, and in Garo, a suffix glossed as "still", but in both cases, no other general aspects are mentioned, so it is difficult to learn what these morphemes contrast with. In Tiwi and Kiwai, a *continuous* inflection contrasts with a *repetitive*. (But see footnote 2). Pawnee has what Parks labels a Usitative in addition to a Habitual. The two aspects differ in form: the first is a preverb and the second a suffix, but both usually occur with the Imperfect verb form. The Usitative is for activites that are usual or customary, even if they occur only now and then.

2. *Formal correlates of generality of meaning*

An *imperfective* morpheme that covers both *habitual* and *continuous* functions is semantically more general than a morpheme that covers only one of these functions. This follows from the fact that if the morpheme covers both of these meanings, it can be used in more contexts than one that is restricted to one or the other meaning. The diachronic progression here, and generally in the development of grammatical meaning, is from the more specific meaning to the more general. For this particular case, Comrie 1976 reports that one diachronic source for a general imperfective marker is a periphrastic continuous or progressive that has generalized to cover habitual functions as well. He cites this development in Celtic, and Yoruba, and Marchese 1979 discusses cases of similar developments in Kru languages. If this semantic generalization is paralleled by phonological reduction and fusion, then we can expect to find a correlation between the degree of semantic generalization of a morpheme and its mode of expression. Comparing the more general *imperfective* with the more specific *habitual* and *continuous*, the languages of the sample give evidence for the following three predictions made by this hypothesis:

First, if imperfectives have undergone more development than habitual or continuous morphemes, then they will exhibit a greater morpho-phonemic fusion with the verb stem. In particular, stem changes conditioned by the *perfective / imperfective* distinction will be more common than stem changes associated with the *habitual / continuous* distinction. This prediction is strongly confirmed in the language sample. In Burushaski, Kiwai, Nahuatl, Pawnee, Sierra Miwok, Serbo-Croatian, Temiar, and Touareg there are stem changes mentioned in connection with forming the general *perfective / imperfective* distinction. However, Sierra Miwok is the only language in the sample that also has a stem change associated with the *habitual / continuous* distinction.

Second, in languages that have both the general contrast, *imperfective / perfective*, and the more specific contrast, *habitual / continuous*, there might be evidence that the more specific morphemes have developed more recently. In a few languages, the fact that the *habitual / continuous* distinction is a subdivision of the *imperfective* is neatly diagrammed by the formal morphology. In Nahuatl, the Imperfective is formed by changes on the end of the stem (in the following example from *a* of the Imperfective to *h* of the Perfective), and in addition to this the "customary present" is marked with a suffix, to distinguish it from the unmarked present.

1s Present Indicative: ni + choloa "I flee, I jump"
1s Customary Present: ni + choloā + ni
1s Preterite Indicative: ni + choloh

In Pawnee, the Habitual suffix is added to a verb that is already marked with the Imperfective suffix, and it follows the Imperfective suffix. In both of these cases, the imperfective marker is closer to the stem than the habitual marker. These facts suggest a more recent development for the *habitual / continuous* distinction, and perhaps a different source for it as well.

A third correlate of generality of meaning is membership in a smaller contrast set: the more general a meaning is, the fewer items it contrasts with. However, since *perfective / imperfective* and *habitual / continuous* each form a two-way contrast, it would seem difficult to show that the more specific markers belong to larger contrasts sets. However, it turns out that whenever aspectual distinctions occur in the same distribution set as mood markers, that is, whenever they occur in the same position as mood markers, and are mutually exclusive with them, it is the more specific meanings that are coded. For instance, in Zapotec, aspectual morphemes belong in a contrast set that contains six prefixes. The meanings of these prefixes are Potential (*s/he'll probably write*), Perfective (*s/he has written*), Incompletive (*s/he will write*), Completive (*s/he wrote*), Habitual (*s/he writes*), Unreal (*if only s/he would write* or *s/he ought to have written*), and Continuative (*s/he is writing*). Thus in this large distributional set, the aspectual meanings are the more specific ones — *habitual* and *continuous*. In Pawnee, the Imperfective is divided into the Intentive, Habitual, Inchoative and a zero-marked member. Here the Perfective and Imperfective form a two-way contrast, while the more specific aspects belong in a four-member set. In Sierra Miwok there is more than one verb formation that codes aspect. In one of these patterns, a general perfective / imperfective distinction contrasts only with the "Volitional", which is a very general mood used for commands, requests, etc. In another pattern, the Continuative and Habituative occur, and they contrast with a Future, Recent Past, Andative ("going to do"), Venitive ("coming to do"), Revenitive ("coming again to do") and a Negative. In all of these examples, the general *imperfective* occurs in a distribution set that includes only one other member — the *perfective*, while the *habitual* and *continuous* occur in distributional sets that contain more members with more specific meanings.

These facts suggest a correlation between meaning and mode of expression that goes beyond those discussed in the preceding chapters. Here the relevant parameter is generality of meaning — a parameter that is not clearly defined for all categories, but one that is surely worth further inquiry. Note that here we have only discussed differences among markers that are inflectional, i.e. that are bound to the verb. But our findings make predictions for the meanings expressed periphrastically as well, because just as we found the more general meanings to be more common in inflection, we would expect to find the more specific, less-reduced meanings to be more common in periphrastic constructions. Thus a survey of the meanings expressed in verbal auxiliary constructions should turn up the *habitual / continuous* distinction more often than the more reduced *perfective / imperfective* distinction.

3.   *Perfective / imperfective* and the inflectional - derivational scale.

As pointed out in Chapter 4, the expression of the *perfective / imperfective* distinction can range from derivational to inflectional. Furthermore, this distinction can apparently arise diachronically either through the grammaticization of periphrastic constructions or through the generalization of derivational morphology. For the former case, Comrie 1976 cites the Scots Gaelic construction of a locative preposition with a verbal noun, which originally had a progressive meaning, but which now is used as a general imperfective. In addition, a perfective can develop, as the French *passé composé* has, from an auxiliary verb (such as *have*) construction with a past participle. Examples of aspect developing from derivational morphology are found in Serbo-Croatian and Georgian, where locative prefixes generalize lexically and take on aspectual meaning, coming progressively closer to being inflection. These latter examples are comparable to the perfectivizing particles in English, such as *up* in *drink up* versus *drink*; *eat up* versus *eat*, etc. Not surprisingly, then, the languages surveyed lie at various points along the scale which ranges from derivational to inflectional.

On the inflectional end are Iatmul, Pawnee and Yanomama, which each have simple suffixes that indicate the *perfective / imperfective* distinction, with little allomorphy (although the Pawnee suffix for Imperfective lengthens the preceding stem vowel). In Logbara, aspect is signalled by a change in the tone pattern of the verb (there are no other inflections on verbs in Logbara), and conditions a different word order for subject, object and verb.

In Nahuatl, Burushaski and Touareg, the *imperfective / perfective* distinction is central to the whole conjugational system. In Nahuatl and Burushaski the aspects are derived by making changes to the end of the verb stem, while in Touareg different vowel patterns are found interdigitated with the consonantal root. All three of these systems are characterized by a great deal of irregularity in the formation of the aspects, which makes them resemble derivation.

Georgian, Serbo-Croation and Temiar also have highly irregular formations of the perfective / imperfective distinction, and in these languages aspect would appear to be at least partially determined lexically, since there are verbs that do not have both aspects. In Serbo-Croatian and Georgian the Perfective, which is formed with prefixes, more closely resembles derivation, because the prefixes often add meaning other than that of aspect. On the other hand, the Imperfective in Serbo-Croatian, formed by suffixation, appears more like inflection.

In Kiwai the aspect of a verb is determined by its final vowel, and not all verbs can be used in both aspects. At this point on the scale it is very difficult to decide whether the perfective / imperfective distinction should be considered derivational or inflectional. In Quileute the distinction was considered derivational because the verbal classifiers associated with aspect do not appear with all verbs, and they do not always have the same predictable meaning.

The *perfective / imperfective* distinction can be contrasted, then, with the *habitual / continuous* distinction in that the former can be expressed derivationally, or have properties of derivational expression, while the latter distinction seems never to be expressed derivationally. In 4.5.1, it was argued that this difference is due to the difference in the *relevance* of these meanings to the meanings of verb stems. *Habitual* and *continuous* meanings do not combine with semantic components denoting events or activities to produce meanings that describe distinct events or activities, while *perfective* (and perhaps *imperfective*) meaning does.

4. *Markedness values*

Several authors (Jakobson 1957, Friedrich 1974, Comrie 1976) have tried to establish markedness values for aspect in particular languages. All have agreed that the various indicators of markedness are often in conflict when applied to aspect. Indeed, the data presented in Chapter 3 concerning the distribution of zero-markers in the various categories show that the distribution of zeroes in aspect is the *least* consistent of all the categories tested. (Perfective is zero-marked 41% of the time, imperfective 15%, habitual 12.5%, and continuous not at all.) The reason for this lies in the fact that aspect is closely related to the inherent lexical meaning of the verb. Languages do not show one aspect as clearly unmarked and the other marked because for some verbs (in particular, activity verbs and stative verbs), imperfective is the conceptually unmarked member, while for other verbs (in particular, telic or event verbs), perfective is the conceptually unmarked member.

Aspect, then, is highly subject to "local markedness". In fact, the more a morphological distinction affects the inherent meaning of the verb, the less clear the general markedness values will be. For instance, since *valence* is an extremely important component of the meaning of any verb, the question of whether transitive or intransitive is the unmarked member of the category simply cannot arise: some verbs are inherently transitive and may have intransitivizing morphology, while others are inherently intransitive and have transitivizing morphology. On the other extreme, a category such as *mood* usually has an identifiably zero-marked member, most commonly the indicative (61% in the present sample), but also often the imperative (28% in the present sample). This is because verbs do not differ lexically as to their mood. The evident conclusion is that general markedness theory should not be applied to categories that may have lexical expression. For these categories the notion of local markedness should be further developed.

5. *Inceptive aspect*

This section concerns morphological elements that indicate the beginning of a situation, or entrance into a state. Inchoative, Ingressive and Inceptive are all terms used for such a meaning. For example, Latin had a suffix -*sc*-, with the meaning "to become" or "to begin to". When applied to a verb such as *dormiō* "I sleep" it produced *obdormiscō* "I fall asleep", and when applied to *amō* "I love" it produced *amascō* "I begin to love". Such morphemes are common in the languages of the world, and yet they rarely qualify as inflectional morphemes, and they rarely form contrasts with other aspectual morphemes in the same language.

Comrie 1976 points out that one of the meanings covered by a general *perfective* in many languages is precisely this inceptive meaning. When a perfective inflection occurs with a stative verb, the resulting meaning refers to the onset of the state. Thus the Spanish verbs *saber* "to know" and *conocer* "to know a person or place", when used in the Preterite mean "found out" in the former case, and "got to know" or "became acquainted with" in the latter. But there are also specific morphemes in various languages that handle only this function. In the current sample there were at least five languages with bound markers of *inception*.[3]

In the previous section we pointed out that *habitual* and *continuous* are subdivions of the *imperfective*, and that in some languages of the sample their formal marking diagrams this relation. If the *inceptive* is similarly a subdivision of the *perfective*, then the formal marking of *inceptive* would show its subordinate relation to the *perfective*. On the contrary, however, the marking of *inceptive* shows it to be thoroughly independent of the *perfective*, and in most cases, to be independent of the rest of the aspectual system of the language. For example, in Pawnee, there is a different Inchoative formation for verbs of state versus other verbs. The Inchoative for verbs of state is further inflected for the Perfective / Imperfective distinction. The following examples are from Parks 1976 :200, 205-206.

/ti + kahuru:s + a:r + Ø/ → tikahuru:sa "it got pithy"
ind + pithy + incho + perf

/ti + rikau:s + a:r + i/ → tirika?u:sa:ri "he is becoming greedy"
ind + greedy + incho + imp

The Inchoative for active verbs is added to the *imperfective* form of the verb.

/ta + t + karu:ci + hus + itik/ → tatkaru:ci:usitit "I started putting it in"
ind + 1s + put + imperf + incho

This would hardly be the case if the Inchoative was in a subset relation with the perfective.

A typical interaction of the inceptive with other aspects is shown in Yugakhir, where an inceptive suffix may be used with both stative and active verbs, and these verbs are further inflected for perfective / imperfective. Here the inceptive is formed with a bound form of the verb "to do" placed between the stem and the suffixes. In Maasai, stative verbs occur only in the present (habitual) tense, the addition of the inceptive suffix makes it possible for the verb to occur in the past tense. In Kiwai, a prefix added to the Past tense form of the verb signals an action begun but not completed. This prefix may appear on verbs of either perfective or imperfective aspect. In general, then, it appears that the inceptive does not form a part of the general aspectual systems of these languages, and certainly does not form a subpart of the perfective in the sense that the habitual forms a subpart of the imperfective. Indeed, in Maasai and other languages the inceptive is explicitly designated a derivational category.

In general, inceptives are not integrated into the inflectional aspect system. An example to the contrary is Pawnee, where the Inchoative seems to contrast with the Habitual in the Imperfective. Another possible case is Tiwi, where the inceptives are described as inflectional. The aspectual system of this language is highly unusual in that it has a Durative, Repetitive, Moving (meaning "to do while moving about"), a Beginning and an Inceptive aspect. These latter two inceptive aspects are produced by adding markers to the Moving aspect. The Beginning aspect is glossed as "to be just starting to do something" and the Inceptive is "to be just about to do something". Neither of these can occur in the past tense, and indeed, the Beginning aspect always co-occurs with the Future prefix. These restrictions suggest that these inceptive aspects are not fully integrated into the aspectual system.

While the survey reported on here concentrated on verbal inflection, in a few cases I noted that inceptive meaning was coded grammatically by auxiliaries, some of which were very similar in their original meanings. For instance, in Iatmul, an Inceptive construction, glossed "to be about to" is formed with the verb "to go". Interestingly, in some languages, the source of the inceptive as a verb of movement is also evident in some of the bound morphology. For example, the Inchoative for active verbs in Pawnee is identifiable as the verb "to go down". The morpheme referred to above in Kiwai is the same as the verb "to go", as noted by Ray 1933. And, as we noted just above, the two inceptives in Tiwi are both formed using the suffix that indicates movement. In contrast to these formations, however, the inceptive suffix in Yukaghir comes from the verb "to do". Finally, note that the source of the inceptive or inchoative for stative verbs is a verb meaning "to become" in Pawnee.

The grammatical expression of inceptive meaning is not as frequent as other meanings related to aspect, but it occurs often enough to justify its consideration as a universal of grammatical meaning. Furthermore, a distinction between inceptive for active verbs, and inceptive for stative verbs also appears justified since different forms are used for the two in Acoma and Pawnee, and in Maasai and Ainu inceptive applies only to stative verbs. On the other hand, the distinction made in Tiwi between "to be just starting" and "to be just about to" seems to be unique. Again we have found a correlation between meaning and expression type in that inceptive meaning is usually expressed by derivational rather than inflectional morphology.

6. *Iterative aspect*

A verbal marker that gives *iterative* or *repetitive* meaning to the verb was found in fifteen of the 50 languages of the sample. This aspect is also usually derivational and usually is not integrated fully into the inflectional aspectual system. The languages that have a bound marker of *iteration* are: Acoma, Diegueño, Garo, Kiwai, Kutenai, Kwakiutl, Nahuatl, Navaho, Ojibwa, Pawnee, Sierra Miwok, Songhai, Susu, Tiwi, and Yukaghir.

As an example, consider the suffix *-ti* in Kiwai (Ray 1933), which gives *arigiti* "to scratch one repeatedly" from *arigi* "to scratch", and *iiriti* "to put in a bag often" from *iiria* "to put in a bag". Or, the Garo suffix *dap-dap*, which means "more and more, again and again", as in *c'a-dap-dap-a* "to eat more and more, this and that" (Burling 1961). In Diegueño, Nahuatl and Pawnee the iterative can also at times signal distribution of action, as in the Pawnee example with the prefix /wa:/, [wa:wius] "to defecate here and there".

In all but one of these languages, the iterative morpheme is clearly a derivational morpheme. It is either described as being derivational, or it is described as having unpredictable meaning or restricted distribution. Only in Tiwi is it described as an inflectional morpheme of aspect. However, this morpheme, which Osborne labels a Repetitive, may also be used for *habitual* meanings, and thus probably has a more general meaning than the other iteratives found in the sample.

The reason that iterative morphemes are derivational rather than inflectional is that the meaning of iteration or repetition, strictly speaking, is only applicable to active verbs, and then only to certain types of active verbs, i.e., those which describe telic events, events that have identifiable endings. In fact, the range of use of some of the morphemes described as iterative may be broader, as for instance, in the case of the Garo suffix attached to the verb "to eat", but we would have to know whether the suffix forces a telic interpretation on "eat". The gloss given by Burling "to eat more and more, this and that" suggests that it does.

As pointed out by Moravcsik 1978, iteration is sometimes signalled by reduplication. In the sample of languages surveyed, Kwakiutl, Nahuatl, Ojibwa, Sierra Miwok and Songhai have reduplication of the verb stem to signal iteration, and in Garo, the suffix itself is formed with two identical syllables. In Yukaghir, the suffix -nu signals iteration, and the reduplication of this suffix signals intense iteration. There is, furthermore, in Quileute the use of the reduplication of the verb as a frequentative, which is once in a while used with a true iterative meaning of repetition on a single occasion. Moravczik 1978 points out the correlation between reduplicative constructions and meanings having to do with increased quantity, and the iconicity of this relation seems very obvious. However, it should be stressed that in this stratified probability sample of languages, reduplication of the stem for iteration occurs in only five out of the fifteen languages identified as having an iterative. In the other ten, a non-iconic marker, such as a suffix or a prefix, is used to signal iteration.

Thus we see that *iterative* is a frequently-occurring grammatical meaning across languages. Unlike habitual and continuous, however, iterative is not integrated into the general inflectional aspectual system in the languages just discussed. Despite the conceptual affinity of iterative to the general imperfective, I did not find cases of iteratives marked as subdivisions of the imperfective. Indeed, an iterative morpheme may occur in a language that has no inflectional aspect at all, as is the case in Acoma, Diegueño, and Susu. And where there is inflectional aspect, the iterative stands outside the general system as a derivational rather than an inflectional category.

7. *Less usual meanings for "aspects"*

Occasionally one finds other meanings listed in grammars as "aspects". None of these qualify as aspects in the context of the present study, because they do not have anything to do with the temporal contours of the situation. For instance, the suffix in Tiwi that means "to do something while moving about" is classified as an aspect by Osborne, but conceptually it does not fit in with aspect, and indeed, it co-occurs rather than contrasts with the other aspects of Tiwi.

There are quite a variety of derivational morphemes classified by authors as "aspect". Quileute has a morpheme that signals a "sudden jerking action", and Nicoborese (Car dialect) has a morpheme that signals completed action, with the goal destroyed, and the action taking place in the direction of the jungle. One meaning that showed up in six different languages could be called a "diminutive". It means "to do something a little", as for instance, the Yukaghir suffix -*či*, as in *pande-či* "to cook a little". In Songhai, Maasai, Vietnamese and Tongan diminutive meaning can be signalled by reduplication. For example, Tongan *kata* means "to laugh", while *katakata* means "to laugh slightly or to smile". In no case, however, is this the only meaning signalled by reduplication. And it is clear that such meanings do not modify the temporal contours of a situation.

8.   *Aspect as a grammatical category*

On a language-specific basis, a grammatical category is identified by its formal or expression properties. For the purposes of cross-linguistic comparison, grammatical categories are classified according to the functions served by their members. To show that a category has cross-linguistic significance, one would have to show that a coherent set of concepts or functions have grammatical expression in a number of languages. When *aspect* is defined as distinguishing different ways of viewing the internal temporal constituency of a situation, it clearly qualifies as a grammatical category of cross-linguistic significance. Moreover, the particular contrasts expressed in this category when it is inflectional are cross-linguistically significant. Thus it is possible to give an even more specfic definition to *inflectional aspect*, as expressing one or both of the following two contrasts: that between a bounded or limited situation and an unbounded or in-progress situation, and that between an habitually-occurring and a merely continuing situation. Furthermore, as we saw earlier in this chapter, these two distinctions tend to be expressed in slightly different ways, i.e. the habitual / continuous distinction has more peripheral or less fused expression than the perfective / imperfective distinction.

I do not mean to suggest that other aspectual systems do not exist, for surely in detail aspectual systems differ from one another a great deal. The cross-linguistic evidence converges, however, to point to this system as the typical or core aspectual inflectional system. It is important to remember that only bound morphology has been considered here; that is, the generalizations made above hold for *inflectional* morphology. They will not extend in a direct way to non-bound grammatical markers.

There is also evidence for an *inceptive* meaning and an *iterative* meaning expressed cross-linguistically. Do these also qualify as members of the category *aspect*? While we can easily see a conceptual relation, as well as a functional overlap, in that imperfectives can have an iterative interpretation, and perfectives can have an inceptive interpretation, there is not much evidence to support the view that grammatically these two meanings are related to the general perfective / imperfective distinction.

NOTES

1. The major difficulty in identifying languages with inflectional aspect lies in distinguishing inflectional aspect from derivational. In some cases, in particular in Kiwai and Serbo-Croatian, it is not clear whether the perfective / imperfective distinction is inflectional or not.

2. The aspect in Tiwi that is labelled "Repetitive" by Osborne 1974 seems to be used as an habitual, and perhaps should be included in this list. This is mentioned again below.

3. Since inceptive markers are often derivational, and since some of the grammars used do not give an exhaustive listing of all derivational morphemes, the data in this case are not reliably quantifiable.

CHAPTER 7: TENSE

Inflections were considered to be tense markers only if their functions, as explicated by the author of the grammar and shown in the examples, indicated the relative *time* of the situation described by the verb. The functions included under tense were *present, past, future* and *anterior*. The appropriateness of this grouping will be examined in this chapter.

1. *Present and past*

An inflectional distinction between time simultaneous with the speech event and time prior to it was coded as a *present / past* distinction. Such a distinction was found in 36% of the languages in the sample. The languages that have this distinction marked as a verbal inflection are:

> Andamanese, Basque, Burushaski, Garo, Georgian, Iatmul, Kiwai, Korean, Kutenai, Maasai, Malayalam, Nahuatl, Ojibwa, Sierra Miwok, Tarascan, Timucua[1], Tiwi and Wappo.

The actual range of meaning covered by past and present morphemes across languages is fairly consistent. Some deviation from the meaning "simultaneous with the speech event" is found when presents are used for generics, for immediate futures, and for narratives in the past ("the historical present"). Past morphemes can be found in non-past contexts when they are used in conditional clauses.

In most cases the present tense is the unmarked or zero form. This is the case for at least some allomorph of the present in Basque, Garo, Georgian, Kutenai, Maasai, Nahuatl, Ojibwa, Sierra Miwok, Timucua, Tiwi and Wappo. The only two examples in the 50 languages of an unmarked past tense are in Gilyak and Iatmul.

Very few gradations in past time were found among the languages examined. Some languages were described as having a *remote past* and a *recent past*, but when the actual usage of the recent past was examined, it could be seen that it functioned as an *anterior* tense, (as for example in

Freeland's 1951 description of Sierra Miwok), and so was coded as anterior. These forms will be discussed in section 3. Finer gradations in temporal reference may also be derived from the interaction of the aspect markers with the tense markers in some languages, or by the combination of *anterior* with the other tenses. Comrie 1983 discusses examples of languages with as many as five degrees of remoteness from the moment of speech that do not result from combinations with aspects or with anterior. In some of his examples, the degrees of remoteness are signalled by auxiliary verbs. Examples of such fine distinctions in inflection are very rare.

2.   *Future*

Inflections placing the situation described by the verb at a time subsequent to the moment of speech are even more frequent than past tense inflections. Future inflections are found in 44% of the languages of the sample. They are:

> Andamanese, Basque, Burushaski, Diegueño, Garo, Georgian, Gilyak, Iatmul, Kiwai, Korean, Kutenai, Malayalam, Nahuatl, Navaho, Quileute, Sierra Miwok, Susu, Tarascan, Temiar, Tiwi, Yanomama, and Wappo.

Note that there are languages that have future inflections that do not have an inflectional *present / past* distinction. We will return to this point below.

Ultan 1978 surveyed future markers in a large number of languages. One of the findings that he reports is that future markers are often used in atemporal functions, especially functions associated with mood or modality. This was also quite clear in the present survey: several languages were found with markers whose primary function appeared to express *mood*, but which could also be used to express *future* time. Examples of such combinations of *mood* and *future* functions include markers of *possibility* or *probability* in Kiwai, Pawnee and Zapotec, markers of *intention* in Garo, Kiwai, Pawnee and Zapotec, markers of *desire* or *volition* in Goajiro, Quileute and Yanomama, and a marker of *incomplete action* in Zapotec. In the present survey, these forms were considered as coding moods rather than tense, unless their primary function was a temporal one. Admittedly, the decision regarding the "primary" function of a morpheme must be arbitrarily made in some cases. The results of any errors of this type in the present case would probably be that *fewer* inflections were coded as futures than are actually used as futures.

With these possible combinations of meanings, one can imagine that a language might have two or more future markers which differ from each other according to which of these modal nuances are included in their meaning. Indeed, this is the case in a few languages. Garo has a general future-time suffix which has an allomorph for positive contexts and one for negative contexts. In addition, Burling lists for Garo three suffixes which he says have approximately the same meaning, which is "immediate or intentional future", and a fourth suffix which corresponds to these but is used in negative sentences (Burling 1961:27). A dialect of Yanomama mentioned by Migliazza (1972:109) has a distinction between an "expected" future (which I assume is a plain future), and a "desired" future, one which implies some volition. Kiwai has three inflections labelled as futures: an Indefinite Future, an Immediate Future, and a Remote Future. The differences in the uses of these three futures is not explicated in any detail, and the examples are not particularly revealing. The distinctive features involved seem to be a certain versus a probable action in the future, and a very immediate (perhaps intentional) future versus a remote one. All three share a suffix, -ri, and differ from one another according to the person / number markers used, and by the occurrence of a prefix in the Remote Future.

The cross-linguistic data make it very clear that *future* inflections are independent of *present* and *past* inflections. There are seven languages in the sample that have a future inflection, but no present / past inflection: Diegueño, Gilyak, Navaho, Quileute, Susu, Temiar, and Yanomama. On the other hand, of the eighteen languages with a present / past inflection, only three lack an inflectional future: Ojibwa, Timucua (about which the data is very poor), and Maasai. While there is no general inflection for future in Maasai, there is what appears to be a residual future inflection, because some verbs have a special future form, which, incidentally, corresponds with the inceptive form used with stative verbs (Tucker and Mpaayei 1955: 62-63; 140-141). One could almost state that the presence of a present / past inflection in a language implies the presence of a future inflection, while the converse implication does not hold.

The independence of future inflections might indicate that the future does not belong in the same grammatical category as the present and past. The fact that futures often cover meanings that are not strictly temporal would support this view. If future is a separate category, then we might expect to find it marked differently in the languages that have future, present and past. For instance, we find that in Kiwai, Sierra Miwok and Tarascan, the future is not marked in the same affix position as present and past. However, there are a number of languages in which the future marking is parallel to the other tenses. Such is the case in Basque, Georgian, Garo, Iatmul, Kutenai, Korean, Malayalam, Nahuatl and Tiwi. For instance, in Malayalam, present, past and future are indicated by suffixes, as follows (George 1971:43):

	present	*future*	*past*
come	varunnu	varum	vannu
see	kaaNunnu	kaaNum	kaNTu
do	ceyyunnu	ceyyum	ceytu

In these languages, it appears that *tense* forms a coherent category consisting of present, past and future. So the data indicate that the future often forms a coherent formal category with the other tenses, although this is not necessarily the case.

Some authors have observed that the future is rather unstable as a grammatical tense. Fleischman 1982 studies the cyclic development of future markers in Indo-European languages, with a special emphasis on Romance languages. In Romance languages, such as Spanish and French, the earlier Latin synthetic future was replaced by a periphrastic construction of an infinitive plus a form of the auxiliary *haber*, as in Spanish *cantaré* or French *chanterai* "I will sing". But this form of the future is now being replaced in both Spanish and French by a new periphrastic construction with the verb *to go* (*aller* in French, *ir* in Spanish), the preposition *a* 'to', and the infinitive. Fleischman suggests that the rapid replacement of one future construction by another is due to the incorporation in the future meaning of modal and other notions which make meaning changes away from the temporal more likely.

Ultan 1978 also observes a difference in the expression types associated with future tenses. He finds in his cross-linguistic survey that future markers are more likely to be periphrastic than are past or present markers. In my survey, I looked for evidence that future affixes were less fused to the verb stem than past affixes, but was unable to find any clear differences.[2] However, I did note that there were more cases where the etymology of a future affix was still identifiable, while the source of past affixes is usually obscure. This suggests a more recent formation of the future, and converges with the idea that futures are reformed frequently, which would also explain their frequent occurrence as periphrastic forms.

The modal nuances, such as intention, desire or obligation that are sometimes associated with future tenses, are the residues of the meaning originally expressed by the construction from which the future evolves. Futures most commonly evolve from constructions expressing *obligation* or *necessity*, *desire*, and *movement* or *intention* (Ultan 1978, Fleischman 1982, Bybee and Pagliuca 1984). Modalities expressing these notions predicate conditions on the agent of the clause. As these modalities develop into future markers, they change to apply less specifically to the agent of the clause, and begin rather to take the whole clause in their scope, as illustrated in the introduction to Part II with the example of English *gonna*. We will see when we discuss mood in Chapter 9 that the development of deontic modalities into epistemic moods parallels the development of future tenses. This parallelism is discussed in detail in Bybee and Pagliuca 1984.

If one views future tenses as just a stage in the development of certain modalities, then it follows that futures may develop quite independently of the present / past distinction. Thus there would be many languages that have a future without having other tenses, which indeed there are. Also, if futures develop independently, then their status as members of the *tense* category would be ambiguous, which it is.

3. *Anterior*

The *anterior* or *perfect* is an inflection used to signal a situation or event that is relevant to another situation or event[3]. Very often, it is the present situation to which the anterior event is relevant. Thus the term "current relevance" is sometimes applied to markers with this meaning (McCawley 1971, Li, Thompson and Thompson 1982, L. Anderson 1982). The following examples illustrate some of these uses:

I've just run four miles (so now I'm tired and I want a shower).
Nixon has just resigned!
Have you seen the Leonardo exhibit?

As McCawley points out, the last example implies that the exhibit is still available, and so whether you have seen it or not is still currently relevant. Compare this to:

Did you see the Leonardo exhibit?

which implies that it is over, and it is too late and just a question of fact, not current relevance.

In several languages of the sample, the *anterior* is specifically described as signalling a past event whose results still exist in the present (Garo, Georgian, Susu). In these languages, then, the anterior signals current relevance. In Sierra Miwok and Kiwai, this tense is called the Recent Past. In Sierra Miwok, its use as an anterior in subordinate clauses is specifically mentioned. In the other languages of the sample (Basque, Burushaski, Korean, Tarascan, and Zapotec), the tense is called a Perfect, and examples indicate that its use is comparable.

When the anterior is combined with the past tense, the result is a *past anterior*, sometimes called a Pluperfect. This signals a past event that is relevant to some other past event.

I had just accepted Mary's invitation when I heard about the party.

The anterior occurs in conjunction with the past in the following languages of the sample: Burushaski, Basque, Georgian, Korean and Tarascan.

I have chosen to treat *anterior* under the heading of tense because its meaning deals with the time of an event or situation relative to another time, usually the moment of speech. It seems to resemble a tense more than an aspect, since it does not affect the internal temporal contours of the situation. Since *anterior* deals with time, it does not seem to be a mood. However, one of the purposes of the survey was to determine whether *anterior* behaves formally like a tense, an aspect, or neither. I have just mentioned one way in which anterior does not behave like a member of the tense contrast set: it cross-classifies with present and past tense. That is, an anterior in some languages may be in the present or past. This would suggest that it is a category which is independent of the present and past.[4]

On the other hand, one indication of a possible relation to the other tenses is the fact that the *anterior* does not occur in languages that do not have other tense distinctions marked inflectionally. It will be recalled that there are languages in the sample that have a future inflection, but have no past tense inflection. In eight of the languages that have anterior, a present, past and future also occur. In the ninth language, Susu, a future and anterior occur as inflections, and other tenses are marked with non-bound morphology. And in Zapotec, there are two inflections that refer to future time (the Incompletive and the Potential), although it is not clear that either of them is a simple future, because they both have uses as modalities. So it seems that the occurrence of an inflectional anterior implies the presence of other tense inflection.

Another criterion for determining whether the *anterior* is a tense depends upon whether its formal marking is parallel to the marking for other tenses. But the results here are ambiguous for our small set of languages with the anterior. In Burushaski, Basque, Garo, Georgian and Zapotec, the anterior is integrated with the other tense inflections, but in most of these languages aspect and/or mood also occur in the same affix positions, or intermeshed in such a way that they are difficult to distinguish. In Kiwai and Korean, anterior seems to occur in a position that is specifically for tense. In Sierra Miwok and Susu, the anterior is marked in a fashion parallel to the future. In Tarascan, the anterior suffix occurs farther from the verb stem than the other markers of tense, but the latter often express aspect as well as tense. Thus the evidence does seem to indicate that anterior can be a part of a general tense category, although it is not always mutually exclusive with other members of the category.

4.   *Tense as a grammatical category*

Tense very rarely occurs as a derivational category. In the present sample of languages, non-inflectional affixes coding temporal notions were found only in Kwakiutl. Kwakiutl has a very large number of non-obligatory suffixes, covering a wide variety of meanings. Included in this group are a few that code temporal notions, such as remote past, recent past and future (Boas 1947:240). These suffixes may occur on both nouns and verbs, for example *εompεwεel* "the late father", and *g:a'xεwεlεn* "I came long ago". Such derivational suffixes for verbs are not very common, because in general tense is not applicable to nouns, and does not affect the inherent semantic content of verbs.

One consequence of the rarity of derivational categories related to tense is that derivational morphology is very unlikely to be the source for the creation of tense inflection. (Compare aspectual inflection, which apparently does sometimes arise from derivational morphology.) The sources for tense inflection, then, would be inflections for other categories, such as aspect, or the semantic and phonological reduction of periphrastic constructions. I have already alluded to this process for the future, which seems to have a variety of sources, including motion verbs, verbs of desire, and verbs of obligation. The sources of *anterior* and *past* tense inflections have not been widely studied in a cross-linguistic perspective. From European languages we know that anteriors develop from a combination of the auxiliaries *have* and/or *be* plus a past participle, as in English *have done*, Dutch *hebben gedaan*, Spanish *ha hecho*. Some Romance languages, such as French, show that an anterior may continue to develop into a perfective aspect (Harris 1982, Fleischman 1983).

Since *pasts* and *anteriors* on the one hand, and *futures* on the other, develop from such different sources, there is no particular reason to suppose that they would be expressed in a parallel fashion and form a coherent category. Indeed, the original Romance future was formed with the auxiliary following the infinitive, while the anterior was formed with the same auxiliary preceding the participle. Where the tenses are expressed in parallel fashion, it may be because they have developed from the same type of periphrastic constructions at approximately the same time. If this is so, then there is no point in claiming that there is a grammatical category *tense*. Rather, various grammatical morphemes can develop, and each of these covers an area of the conceptual space having to do with time. The area not covered is then the province of the zero-mark, or is partially occupied by some other grammatical morpheme, if there happens to be one. This view is consistent with the independence of the *future* from other tenses. It may be, though, that *anterior* and *past* are not independent, owing to the overlap in their conceptual domains, which leads at least to a diachronic relation between them.

To claim that the various ways that tense is expressed in natural languages is the result of historical developments is not to claim that there is no synchronic significance to the grammatical notion of tense. On the contrary, the fact that so many languages do express quite comparable notions of tense by verbal inflection indicates that relative time is an extremely important grammatical notion synchronically. The diachronic developments mentioned here would be impossible unless this were so. What I am claiming, however, is that the conceptual coherence and salience of grammatical tense does not always correspond to a structural coherence in the mode of expression of tense, since the various tense markers of a single language must develop from different sources, and that these developments may not correspond in structure or timing in a way that produces a structurally-coherent category.

NOTES

1. The data on Timucua were poor, and I am not confident that the markers in this languages code tense.

2. This difference in findings between Ultan's survey and my own is due to differences in sampling. Ultan apparently chose languages known to have tense markers, while the languages I used were selected randomly. Ultan says he uses "approximately 50 languages", and I count at least 15 Indo-European languages among these.

3. I have chosen to use the term *anterior* rather than *perfect* to avoid confusion with the perfective aspect. I am not claiming that there is no distinction to be made between an anterior and a perfect, it is only that I could not make this distinction clearly on the basis of the available data.

4. The way that *anterior* cross-classifies with the *present, past* and *future* is different from the way that *habitual* and *continuous* subdivide *imperfective*, because the *habitual* and *continuous* are restricted to the *imperfective* and do not occur with the *perfective*, while the *anterior* may cross-classify completely.

CHAPTER 8: MOOD

Mood, modality and mode are terms used to designate a wide variety of linguistic functions, functions that have been much discussed from a logical and semantic point of view. This chapter concentrates primarily on those modal functions that are marked by verbal inflection in the 50-language sample. We will first see that many of the meanings associated with "modality" do *not* commonly occur as inflectional affixes on verbs. When we turn to an examination of those meanings that *do* occur as inflections, we will take them up in sets of conceptually-related functions. It is often the case that a particular grammatical meaning has a similar mode of expression across languages (e.g. interrogative as a final suffix). It is also often the case that two or more grammatical meanings (e.g. imperative and subjunctive) have similar modes of expression *within* a language. Using the criterion of similarity of expression type both language-internally and cross-linguistically, I will try to discover a coherent conceptual domain for the category of mood. I will also examine attempts to divide the broad category of mood into smaller conceptual domains.

1. *Mood and modality*

The working definition of *mood* used in the survey is that *mood* is a marker on the verb that signals how the speaker chooses to put the proposition into the discourse context. The main function of this definition is to distinguish *mood* from *tense* and *aspect*, and to group together the well-known moods, *indicative, imperative, subjunctive* and so on. It was intentionally formulated to be general enough to cover both markers of illocutionary force, such as *imperative*, and markers of the degree of commitment of the speaker to the truth of the proposition, such as *dubitative*. What all these markers of the mood category have in common is that they signal what the *speaker* is doing with the proposition, and they have the *whole proposition* in their scope. Included under this definition are epistemic modalities, i.e. those that signal the degree of commitment the speaker has to the truth of the proposition. These are usually said to range from certainty to probability to possibility.

Excluded, however, are the other "modalities", such as the deontic modalities of permission and obligation, because they describe certain conditions on the *agent* with regard to the main predication. Some of the English modal auxiliaries have both an epistemic and a deontic reading. The following two examples illustrate the deontic functions of obligation and permission respectively:

Sally must be more polite to her mother.
The students may use the library at any time.

The epistemic functions of these same auxiliaries can be seen by putting them in a sentence without an agentive subject:

It must be raining.
It may be raining.

Now the auxiliaries signal the speaker's degree of commitment to the proposition "it is raining". Along with deontic modalities, markers of *ability*, *desire* and *intention* are excluded from the definition of mood since they express conditions pertaining to the agent that are in effect with respect to the main predication. I will refer to obligation, permission, ability, desire and intention as "agent-oriented" modalities.

The hypothesis implicit in the working definition of mood as an inflectional category is that markers of modalities that designate conditions on the *agent* of the sentence will *not* often occur as inflections on verbs, while markers that designate the role the *speaker* wants the proposition to play in the discourse will often occur as inflections. This hypothesis was overwhelmingly supported by the languages in the sample. Hundreds of inflectional markers that fit the definition of mood were found to occur in the languages of the sample. In fact, such markers are the most common type of inflection on verbs. However, inflectional markers of obligation, permission, ability or intention are extremely rare in the sample, and occur only under specific conditions. We will examine these few examples before turning to our more general discussion of mood.

Many languages have *optative* or *hortative* forms which signal a speech act by which the speaker grants permission to a 2nd or 3rd person, as in "let him come in", or expresses a wish (e.g. "would that he were here") or an indirect command. These forms are considered *mood* by our definition, because the verb inflection signals a speech act type — something the *speaker* is doing with the whole proposition. However, a form which predicates that the subject or agent has permission or an obligation whose source might be some authority *other* than the speaker does not come under the definition of *mood*. These are the functions that are very rare as inflection. In the sample, the only examples that have emerged are in Tiwi and Malayalam. Consider the form called the Compulsional in Tiwi. According to Osborne, this form may occur either in the non-past or the future. Its form is the prefix [u]:

a - u - kərimi   "He has to do it"
he - comp - do

a - u - ra - kərimi   "He will have to do it"
he - comp - fut - do

(Osborne 1974:44) Judging by the translations of these sentences, the Compulsional is not a speech act type by which the speaker imposes an obligation on the agent, but rather an assertion that the agent has an obligation.

Malayalam has a number of suffixes indicating mood, of which two fit our definition of agent-oriented modality. The suffix *-aNam*, which George 1971 labels the Optative corresponds to English "must, should or ought". It derives from the verb *ventum* meaning "it is necessary" (Subrahmanyam 1971). This suffix can be used with 1st, 2nd or 3rd person. However, it can also be used in an imperative sense with a 2nd person subject. Thus *pookaNam* with a 3rd person subject means "he must go", but with a 2nd person subject it may be used as an imperative (George 1971:33-34). A second suffix of agent-oriented modality in Malayalam, *-aam*, is used in a Permissive sense. It derives from the future tense of the verb "to become". This suffix indicates both permission and possibility, and can also be used to *grant* permission. Thus *pookaam* with a 2nd person subject means "you may go" in the sense that "I give you permission to go". With a 1st person subject it signals agreement, a promise or willingness, as in "I agree to go, I am willing to go" (George 1971:161, Subrahmanyam 1971:462). Both of these suffixes, then, have in addition to their uses as agent-oriented modalities, uses that fall under our definition of mood, in that they can be used to indicate a speech act by which the *speaker* grants permission or issues a command.

Examples of agent-oriented modalities expressed in bound morphology can be found outside the sample as well. For instance, Turkish has a Necessitative verb form that signals an obligation on the part of the subject (Lewis 1967). All indications are that this is an inflection. Other examples of agent-oriented modalities seem to be derivational. For instance, Luiseño has a Desiderative suffix meaning "the subject wants or wishes", and a Potential, which means "the subject is able to" or "it is possible" (Kroeber and Grace 1960). These suffixes appear to be derivational (Langacker 1972). The possibility of derivational markers of agent-oriented modality points to the further possibility of their occurrence in polysynthetic languages as incorporated adjunct verbs. (See 4.6 for a discussion of incorporation as a morphological process.) Indeed, Quileute has incorporated adjunct verbs (postpositives) meaning "to wish or want" and "to have an obligation".

No inflectional markers designating *ability* of the subject were found in the sample. The few markers of the subject's *intention* in the sample are also used to mark the simple future. (See the discussion in 7.2.)

Since these were the only examples of agent-oriented modality that turned up in the survey, it is clear that inflectional *mood* markers that have the whole proposition in their scope and mark the role the proposition plays in the discourse are quite common, while inflectional markers of modality that express conditions on the agent are very rare. Why should this be so? The answer can be found by examining the diachronic development of modal auxiliaries and mood markers. It is generally the case in diachronic change that deontic modalities develop into epistemic modalities. For instance, the English modal *may* developed from a verb that originally meant "to be strong or able, to have power" according to the Oxford English Dictionary. From that agent-oriented sense, it later developed the sense of "possibility", an epistemic notion. This process was paralleled by English *must*, which has the agent-oriented meaning of "obligation," and has also developed the epistemic meaning of "inference" or "strong probability" as in "It must be raining." The development from agent-oriented to epistemic modality is another case of *generalization* of meaning. The range of contexts in which an epistemic marker can be used is wider than the range of contexts in which an agent-oriented marker can be used. An agent-oriented modality is restricted to clauses with an animate agent — someone with whom conditions of obligation, permission, ability or volition may be associated. Epistemic markers are appropriate in a clause with any type of subject, even the *it* of "It is raining". We might generalize, then, and suppose that as modals develop, they move in the direction of becoming markers that have the whole proposition in their scope, a generalization which also holds for the development of future markers out of verbs meaning "to want" or "to go". (For further arguments and examples, see Bybee and Pagliuca 1984). The Malayalam suffixes discussed above, which historically derive from verbs, have both deontic uses and uses as speech act markers, and so appear also to be moving in this direction.

As mentioned before, the general reduction of grammatical meaning is paralleled by the phonological reduction and fusion that creates inflection. There is no specific prohibition against agent-oriented modalities as verbal inflections, but they are rare because in most cases by the time a marker (usually an auxiliary verb in this case) is reduced enough phonologically to be fused to the main verb, its meaning has also been reduced: it has lost the part of its meaning that expresses conditions on an agent, and has come to have the whole proposition in its scope.[1] If this view is correct, then we would expect agent-oriented modality to be expressed in inflectional morphology only where it is "new" morphology, which appears to be the case in Malayalam, where the verbal source of the modal suffixes is still transparent, or where the language in general incorporates a large number of meaningful elements into a single word, as in Tiwi, which is polysynthetic, or Turkish, which is highly agglutinative.

The cross-linguistic data suggest, then, the following uses of the terms *modality* and *mood*. *Modality* designates a conceptual domain which may take various types of linguistic expression, while *mood* designates the inflectional expression of a subdivision of this semantic domain. Since there is much cross-linguistic consistency concerning which modalities are expressed inflectionally, *mood* can refer both to the form of expression, and to a conceptual domain. The question to be considered in the following sections is whether or not this conceptual domain is coherent in a single language, or across languages.

2. The functions of mood

Since agent-oriented meanings are not usually expressed inflectionally, the *moods* to be examined here are only those that have the whole proposition in their scope and signal the *speaker's* intention with respect to the proposition in the context of the speech situation. However, even this characterization of the conceptual domain of *mood* is extremely broad, so it is useful to attempt to further subdivide it. In the following we will consider whether certain suggested conceptual subdivisions are supported by the cross-linguistic data. One particular subdivision we will examine has been proposed recently by Foley and Van Valin 1984.

This distinction is between markers designating the type of speech act being performed, i.e. the illocutionary force of the utterance in which the proposition occurs, and markers indicating the speaker's commitment to the truth of the assertion. Whorf 1938 suggested such a distinction for Hopi categories, using the term "status" to cover the markers of illocutionary force, and the term "modality" for the indicators of the speaker's commitment to the assertion. Hare 1970 also distinguishes the propositional content of an utterance from the sign of its illocutionary force, and the sign of the "speaker's subscription" to the speech act. (See also Lyons 1977 discussion of this point.) Foley and Van Valin 1984 propose that such a distinction is cross-linguistically significant in ways to be discussed below.[2]

Applying such a distinction to some of the verbal inflections discovered in the 50-language sample, we might propose the following dichotomy:

Illocutionary force: Imperative, Optative, Admonitive, Prohibitive, Interrogative.
Commitment to truth of assertion: Subjunctive, Dubitative, Probable, Potential, Conditional.

This division is useful in that it helps to explain the diverse functions of the *indicative* across languages. In some languages (such as Quileute) the Indicative is the sign of declarative sentences, since it contrasts with an Interrogative, while in other languages, the Indicative contrasts with a Subjunctive or a Conditional and thus is used both in declarative assertions and questions. If the unmarked or basic utterance is a declarative assertion of truth, then contrasts with this basic utterance can develop along the two parameters — the speech act type can be modified, and the degree of assertion can be modulated. Different languages have inflectional markers for different points on each of these parameters. Whatever is left over is called the Indicative Mood.

The conceptual motivation for the proposed distinction seems sound. One possible conceptual problem with the distinction is that a qualified assertion might be considered a different sort of speech act than an unmarked assertion. Still, one could maintain a distinction between a qualified assertion and other types of speech acts. The important question now is whether this distinction is coded in grammatical systems in a coherent way. What we must look for are cases in which the two types of moods are marked differently in languages. Foley and Van Valin 1984 make a very specific prediction: they predict that markers of illocutionary force will occur farther away from the verb stem than tense, and that markers of degree of assertion will occur closer to the verb stem than tense. This is a prediction that is easily testable on our data. We will be considering this and other possible evidence for the proposed distinction as we discuss mood markers.

3. *Imperatives and related moods*

The *imperative* mood is the form of the verb used in issuing direct commands or orders. Direct commands are restricted to a second person subject, so in many languages the *imperative* has only two forms, one for singular and one for plural. If first and third person forms also exist, they will translate into English as "let him (them, us) go", or "may he (they, we, I) prosper", for example. If there is a full set of subject-agreement forms, the authors of grammars usually refer to the mood as the Optative as, for example, in Nahuatl, which has no separate imperative. Furthermore, in Nahuatl, the Optative has both a Present and a Past tense. The following forms, accompanied by a pre-verbal particle *mā*, would be translated in the 3rd singular Present as "if only he would weep", and in the Past as "if only he had wept" (Andrews 1975:52, 384):

	Present Optative	*Past Optative*
1s	nichōca	nichōcani
2s	xichōca	xichōcani
3s	chōca	chōcani
1p	tichōcacān	tichōcanih
2p	xichōcacān	xichōcanih
3p	chōcacān	chōcanih

The same sort of mood may also be referred to as the Hortative (for example, in Acoma), or the Volitional (as used in the description of Iatmul and Sierra-Miwok). The latter is very similar to the *optative* in that it expresses a wish or desire of the *speaker*, and thus signals a type of speech act. In some grammars, such as Lorimer's grammar of Burushaski, the Imperative is given as having only 2nd person forms, while the Optative has only 3rd person forms (Lorimer 1935:246):

	Imperative ɛtas "to do, make"		
2s	ɛti, ɛ	2p	ɛtin
	Optative		
3s	ɛtiš	3p	ɛtiš∧n

A strict distinction is made between Imperative, Optative and Exhortative in Boas' grammar of Kwakiutl. Imperative is for a direct command, Optative for a wish of the speaker, and Exhortative for "let me (come), let him (come)" etc.

The *imperative* and other related moods are expressed similarly both language-internally and cross-linguistically. Among the languages of the sample that have explicit markers for the *imperative*, or another mood that is used as an imperative, there are some striking regularities in the mode of expression:

1. An areal trait among the native languages of North America, is to have special person/number forms that indicate imperative or optative. This occurs in Acoma, Diegueño, and Nahuatl, where the person/number markers are prefixed to the verb (see the Nahuatl examples above), and in Ojibwa, where the person/number markers are suffixed to the verb.

2. A more widespread phenomenon is the use of an unmarked verb form for the imperative. This occurs in Basque, Burushaski, Kiwai, Kwakiutl, Pawnee, Tarascan, and Touareg.

3. An equally common expression type for the imperative or optative is the use of a suffix that occurs immediately before the person/number marker. This arrangement is found for moods used in commands in Serbo-Croatian, Sierra-Miwok, Yukaghir and Yupik. Consider the Volitional forms in Sierra Miwok, where the Volitional suffix -e:- precedes the person / number suffixes (Freeland 1951:46):

hïwá:te:mà?	let me run!	hïwá:te:mà:š	let us run!
hïwá:tè?	run, thou!	hïwá:tè:č	run, ye!
hïwá:te:tì:	let us two run!	hïwá:te:tì:č	let us all run!
hïwá:te:nì:š	let him run!	hïwá:te:niškò:	let them run!

In addition to their Imperative forms, Iatmul has a Volitional, Ojibwa a Delayed Imperative, and Kwakiutl an Optative, that are marked with suffixes occurring just before the person/number suffixes. There were no languages found in which a suffixed imperative or optative marker occurred *after* the person/number suffixes.

4. Some languages have an imperative suffix that does not interact with person/number marking, either because the language does not have person/number marking — Garo, Gilyak, Korean, Malayalam, and Wappo (all SOV languages), or because the person/number marking is prefixed to the verb — Goajiro and Kutenai (both VSO languages).

5. Prefixes are relatively uncommon as imperative markers. A prefix occurs in Maasai, where it precedes the person/number markers; in Kutenai (for the Optative) and in Tiwi, where it follows the person/number marker. In Zapotec, the Imperative is a prefix and the person/number markers are suffixes. Maasai, Kutenai and Zapotec are VSO languages. Tiwi has a basic word order of SVO, with a number of other orders possible, but VSO is not one of them. However, Tiwi is largely prefixing in its inflectional morphology.

6. Two miscellaneous cases are Iatmul, where the imperative is marked by a prefix, an optional suffix and a special set of person / number forms, and Logbara, where the imperative verb has a different tone pattern from the indicative.

The generalizations that emerge from these data are that it is much more common to have an imperative *suffix* than a *prefix*, and an imperative prefix that is not also a person/number marker occurs only in VSO languages or highly prefixal languages. Zero-marking is common in the imperative. With one exception (Maasai), imperative markers occur closer to the verb stem than person/number markers. We will compare these generalizations with generalizations about other mood markers in upcoming sections.

Markers that modify imperative meaning are found in some languages. Sierra Miwok, Kiwai and Ojibwa have special forms that signal a Delayed or Future Imperative. Garo, Malayalam, Yupik and Ojibwa have a special form for the negative of the imperative, which is often called the Prohibitive. Burushaski has a "Deprecatory Imperative", while Kiwai and a number of other languages have inflectional means of producing a milder or more polite imperative. Nahuatl is the only language in the sample that has an Admonitive inflection. The Admonitive means "let (subject) beware of (verb)-ing". Compare, for example the indicative *nitzahtzi* "I am shouting" to *mā nitzahtzih* "Let me beware of shouting. I must be careful not to shout. I mustn't shout. I'd better not shout" (Andrews 1975: 56).

Is there any evidence that the *imperative*, which designates a speech act, is expressed differently than moods which have other functions? At this point, there is only evidence to the contrary — evidence that one and the same form can be used in commands, and in statements to express other functions. In some languages the imperative is related to or expressed by a *subjunctive*, or a form that has general uses in subordinate clauses of certain types. For example, commands are given with a form of the Subjunctive in Basque, Maasai and Tarascan. On the other hand, in Tiwi, it is the so-called Future prefix that is the sole marker of commands. These examples indicate that it may be difficult to separate the speech act functions of mood from its other functions.

4. *Interrogatives*

Interrogative markers are uncontroversially markers of a speech act type. They occur bound to the verb in about one third of the languages that have mood markers. The distinction between indicative and interrogative occurs much less frequently as an inflectional distinction than the distinction between indicative and imperative.[3] This simply means that there are more often non-inflectional ways of signalling interrogation, such as with particles that may occur on various elements in the sentence. However, when interrogation is marked inflectionally, its marking is much more uniform across languages than that of imperative. In all ten languages of the sample that have interrogative inflection, it occurs as a *suffix* on the verb, as in these examples from Diegueño (Langdon 1970: 161):

ma:y nyəway = a	"Where are they?"
where they - are = ques	
ma: = c ma:yp = a	"Do you talk?"
you = subj you - talk = ques	
wa:m = x = kəx = a	"Might he go?"
go = fut = prob = ques	

The languages that have an inflectional interrogative are Burushaski, Diegueño, Garo, Kwakiutl, Santa Cruz, Tarascan, Quileute, Yukaghir, Yupik and Zapotec. Six of these languages are SOV languages, so that suffixes are to be expected. However, prefixes do occur in four of these six SOV languages. Four of the languages — Kwakiutl, Tarascan, Quileute and Zapotec — are VSO languages, so that the occurrence of the interrogative as a suffix in these languages is not predictable from their word order typology. There must be something inherent in the nature of interrogatives, or the sources from which they develop, that causes them to occur only as suffixes. Note further that inflectional markers of interrogative occur only in SOV or VSO languages in the 50-language sample. There are no SVO languages with interrogative suffixes in the sample.

Interrogatives resemble imperatives in the preference for suffixation, but the preference is stronger in the case of interrogatives. An important difference is that the imperative suffixes tend to occur *before* the person/

number suffixes, and the interrogative suffixes tend to occur *after* the person/ number suffixes. In fact, the interrogative marker is usually the last suffix on the verb. Such is the case in Burushaski, Diegueño, Garo, Tarascan, Quileute, Yukaghir and Zapotec. Only in Santa Cruz, Yupik and Kwakiutl are the interrogative suffixes followed by person/number forms. In Kwakiutl, Boas reports, the interrogative marker precedes the person marker, but is often *repeated after* the person suffix as well. Thus there is a strong universal tendency for affixed interrogative markers to occur as the *final suffix* on the verb.

Since *imperative* and *interrogative* both signal speech act types, we might expect that their expression types would be the same: we would expect, for example, that markers for these two functions would occur in the same affix position across languages. The data just presented, however, show that this is not the case: imperative suffixes occur before person/number suffixes, while interrogative suffixes tend to occur after them. This suggests that the mode of expression of inflectional categories is less a matter of their synchronic conceptual structure, and more a matter of the diachronic source from which the markers developed. I suspect that imperative (and optative and hortative) affixes tend to develop from auxiliary verbs, which carry person/number suffixes themselves. This would result in final person/number marking. Interrogative markers very likely have a different source, but it is beyond the scope of the present study to determine what that source is.

An uncommon feature of inflectional languages is to have a certain inflectional form used both in questions and in other contexts as well. For instance, Tarascan has a Clarificational mood that is used to ask questions, but also used in the answer to questions in certain tense/aspect categories. This inflection is accompanied in questions by an Interrogative enclitic (which amounts to the voicing of the final vowel of the verb). Consider the following sentences in which the suffix *-pi* marks the Clarificational (Foster 1969: 57):

  né ka=ma-an-pi /né kámaampi/ "Who brought it?"
  xí ka=ma-an-pi-ni /xí kámaampini/ "I brought it (reply)"

In Acoma, the Dubitative mood, which is signalled by a special set of pronominal prefixes, is used in statements about which there is an element of doubt, to report unwitnessed occurrences, and in questions.

Since interrogative markers are usually the *final* suffix on the verb, there is little interaction or fusion with tense or aspect morphemes.

5. *Negatives*

Negation is not a member of the mood category according to the definition used here, but it does occur as a verbal inflection in a substantial number
of languages, and will be treated here because of its affinity to other mood
meanings. Negation is not a type of speech act, since a statement, question
or command may be either affirmative or negative. Nor can negation be
considered to modify the degree of commitment of the speaker to the proposition, since the negative sentences can be asserted, strongly or weakly,
doubted, and so on. Yet in some uses negation can resemble what we are
calling mood, in that it can have the whole proposition in its scope. And in
some theories of grammar (such as early transformational grammar), negative sentences are analyzed in a very similar way to interrogative, imperative
and emphatic sentences.

A major difference between the conceptual category of negation and
other moods is that the scope of negation is highly variable, and in some
cases it can have a single lexical item in its scope. This, and the fact that
negation accomplishes a substantial meaning change in the word it modifies,
leads to its expression in derivational morphemes, and even in lexical combination with predicates. In this respect, negation is unlike mood, which
ordinarily does not have derivational or lexical expression. A common derivational expression of negation affects stative predicates or adjectives. The
English examples of *unhappy, unbelievable, unwed* are paralleled by such
examples in numerous languages (Zimmer 1964). Inflected verbs can also
incorporate a negative meaning in lexical expression. For instance, Korean
has several pairs of positive / negative verbs: *cota* "to like", *silta* "to dislike,
not to want", *itta* "exist, be present", *ɔptta* "not to exist, be absent".

Negative inflections occur in fifteen languages of the sample. This is a
little less than one-half of the languages that have mood inflection. It is thus
more common than interrogative inflection and less common than imperative
inflection. Consider the example of negation in Maasai (Tucker and Mpaayei
1955: 67):[4]

a-rany	I sing	m-a-rany	I do not sing
kɪ-ranyɪta	we are singing	m-kɪ-ranyɪta	we are not singing
e-ɪrrag	3rd lies down	m-e-ɪrrag	3rd does not lie down
ɪrrag-ɪta	you are lying down	m-ɪrragita	you are not lying down

Negation presents a striking contrast to imperative and interrogation, which are much more commonly expressed as suffixes than prefixes, because for negation there is a slight preference for prefixal expression. Negation occurs as a prefix in seven languages, three of them VSO, where prefixation is more expected (Maasai, Pawnee and Zapotec), and four of them SOV, where suffixation would be expected (Acoma, Burushaski, Gilyak and Yukaghir). The five languages in which negation occurs as a suffix are all exclusively suffixing, except for Ojibwa, which has some pronominal prefixes. Three of these languages are SOV (Garo, Malayalam and Wappo), and two have variable or undetermined word order (Ojibwa and Sierra Miwok). Two languages remain to be mentioned. Santa Cruz (SOV) uses both a prefix and a suffix to negate verbs (Zapotec also has an optional suffix that may accompany the negative prefix), and Touareg has a special form of the stem for negative verbs, but these are accompanied by a preverbal particle in negative sentences.

Dahl 1979 presents the results of a large-scale cross-linguistic study of sentence negation. He uses 240 languages, but states with regret that the sample is not free of areal or genetic bias. He studied both bound and non-bound markers of sentence negation. His general conclusion was that negative markers tend to occur early in the sentence. This conclusion is also supported by the present finding of a preference for prefixes. However, there is an anomaly in Dahl's data, which he does not note. It is that *suffixing* is preferred for the bound expression of negation in his sample at a ratio of two to one, but *pre-posing* (to the verb, verb phrase or sentence) is preferred for non-bound markers at a ratio of about three to one. If the diachronic source of bound markers is non-bound markers, as we suppose it to be, then there should not be a great difference in their positional tendencies. Dahl himself suggests the cause of the preponderance of suffixed negatives: his sample is heavily biased toward SOV, suffixing languages. We have seen in our sample that purely suffixing languages can have suffixal negation, so the inclusion in his sample of nineteen Altaic languages which are purely suffixing biases his results. If eighteen of these closely related languages are removed, then Dahl's results will be much like those gained from the sample used here.

The preference for prefixal expression of inflectional negation is even better underscored in the present study than in Dahl's because we can compare the ratio of prefixes to suffixes in negation to the same ratio in other categories. For instance, we have already seen that imperatives and interrogatives are nearly always expressed by suffixes. Thus the slight edge that prefixes have over suffixes in negation is all the more significant.

Other details point to a marking of negation early in the verb form: in Yukaghir and Burushaski, the negative prefix appears to be the *only* inflectional prefix. In Maasai, Pawnee and Zapotec, the negative prefix precedes all other prefixes. In languages where negation is a suffix, it occurs closer to the stem, and thus earlier in the verb form, than other inflectional suffixes (e.g. in Garo, Ojibwa, and Zapotec). Thus negation is a category where position with regard to other categories tends to be determined not in relation to the verb stem, but in an absolute left-to-right fashion.

6. *Potential, dubitative and related functions*

Let us turn now to a consideration of those markers that qualify the speaker's commitment to the truth of a proposition. In this section those markers that occur freely in main clauses and have among their functions the expression of epistemic possibility are discussed. In the next section, we will take up verbal inflections that sometimes have similar functions, but are restricted to certain clause types, in particular, subordinate, conjoined or conditional clauses.

While the meaning of epistemic modalities for languages such as English has received considerable attention in the literature on semantics, Lyons 1977 points out that the distinctions among epistemic modalities that are grammaticized in the languages of the world have not been studied. The current report will help to fill this gap, but it necessarily suffers from certain limitations. First, the comments made here will refer only to bound markers of epistemic modalities, and will not be applicable to non-bound markers such as modal auxiliaries, which often code more distinctions. Second, although such markers are found in twelve different languages, in no case in the sources is the description of the functions of these inflections very detailed. Thus the generalizations that emerge must be considered tentative and suggestive rather than conclusive.

Among the labels given for the inflections to be discussed here are Potential, Suppositional, Indecisive, and Dubitative. The descriptive statements attached to the first three of these labels include terms such as "probable, possible, potential" and sometimes "future". The English translations use "may, might, probably, I think, it seems". Consider the following sentences from Diegueño, where the suffix /kəx/ "conveys doubt or imprecision" (Langdon 1970: 160):

Darrow kurak = vu   xuma:y = kəx
Darrow old-man = specfic   man's-son = must-be
"He must be old man Darrow's son"

wa:m = x = kəx
he-goes-away = will = must-be
"He might go"

In some cases, the translation uses the future, with "probably" added, as in the case of Zapotec verbs in the Potential (Pickett 1955: 220):

gu - kaʔa - beé   "s/he will (probably) write"
Potential - write - 3s human

zu - kaʔa -beé   "s/he will write"
Incomplete - write - 3s human

A Dubitative (and sometimes moods labelled differently) is usually described as expressing an element of doubt that the event described in the proposition occurred or will occur (Acoma, Diegueño, Ojibwa and Pawnee). Note, however, that it is only an *element* of doubt, for these sentences never translate "I doubt that ..." but rather "probably" or "it seems". Consider Bloomfield's translation of the Ojibwa sentence in the Dubitative: *kenapac uwaya pi-eya:tik* "someone seems to be coming here". (The Dubitative marker is the final -*tik*.) None of the languages in the sample had an inflection that expressed the meaning "the speaker doubts that ...".

Epistemic inflections found in the languages of the sample can be divided into two types, depending upon whether the inflection itself implies future time, or whether it is freely combinable with present and past tense. The Zapotec Potential seems to express probability, but only in the future. The Malayalam Permissive, which expresses possibility also refers to future events. The Yukaghir Potential is restricted to future, and one of the Garo suffixes for "probable", -*nabadoŋa* refers to an "uncertain future". Kiwai has an Indefinite Future, which may be similar, but is not described well enough for me to be certain.

On the other hand, the Dubitative in Acoma, Pawnee, and Ojibwa can be used to describe past events, but in such cases it signals that the event described was not witnessed by the speaker. Similarly, the Tarascan marker translated as "probably" in the past indicates a surmise. The Korean Indecisive inflection combines with present, past and future, as does the Garo suffix -*kon* in the following examples (Burling 1961: 34):

sokba - gen - kon   "(s/he) will probably come"
come - future - probable

anti - ci   re'an - aha - kon   "I think he went to the market"
market - to   go - past - probable

In discussions of epistemic modality as it is grammaticized in the languages of the world, it is usual to distinguish several points on a scale from certainty to probability and possibility (Horn 1972, Steele 1975). Steele 1975 suggests that the English modal auxiliaries distinguish as many as five points on this scale:

Weak possibility: That *might / could* be Beethoven.
Possibility: That *may* be Beethoven.
Probability: That *should* be Beethoven.
Contingent certainty: That *would* be Beethoven.
Certainty: That *must / will* be Beethoven.

One could argue that the last example is not simple "certainty", since that would best be expressed by the nonmodal sentence "That is Beethoven". The last example is rather "confident inferral" (Coates 1983). Nevertheless, it is correct to say that English modals permit these five distinctions in epistemic modality. In the present survey of verbal inflections, however, such grading of epistemic modality was not evident. There are no languages in the sample that have more than one inflectional epistemic mood. (But see the discussion of Pawnee and Garo just below.) Rather, the epistemic moods found in this sample cover some range around the possibility - probability area on this scale, and the languages of the sample do not in fact have an inflectional means of making finer distinctions. This is not surprising in view of the general diachronic pattern by which inflections develop from nonbound forms. This pattern leads us to expect that inflections will have broader meanings and present fewer contrasts than free grammatical morphemes.

In some languages, inflectional markers of epistemic mood exist alongside other non-inflectional affixes expressing meanings having to do with epistemic modality, as for example in Garo and Pawnee. Garo has several layers of suffixes for verbs. The suffixes that Burling calls the Principal Suffixes are the ones that were considered inflectional for the purposes of this study, since one of them is required to form a verb. These suffixes code notions of tense and mood. One of these suffixes is labelled "an uncertain future". It is -*nabadoŋa*, as in *re'banabadoŋa* '(he) may come" (p. 28).[5] This contrasts with four other future suffixes: a simple future, and three suffixes that include in their meanings "intentional" or "immediate" future. The suffix, -*kon*, illustrated above, occurs in a more outer layer of suffixes, and may attach to nouns although it usually occurs with verbs. This suffix, Burling says, "injects an element of doubt into the statement" (p. 34). It translates with English "probably, it seems, apparently, I suppose, I guess, I think" and is used in Burling's examples with past, present and future suffixes. The difference between the two markers of uncertainty, -*kon* and -*nabadoŋa*, is that one has an inherently future reference and the other modifies a statement in any tense. This same difference is found among epistemic markers considered cross-linguistically, as we saw above.

The affixes of interest in Pawnee are the Potential, which Parks 1976 considers to be one of several obligatory mood prefixes, and the Evidential prefixes, which are not obligatory. The Potential is a combination of the prefix *kus-*, which precedes the subject prefix, and the prefix -*i-*, which follows it. The Potential expresses simple future, possibility, potentiality and probability (Parks 1976:154). In the following examples, only the verb containing the Potential prefix is given a morpheme-by-morpheme gloss.

iriheriwihat kustuci?a:kaciksta   "They can stay; I'll take care of them"
/kus + t + ut + i + ak + aciks + ta + Ø/
Potential + 1st + Benef + Pot + 3p + verb + Intentive + Perf

para kasiat   "you could have gone"
/kas + s + i + at + Ø/
Potential + 2nd + Pot + verb + Perfective

The Evidential system has a four-way contrast between a prefix used for quoted material, a prefix for unwitnessed events about which there is no doubt, and two that resemble epistemic moods: the Inferential, which "signifies that the speaker knows an act to have occurred on the basis of inference" and a Dubitative, which "indicates that the speaker did not actually see an activity or state and that there is an element of doubt concerning its occurrence" (Parks 1976: 230). Both of these prefixes seem to be used primarily in statements about the past. Combined with the Absolutive Mode, the Dubitative is "one of the most frequently occurring evidentials in narratives" (p. 230). Consider the following examples:

Inferential /tir/:
tihraku:tit ku:ruks   "He must have killed a bear"

/tir + ra + ku:tik + Ø/
Inferential + Absolutive + kill + Perfective
titaku wetihrikska:cuwa   "They must have urinated here"

/we - tir + ra + ir + uks + ka:cu + wa + Ø/
preverb - Inf + Abs + Pl + Aor + urinate + Pl + Perf

Dubitative /kur/:
kuhru pi:ta a ku capat   "It was either a man or a woman"

/kur + ra + u + Ø/
Dubitative + Absolutive + be + Perf

tira:wa:hat kukuhriri:ta:ka "The Creator must have done something for them"

/ku - kur + ra + ir + ri + ut + ak + a:r + Ø/
Indef + Dub + Abs + S-pl + Poss + Ben + O-pl + do + Perf

The difference between these evidential prefixes and the Potential is in the way they interact with the temporal context. The Potential may refer to a possibility or potentiality that existed in the past (as in the example "you could have gone"), as well as the present and future. The evidentials, however, signal only the way the speaker arrived at knowledge about the event, whether in the past, present or future. The evidentials definitely signal how the speaker views the truth value of the proposition. The Potential is more like an agent-oriented modality, since it predicates certain conditions that hold with regard to the main verb, although it is not clear whether an animate agent is necessary for this mood.[6] The close relation between the Potential and the Dubitative meanings is underscored by the fact that the two prefixes for these meanings could have the same diachronic source. The Potential is *kus-*, and the Dubitative, which always occurs before the Absolutive *-ra-*, is *kur-*.

These language-specific examples suggest that if there are further subdivisions to be made in epistemic mood, they will not be along the degree of probability dimension, but rather will concern the scope of the operator, and how it interacts with the temporal context. Further progress on this question will demand better language-specific descriptions than the ones used in this survey.

The question of the relation of epistemic mood to the other moods examined so far can now be raised. The relevant comparison will be between the epistemic moods on the one hand, and the two moods that are uncontroversially indicators of speech act type, that is, imperatives and interrogatives, on the other. Recall, however, that imperatives and interrogatives are not marked in the same way. Thus we must compare epistemic markers separately to imperatives and interrogatives.

Of the twelve languages that have an epistemic mood, seven have this mood marked in the same way as the Imperative, Optative or Hortative. For instance, in Acoma, the Dubitative and Hortative (used for imperative) are formed with special pronominal prefixes; in Garo, the Uncertain Future suffix occurs in the same position as the Imperative; in Basque, the Potential is parallel to the Imperative; in Korean, the Imperative and Indecisive occupy the same suffix position; in Kutenai, the Suppositional is in the same position as the Optative; in Malayalam, all moods are suffixes in the same position; and in Pawnee, the Potential occurs in the same position as the Imperative.

In the remaining five languages, the epistemic marker is found in a different position than the imperative and related moods. In Diegueño, the imperative is formed with a special second person prefix, while the epistemic is a suffix; in Ojibwa, the imperative is a matter of special pronominal prefix arrangement, while the Dubitative is a suffix; in Tarascan, the imperative is unmarked, while the epistemic is a final suffix or enclitic; in Zapotec, the Potential occurs in the same prefix position as the aspectual markers, while plural imperative is an initial prefix: however, the Plural Imperative is formed using the Potential morpheme; in Yukaghir, the Potential is a prefix, while the Imperative is a suffix.

The comparison with interrogative markers is more difficult, simply because fewer languages have inflectional interrogatives. In the sample, Diegueño and Garo have their epistemic suffixes occurring immediately before the interrogative suffixes, which are final. In Tarascan, the epistemic occurs in the same enclitic position as the interrogative. In Korean, the interrogative appears in the same slot as the epistemic. In Yukaghir and Zapotec, the two markers occupy quite different positions.

The survey does not, then, give good evidence for a different type of marking for epistemic moods. In fact, it appears that epistemics and imperatives are more likely to be marked in the same way than imperatives and interrogatives are. This goes against any predictions made by those who propose to distinguish moods that signal a type of speech act from moods that qualify the speaker's commitment to the truth of the proposition. But before leaving the subject of this distinction, let us consider one other hypothesis put forth by Foley and Van Valin 1984, who propose that this distinction is linguistically significant.

Foley and Van Valin suggest that markers of epistemic modality (which they term "status") occur closer to the verb stem than markers of tense. This hypothesis can be tested on the six languages of the sample that have both epistemic mood and tense: five of these six languages (Diegueño, Garo, Korean, Kutenai and Tarascan) have the epistemic mood marker *farther* from the stem than the tense marker. Only in Ojibwa is the epistemic closer to the stem than tense.

It will be recalled from the discussion in Chapter 2, that the *relevance* principle predicts that a marker of epistemic mood will occur farther from the verb stem than a marker of tense. Tense is more relevant to the verb than mood, because mood necessarily has the whole proposition in its scope, while tense places the event described by the *verb* in time relative to the speech event.

7. *Evidentials*

Evidentials have already been mentioned several times, since an epistemic mood, especially when coupled with past tense, may signal that an occurrence is unwitnessed or inferred, and this is a function also often served by an evidential. Evidentials may be generally defined as markers that indicate something about the *source* of the information in the proposition. Evidentials do not occupy a large section of this discussion, however, because their occurrence as inflectional morphology is rare in the languages of the sample: *evidential* morphemes can be identified in Korean, Pawnee, Tarascan and Yukaghir. It appears, however, that this category may be obligatory, that is, inflectional, only in Korean. Ramstedt's 1939 analysis of Korean gives a basic three-way division in the Indicative. He calls the three groups of forms the Declarative, the Regressive and the Indecisive. I have already had occasion to mention the Indecisive, because it seems to be a marker of epistemic possibility. The Regressive is an evidential which Ramstedt says "expresses the verb or the action as in some respect remote in time or space..." (p. 70). Martin 1960 says that the Regressive (which he calls the Retrospective) means roughly "it has been observed that" (p. 225). Pawnee has more distinctions within the evidential category than any language of the sample, but as mentioned above, Parks explicitly states that the evidential marking is not obligatory. The Pawnee evidentials include a Quotative, which is used when the speaker is "relating material that he has been told by someone else, or where the evidence is based on hearsay" (Parks 1976:225), an Evidential Proper, which is used for events that the speaker is certain of, but to which s/he was not an eyewitness, an Inferential, for inferred events, and a Dubitative, which is also for unwitnessed events, but those about which there is some doubt. Yukaghir has only one evidential, apparently, and it is used for unwitnessed events. Tarascan has an enclitic which indicates that the statement is hearsay. It seems that the primary distinction where an evidential morpheme occurs is between events that the speaker has directly witnessed (the unmarked case) and events which s/he is relating without having directly witnessed.

8. *Emphatics*

Morphemes described as *emphatics* were identified in seven languages of the sample, but in four of these, they are not verbal inflections. In Diegueño and Kiwai, the emphatic may attach to elements other than the verb. In Kwakiutl, the emphatic suffix occurs among a large class of non-obligatory suffixes. In most cases the emphatic morpheme is peripheral to the verb, that is, it occurs as one of the first prefixes (as in Kutenai, Pawnee and Kiwai), or as one of the last suffixes (as in Diegueño, Tarascan and Kwakiutl). In Pawnee, the Assertative mode gives emphasis to a statement, and can also be used with the Imperative, but not with any of the Evidentials. An emphatic is not always restricted to expressing the speaker's certainty of the truth of a proposition, however. In Diegueño, the emphatic suffix may follow the epistemic suffix. In Kutenai, the emphatic is mutually exclusive with the epistemic, but it can also occur in questions. In Santa Cruz, the suffix labelled Emphatic also occurs in questions. The Tarascan emphatic does not occur with any of the other tense or aspect morphemes. It signals surprise, wonder or pleasure at the situation described by the verb. These few facts suggest that emphatic markers may be used for quite different functions in the various languages. An emphatic that simply strengthens the assertion of the truth of the proposition is not very common as an inflection. The only possible example found in the sample was in Kiwai. The reason for this is that in order for a morpheme to become attached to a verb as an inflection, it would have to be very frequent in discourse. However, if a morpheme is very frequent, it would tend to lose its emphatic meaning. Consider, for instance, the discontinuous negative morpheme in French, *ne ... pas*. Originally, the *pas* was an emphatic added to the normal negative, but over time this construction lost it emphatic force, and has become the normal means of negating a verb. So an emphatic marker that strengthens an assertion would tend to become just an assertion marker, or an indicative.

9. *Subjunctives and conditionals*

Subjunctive is the term usually applied to special finite verb forms associated with certain types of subordinate constructions. The range of uses of the subjunctive varies considerably from language to language. A subordinate clause that uses a subjunctive verb in one language might take an indicative verb in another language, a nonfinite construction in still another (Noonan 1981). Since the survey reported on here did not include data on infinitives and participles, it is not possible to provide a full comparison of subordinate clause types. I will only make some remarks about the uses of subjunctives, and how they fit in with other moods.

For the most part, subjunctives are concommitants of particular constructions: that is, they occur in the complements of certain main verbs, or they occur after certain conjunctions. For example, in Maasai, the Subjunctive form is used after verbs meaning "to let" and verbs of commanding. In the following examples the Subjunctive marker is the prefix *m-* (Tucker and Mpaayei 1955: 64):

E-ıshɔɔ   m-e-to-ok-o ɛnkarɛ   "S/He let 3rd person drink some water"
E-tiaak-a m-ɛ-tu -suj-a   "S/He told 3rd person to follow him/her"

When the Subjunctive occurs after other verbs, the Subjunctive form implies purpose, even though no conjunction occurs to specifically indicate purpose:

E-inyo ma-tɔ-dɔl   "He stood up so that we could see him"
E-ta-mayian-a yiook ma-tu-bul   "He blessed us so that we should prosper"

Since the subjunctive is usually a marker of certain types of subordination, it is very difficult to say what the subjunctive "means" in any given language. There is a long literature on this problem in European languages, and no satisfactory solution. At most, it might be said that the subjunctive has a very general meaning such as "non-asserted" and then it takes more specific meanings from the context in which it occurs.

Considered cross-linguistically, there is evidence of a relation between the *subjunctive* and *imperative* or related moods. When subjunctive forms are used in main clauses, they have an *imperative* function in Maasai, Basque and Yupik, and/or a *hortative* function in Tarascan, Pawnee and Maasai, in keeping with their non-asserted subordinate clause functions. The marking of subjunctive parallels that of indicative or imperative in most languages. In Maasai and Pawnee, the subjunctive is a prefix, just as the imperative is, and in Tarascan, Ojibwa and Georgian the subordinating mood is expressed in the same way as the imperative or optative.[7]

In addition to a subjunctive form, some languages have a *conjunctive* form, or a form that is used specifically in conjoined clauses. In our sample, Maasai has such a form. (Tucker and Mpaayei call it the N-Tense.) It is used when the verb is the second verb of a conjunction, and it is unmarked for tense, since its tense will be the same as the first verb. It is also used in the second verb of a command, and after verbs of wanting (which would take a subjunctive verb form in some languages).

Yupik has the largest number of subordinating moods in the sample. In addition to a Conditional and Concessive, whose functions will be discussed just below, Yupik distinguishes a Consequential mood from a Precessive Mood (Jakobson 1977):

Consequential
    neghe + ya + n   /neghyan/   "when s/he ate"
    eat + Consequential + 3s

Conditional
    neghe + ka + n   /neghekan/   "if s/he ate"
    eat + Conditional + 3s

Concessive
    neghe + ghngaa + n   /negheghngaan/   "although s/he ate"
    eat + Concessive + 3s

Precessive
    neghe + vagilga + n   /neghvagilgan/   "before s/he ate"
    eat + Precessive + 3s

In the following sentences, it can be seen that no conjunction is necessary:

kaate + vagilga + ma   neghe + kaa + guq /kaatfagilgama neghegkaagu/
arrive + Prec + 1s   eat + Past + 3s
"Before I arrived, he had eaten"

neghe + nghite + ka + n   aanyaghaghaatek
eat + Neg + Cond + 3s   leave early + Ind + 2 dual
"If he doesn't eat, you two can leave early."

While very few languages distinguish so many subordinate meanings with verbal inflection, it is not uncommon to find a special verb form used in conditional sentences. In the sample, ten languages have such a verbal inflection. Conditional sentences typically consist of two clauses, one, introduced in English by *if*, states the condition, while the other, introduced in English by *then*, states what will or would happen if the condition were met. In Pawnee, Tarascan, Malayalam, Iatmul, Yukaghir, Gilyak, Yupik, Sierra Miwok and Georgian, there is a special verb form that occurs in the *if*-clause of a conditional sentence.[8] This seems to be the most common situation. However, Georgian and Sierra Miwok also have a special verb form, termed the Conditional by the authors, that appears in the *then*- clause of a conditional sentence. In Pawnee the Subjunctive is used in the *then*-clause. In Basque, there is a Conditional for the *then*-clause and it may optionally appear in the *if*-clause as well. The Tiwi Past Subjunctive is used in both clauses of a past conditional sentence.

Verb forms for conditional sentences are formally parallel to the subjunctive and imperative in Pawnee, Malayalam, Basque, Iatmul, Yupik and Georgian. Further, there is some overlap in function between the conditional and other moods. For instance, in Pawnee, Tiwi, Sierra Miwok and Ojibwa, the forms used in conditional sentences are also found in other subordinate clauses. In Pawnee and Sierra Miwok, one of the forms used in conditionals can also be used in hortative or optative functions. These facts suggest that conditionals are related to other moods.

10. *Conclusion*

Our survey of *mood* inflection in the languages of the world has shown, then, that the following four conceptual domains have very similar expression in verbal inflection:

1. Imperatives and related moods
2. Epistemic moods
3. Subjunctives or subordinating moods
4. Conditionals

On the other hand, we have also seen that *interrogatives* and *negatives* have very different expression types, and are in general unrelated to mood. In the next chapter we will discuss the consequence of these findings for the notion of *mood* as a univeral grammatical category.

NOTES

1. Givón 1973 argues that the epistemic notion of possibility is already present in the notion of "ability", and that a change from a meaning of "ability of the agent" to "proposition is possibly true" is a loss of meaning. Perhaps the same argument can be made for the development of epistemic moods from other sources.

2. Foley and Van Valin seem to confuse Whorf's terminology, since they adopt the term "status" for the speaker's commitment to the truth of the proposition, while Whorf used that term to refer to markers of illocutionary acts.

3. Lyons 1977: 748 speculates "possibly in no attested language, is there a distinct mood that stands in the same relation to questions as the imperative does to mands." Clearly he is wrong.

4. The *m-* prefix for negation is phonetically longer than the *m-* prefix for subjunctive, which appears in an example in section 9.

5. Burling suggests that this long suffix may perhaps be further analyzable into morphemes, but he adds that it functions just like any other Principal Suffix.

6. The Pawnee Potential may be described as expressing *root possibility*, in the sense used by Coates 1983.

7. In Ojibwa and Georgian this mood is called the Conjunctive, but it functions more like a *subjunctive* than does the *conjunctive* of Maasai, which will be described just below.

8. In both Pawnee and Tarascan, the Conditional is described as indicating an action or event that is contingent upon some other action or event. Yet in the examples given by the authors (Parks 1976 for Pawnee, and Foster 1970 for Tarascan), the Conditional verb form appears in the *if*-clause, rather than the *then*-clause, as would be expected from the author's explanation.

CHAPTER 9:
ASPECT, TENSE AND MOOD AS GRAMMATICAL CATEGORIES

1. *MOOD as a cross-linguistic grammatical category*

Let us consider the question of whether the inflections that fall under our working definition of mood form a cross-linguistically coherent grammatical category. This case is more complex than that of tense or aspect, so it is worthwhile to reconsider what it would mean for a set of inflections to constitute a grammatical category. The notion of grammatical category is central to all modern linguistics, and has developed over the years in the work of Boas, Whorf, Sapir, Jakobson, Benveniste, Kuryłowicz and many others. The basic idea is that sets of conceptually-related morphemes *contrast* with one another, in the sense that the presence of one excludes the presence of another. Further, these conceptually-related morphemes will ordinarily be expressed in a parallel fashion; that is, they will occur in the same affix position. In explicating grammatical categories, the linguist tries to define the general conceptual domain covered by the category and tries to determine how this domain is divided by the members of the category. For instance, *tense* is the category that covers references to time relative to the time of the speech event. This domain is divided into three parts in some languages: time preceding the speech event, time simultaneous with the speech event, and time subsequent to the speech event. If the three markers for these functions are mutually exclusive in some language, and expressed in a parallel fashion, we conclude that *tense* is a grammatical category in that language.

In order to show that some category is coherent and has cross-linguistic significance, it is necessary to show that a particular conceptual domain behaves like a grammatical category in a substantial number of languages. For *aspect* two two-way distinctions were found to be significant — the perfective / imperfective distinction and the habitual / continuous distinction, and furthermore, these two distinctions are related in some languages. For *tense* some two-way distinctions were identified — between future and non-future, past and non-past, anterior and non-anterior — and a few languages were found in which tense formed a coherent three-member category. When it comes to *mood*, however, we have a large number of distinctions to consider, and we must ask if they all fit into one category, and if this category is appropriately characterized by our working definition.

The working definition, it will be recalled, covered any markers that indicated what role the speaker meant the proposition to play in the discourse. This includes all markers that indicate illocutionary force, as well as markers that signal that the speaker is qualifying the assertion. The evidence that we have examined here indicates that the markers that fall under this definition do not form a coherent category cross-linguistically. First, it is clear that markers of illocutionary force do not constitute a category or sub-category. While markers of commands and questions are mutually exclusive, they hardly ever have parallel inflectional expression. The only example in our sample in which the interrogative and imperative are expressed in the same affix position is Yupik. In all other cases, interrogative and imperative are expressed differently. Indeed, the interrogative has unique expression properties not paralleled by any other markers. Similarly, inflectional markers of negation are unique in their expression properties. In fact, interrogative and negative inflections show more *cross-linguistic* than language-internal coherence. That is, the expression of interrogation and negation follows universal principles, and neither of these inflections shows much parallelism with other inflections language-internally.

Among other mood inflections, however, there is good evidence for language-internal, as well as cross-linguistic relations. Consider the following facts, discussed in the preceding chapter:

1. Imperatives and subjunctives are related in that there are languages in which one form serves both for forming commands and for marking subordination. Further, where the imperative and subjunctive are distinguished, they are sometimes marked in a parallel fashion.

2. Another set with some internal relations are the epistemic markers and evidentials. In some cases, epistemics in the past tense function very much like evidentials of "unwitnessed" events.

3. More than half the languages that have an inflection for epistemic possibility or probability mark this function in a way that is formally parallel to the mood used for commands.

4. The subjunctive and conditional are related in the following way: some languages have a special verb form for *if*-clauses, while others use a general subordinate verb form (a subjunctive) in *if*-clauses; some languages have a special verb form used in *then*-clauses, and in these languages, the

same form can usually also be used in the *if*-clause (Tiwi, Serbo-Croatian, Sierra Miwok, Basque). (Cf. English: *It would please me if it would rain hard.*) In other words, subjunctives and conditionals, when compared cross-linguistically, are used in the same contexts.

5. In some cases, conditionals are related to optatives, in that the same form is used for both. This is the case in Pawnee and Nahuatl.

To summarize, there is evidence for a set of intricate relations among the inflectional markers of *imperatives* and related moods, *subjunctives*, *epistemics* and *conditionals*. Furthermore, these markers are almost all mutually exclusive. Thus we might propose that these inflections form a grammatical category. But how would we describe the conceptual domain of this category?

All of these markers have propositional scope, are relevant only in non-interrogative clauses, and contrast with an unmarked function which is an unqualified assertion. Imperatives and subjunctives occur in non-asserted clauses, while epistemics and evidentials, which occur in asserted clauses, serve to qualify the assertion in some way. Thus we could define a cross-linguistic category of *mood* as indicating the discourse function of non-interrogative clauses.

This is not a very satisfying definition — certainly in no way as coherent as the definitions of aspect and tense. But then the number of contrasts that aspect and tense must cover is much smaller, and the expression types in these categories more consistent. The truth is that there are very few languages in which more than two of the inflections that come under this definition of mood occur in the same affix position. In the present sample, Malayalam, Pawnee and Yupik are the only languages with a large selection of moods expressed in the same affix position.[1]

Referring again to the discussion of *tense* and *aspect* as categories, it appears that in most cases a "category" arises diachronically because a single grammatical marker develops to cover a range of meaning in one domain, with the other "member" of the category just the unmarked remainder of the domain. The lack of uniformity in the expression of the various "moods", including the uniqueness of the expression of interrogation and negation, can also be explained diachronically, for if the different markers develop from different sources at different times, then a variety of expression types is to be expected. The uniformity of expression of the various moods in Malayalam, Pawnee and Yupik is perhaps due to the simultaneous development of a number of moods from a set of syntactically parallel sources, such as a set of auxiliary verbs. Comparative and historical evidence makes it clear that this is correct for Malayalam (George 1971), and the Yupik and Pawnee cases appear synchronically very similar.

If this diachronic picture accounts for the differences in the expression of the mood category, it also provides a means of exploring the complex relations of similarity that are found to exist among mood markers. Rather than trying to define a large conceptual domain with language-internal synchronic validity under the label of *mood*, we should recognize that what we see in any one language at any one time are only a few links in a larger developmental chain. Under this view, the similarities among mood inflections are either relations of parallelism due to developments from a similar or identical source, or relations of contiguity — two mood meanings representing contiguous links in a single chain. I will illustrate these relations by discussing a few of the known diachronic developments affecting modality and mood.[2]

Obligation: Markers of the modality of *obligation* tend to develop into *epistemic* markers, as illustrated earlier with the examples of the epistemic uses of the English modals *must, should* and *ought to*. A similar development can be seen in Catalan *deure* which derives historically from Latin *debere* "to owe", but which now, when used with an infinitive, only signals probability (Yates 1975:83).

Markers of obligation also develop into *futures*, as in the case of the English *shall*, which earlier meant "to owe", and the Romance future, which developed from a construction with the verb *habere* "to have" that originally signalled obligation when used with an infinitive. Similar examples are found in Kru dialects (Marchese 1979) and in Ukrainian (Ard n.d.).

A notion related to *obligation* — *necessity* — yields the optative and imperative in Tamil and Malayalam (Subrahmanyam 1971).

Ability: Markers of the agent-oriented notion of ability can develop into markers of *potentiality* or *possibility*, as illustrated by the English modals *may* and *can*, and by the Haitian form *cap* (from French *capable*), now used to mean both ability and possibility.

Alternatives for further diachronic development from markers of ability and possibility include the *optative*, as in the use of English *may* (*May you prosper*), and also a *conditional*, as in Sierra Miwok, where the same form serves for potential and conditional.

Future + past: There are several sources for future markers, e.g., modals of obligation or volition, and verbs of movement. A future from any of these sources, when combined with a past tense, can yield a *conditional*. The English conditional *would* is an example, since it is originally the past tense of the future auxiliary *will*. *Should* (the past tense of *shall*) can also be used in conditional sentences (*Should it rain ...*). The Romance conditional is formed from the past tense of the auxiliary *habere*, whose present tense gives the future. In Tiwi, the form used in conditional sentences (both clauses) combines the Past and the Future prefixes. The Nahuatl conditional uses the Imperfective of an incorporated verb meaning *to want, to intend*. In Sierra Miwok, the past tense of the Andative (meaning "to go in order to ...", and used as a future) has a conditional sense.

Conditionals are used as *optatives* in Pawnee and Nahuatl, as well as in more archaic English, where one could say *Would that he were here*.

Apparently, *conditionals* can take on *subjunctive* uses, although only a few examples are available. The English auxiliary *should* has a subjunctive use in embedded clauses in British English (Coates 1983). Consider the following example from British television news, April 17, 1984: *The police are expecting that the Libyans should make the first move*. Similarly, in certain Spanish dialects studied by Silva-Corvalán (1984), the *conditional* verb form is replacing the Past Subjunctive, both in the *if*-clauses of conditional sentences, and in complements to verbs of telling and commanding.

The preceding list is by no means exhaustive. There are undoubtedly other diachronic relations that need to be explored. However, it serves to illustrate the close diachronic relations among the different mood and modality markers. There are two points in particular that should be noted concerning this summary of diachronic developments. The first is that one source may yield a number of different moods — e.g. an epistemic, an imperative or optative, a conditional (usually with past tense) and perhaps eventually a subjunctive may all derive from *obligation* markers. Such developments from the same source, whether linear or parallel, account for some of the structural parallelism found language-internally, and suggest a way of investigating the semantic relations among moods. Second, each mood has a variety of possible sources. An epistemic may arise from a modal of obligation or ability; a future from obligation, volition or movement, and so on. The fact that very similar grammatical notions are arrived at from different sources and independently in many languages suggests that there is some special significance to these grammatical notions that needs to be understood.

A universal study of grammatical meaning, then, could proceed as follows: working within a general area of semantic space (much as in L. Anderson 1982), a number of very specific grammatical functions can be identified on the basis of meaning and contextual factors. (For example, *progressive* and *continuous* markers have similar meanings, but they can be distinguished by the fact that *progressives* are restricted to *active* verbs.) Relations among these very specific functions can be studied, again following L. Anderson 1982, by determining cross-linguistically which functions can be covered by the same grammatical marker, and by studying the diachronic extension of a marker from one function to another. If we understand the nature of a relation of similarity between specific grammatical functions, then we are closer to understanding the nature of grammatical meaning.

Another dimension to this proposal concerns expression types, and the relation between meaning and mode of expression that has been discussed in earlier chapters. Some areas of semantic space occupied by inflectional morphemes overlap with or border on areas occupied by non-bound grammatical morphemes, and there is a certain diachronic relation between non-bound and bound morphemes. Other areas of semantic space covered by inflections border on areas occupied by derivational morphemes or lexical expression. Grammatical meaning can most profitably be studied in the larger context of the study of meanings expressed in other ways.

2. *The ordering of aspect, tense and mood markers*

In Chapter 2 the data on the ordering of inflectional morphemes was presented. There we saw that the regularities in morpheme order can be stated in terms of an ordering with respect to the verb stem: aspect occurs closest to the verb stem, followed by tense, and then by mood. The only exception to this ordering found in the 50-language sample is in Ojibwa, where the Dubitative suffix precedes the Preterite suffix.[3] Otherwise the regularity of this ordering across languages is quite remarkable. In Chapter 2, an explanation for this ordering was offered in terms of the relevance principle. It is necessary to bring up ordering again here, because other linguists have proposed a somewhat different ordering for elements in the verb phrase.

Bickerton 1974 studied the function and ordering of pre-verbal elements in several pidgin and creole languages and concluded that the universal ordering for these elements is as follows:

ANTERIOR - IRREALIS - DURATIVE - VERB

The morpheme referred to as "durative" by Bickerton is an aspect in our terms, so its position closest to the verb conforms to our data. However, the ordering of "anterior", which is a *tense*, and "irrealis", which is *mood* or *modality*, are the opposite of what is found in the current sample of languages. Similarly, the data discussed here do not square with the examples cited by Foley and Van Valin 1984 from Lisu (examples from Hope 1974) in which intransitive verb stems indicating "reality status" in their terms (which corresponds to epistemic mood in our terms) occur after the main verb with tense markers suffixed to them, giving the order

VERB - EPISTEMIC - TENSE:

ása nya ami khwa wa̧-a̧   "It is obligatory for Asa to hoe the field"
Asa TOP field hoe obligatory-NONPAST

ása nya ami khwa da-a̧   "It is acceptable for Asa to hoe the field"
Asa TOP field hoe acceptable-NONPAST

ása nya ami khwa khù-a   "It is normal for Asa to hoe the field"
Asa TOP field hoe normal-NONPAST

Furthermore, if the English modal auxiliary complex is analysed, as it often is, as consisting of the following elements, then here also we find the ordering of the *modal* element closer to the verb than *tense*:

TENSE - MODAL - PERFECT - PROGRESSIVE - VERB

Of course, these constructions in the creoles, in Lisu and in English are not inflections, since they are not bound to the verb. But since bound inflections develop diachronically out of non-bound constructions such as these, one would expect the same ordering of elements, for such grammaticized elements are not likely to change their order as they become bound to the verb. What, then, explains this discrepancy in the facts about the ordering of inflections and non-bound grammatical elements?

The problem lies solely in the attempt to equate inflectional *mood* and non-inflectional *modality*. We have already discussed the fact that inflectional mood rarely expresses deontic notions or other notions we have called *agent-oriented* modalities. We have also noted that the *agent-oriented* modalities develop diachronically into epistemic and other moods, and future tenses. As this happens, tense distinctions marked on modals tend to be lost, or reinterpreted as non-temporal distinctions. This can easily be illustrated for English, where the modals that were formerly past tense can now be used in present contexts:

He could do it now, but he won't.
He might do it now, but I doubt it.
He should do it now, but he won't.

Thus it is not correct to analyse the English modal auxiliary sequence as obligatorily containing an initial tense marker. Indeed, on the surface, where the relevant comparisons are being made, there is no sense in which *tense* could be said to precede *modality* in Modern English. When the modal auxiliary sequence explicitly codes tense, it does so with the *have* + EN construction so that tense actually occurs closer to the verb than modality or mood:

Bill should have heard that lecture.
Brody could have eaten the whole thing.
Randy must have already left for school.

Note that Past plus *must* forces the epistemic, inferential reading of *must*, rather than the deontic one.

Consider now the Lisu examples. In the grammar by Hope 1974, the final -a̧ in these sentences is not glossed as Non-past as in Foley and Van Valin, but rather as Declarative, indicating that it is probably a mood marker rather than a tense marker. Sentences with this final suffix may be translated in the English Progressive, Present, Future or Past (Hope 1974:156). There is another Declarative marker -u̧ which is restricted to past meaning, so one could argue that at least with this marker tense is signalled. However, an examination of the examples in Hope 1974 turned up no cases where -u̧ occurs on the auxiliaries that according to Foley and Van Valin signal epistemic categories. It is possible that no real tense distinction applies to these particular auxiliaries. It should be further noted that the meanings of the final verb auxiliaries are much more specific than any meanings we found coded inflectionally. At least some of these verbs have readings in which the final verb expresses an agent-oriented modality. As, for example, the second sentence, which may also have the reading "Asa is able to hoe the field". Thus the meanings expressed by these non-bound auxiliaries may not be purely epistemic, and may not be truly comparable to inflectional mood.

The pidgin and creole case is more difficult to deal with, because it is less clear what is meant by "Irrealis". Furthermore, Bickerton is generalizing over a number of pidgin and creole languages in which the pre-verbal elements come from different sources and are in different stages of development. If we take just two of the examples that Bickerton discusses, however, we can see that the particular morphemes to which he refers are agent-oriented modalities, rather than mood. The Hawaiian Pidgin examples that Givon 1982 discusses (from Bickerton's transcripts), use the so-called irrealis marker *go*, both in a past context and with the Anterior marker *bin* (or *wen*), as a marker of past intention. Givón (1982: 123, 125) translates these examples as "was/were going to" or "had been aiming to."

> ah, I say... I *wen go* order, see... from da-kine Honolulu Roofing
> ah, so I said I *had been aiming to* order it, see... from Honolulu Roofing.

All the examples with *go* (cited in Bickerton 1974 or in Givón 1982) have human agents and active verbs, suggesting an agent-oriented meaning rather than a mood. If this marker is indeed agent-oriented, then its occurrence after the tense marker *bin* or *wen* is to be expected.[4]

The relevant marker in Haitian Creole, *a*, *ava* or *va* is labelled as a future by Hall 1970, and as a posterior marker by Phillips 1983, who gives a detailed analysis of pre-verbal elements in Haitian Creole, working from transcripts of spoken language. Phillips finds that this morpheme is actually not common in the language of her subjects. It occurs in her data only with first person subjects, and only with active verbs. Phillips states "all the uses of the marker bear a strong sense of 'intention'...". Consider these examples:

> n'a mõtre yo tire   "we will show them how to shoot."
> we POST show they shoot

Unmodified by tense, this marker probably indicates an agent-oriented modality. However, when the same marker occurs in combination with the Anterior marker *t'*, it yields a fused morph *ta* / *tav*. Phillips implies a doubt that the speakers are aware of an internal composition for this form. Like Hall 1970, she labels it a Conditional. Her examples indicate that this is accurate, and that the marker does not necessarily imply a past context. Rather the marker seems to correspond directly to English *would*:

> m ta rẽmẽ se kõsa   "I'd like it like that...
> I COND like it like that

> mwẽta rẽmẽ aysyẽ ta ka al viv   "I'd like Haitians to be able to live like that"
> I COND like Haitian COND able to live

These data show that a tense marker may occur farther from the verb than an agent-oriented modality, but there is no clear evidence for tense occurring farther from the verb than mood, where *mood* refers to a marker that has the whole proposition in its scope. Still, there is an apparent anomaly to be explained: if agent-oriented modalities diachronically develop into moods, then their order with respect to other verbal modifiers ought to remain the same. The explanation for the apparent change in ordering lies in the interaction of tense with modality and mood. Modality markers very often develop out of main verbs, which are originally marked for tense in languages with tense marking. In OV languages, the tense marker will be a suffix, so that the order VERB - MODAL - TENSE results. In VO languages, the tense markers are more likely to be pre-verbal, yielding the order TENSE - MODAL - VERB. However, as the modal auxiliary loses its agent-oriented meaning and becomes epistemic, it can no longer be modified by tense. This was illustrated above for English and Haitian Creole. Similarly in Dutch, where modal auxiliaries may be used in a periphrastic past construction such as *hebben moeten*, in which the tense precedes the modal (which is in turn followed by the main verb), this can only convey the deontic meaning of "had to", and never the epistemic meaning of confident inferral, which *moeten* in the unmarked tense can convey. Thus the order TENSE - MOOD - VERB or VERB - MOOD - TENSE does not develop because where an agent-oriented modal develops into a mood, the real temporal sense of tense is lost.

The order MOOD - TENSE - VERB or VERB - TENSE - MOOD can arise from the preceding situation if some other means is found to indicate tense independently of the mood, as in the English auxiliary, where *have* is used after the modal to indicate past time. Or this order can develop if the mood develops from a non-verbal source, i.e., from a particle or adverbial (which does not have agent-oriented meaning) that comes to modify a tensed verb. In these cases, the original order of non-bound elements follows the relevance principle, so that the sentential modifier, mood, occurs farther from the verb than the tense indicator which is more relevant to the verb.

3. *Factors determining the development of verbal inflection*

The data on verbal inflection from 50 languages discussed in the preceding chapters show a remarkable cross-language consistency in the following:

1. The meanings coded as verbal inflections are very similar across languages of diverse genetic and areal affiliation and distinct word order typology.

2. The mode of expression associated with particular grammatical meanings is also highly consistent across languages. There are correlations between meaning and mode of expression when bound and non-bound grammatical morphemes are considered, as well as when inflectional versus derivational morphemes are considered. There are also correlations between meaning and the preversus post-position of an affix.

3. The order of inflectional morphemes (usually with respect to the verb stem) is consistent across languages. There are also correlations between the meaning of a morpheme and the degree of fusion with the verb stem it exhibits.

These facts point to the existence of strong universal factors governing the development of inflectional morphology. Unfortunately, the actual nature of only some of these factors is known. The following sketch is intended to outline what is known and what is not known about the causes of the development of inflection.

First, the position of a morpheme before it becomes an inflection is important, since a morpheme cannot become fused with a verb unless it is immediately contiguous to the verb. At the beginning of this book, the *relevance* principle was proposed to explain the ordering of inflectional material with respect to the verb stem. The same principle, or a version of it, such as Bartsch's Natural Serialization Principle (Vennemann 1974) that refers to free morphemes, predicts which morphemes will occur close to the verb, and in what order.

Second, I suggested in Chapter 2 that simple contiguous positioning may not be enough to spur fusion, but that *relevance* influences the actual fusion process, since the elements to be fused must have some conceptual unity, so that they can be viewed by speakers as cognitively coherent units.

Third, in order for a morpheme to reach inflectional or even grammatical status, it must undergo an extreme increase in frequency of use. This increase in frequency is concomitant with a semantic generalization, by which the morpheme comes to be used in an increasing number of environments. The semantic generalization and frequency increase continues even after a morpheme has become fused with the verb (as suggested by the data on aspect, discussed in Chapter 7). While this is an extremely well-attested phenomenon, its actual cause is as yet unknown.

The sorts of morphemes that undergo semantic generalization and grammaticization are similar across languages, as are the grammatical meanings that result from this process. That is, there are certain universal paths of semantic change leading to grammaticization. However, beyond invoking the notion of semantic generalization, we do not know how to predict the paths leading to grammaticization.

Finally, an inflectional morpheme is obligatory, so we must also explain how and why a morpheme becomes obligatory. Obligatoriness means that some exponent of a category appears in every finite clause, whether or not the information it conveys is redundant in the context. When a morpheme becomes obligatory, it joins the other automatic grammatical devices that a language employs to give structure to utterances. Asking why morphemes become obligatory is the same as asking why there are obligatory structures of any sort in language. Why can't each utterance be constructed in a new and imaginative way each time out of purely lexical material? Obligatory structures and categories are what allow linguistic productions to be fluently delivered and manageably decoded: they provide a framework with a limited number of variables into which speakers can fit their thoughts. They restrict the number of decisions that have to be made both by the speaker and the hearer.

Obligatoriness in itself places certain constraints on grammatical meaning. Generality has been discussed in this regard since only highly general meanings can become obligatory. But the specific content of the material that becomes obligatory must also be widely applicable. This in itself opens many questions. Why are temporal notions so much more often obligatorily expressed (as either tense or aspect) than spatial notions? Why are indicators of the speaker's degree of commitment to the truth of a proposition grammaticized while emotional responses are not? Why aren't there mood inflections that mean "the speaker is sorry that ..." or "the speaker is surprised that ..."? These are questions that require answers if we are to understand fully the development of inflections.

This sketch shows that there is much yet to learn about the causes of the development of inflection. I cannot emphasize enough the point that the data presented in this book argue strongly for *universal* causes of grammatical development. This view contrasts with the cause usually cited for the development of inflection — language-specific cases of particular "communicative needs". Consider, for example, the statement by Givón (1982: 117):

> grammatical subsystems and their attendant inflectional morphologies ('coding devices')...*arise* when the specific communicative need arises, normally when the older system coding a particular function has eroded beyond a certain threshold of communicative coherence ('transparency')...

This statement gives the impresssion that inflection develops because certain gaps appear in the grammatical system, and morphemes move, in drag-chain fashion, to fill these gaps. There are several reasons why communicative need cannot be invoked in this way as an explanation for the development of inflection:

First, this view assumes that there is a set of communicative functions (which presumably vary little across cultures) for which languages must supply grammatical expression. The normal state for a language, then, would be to have all of these needs fulfilled, so that the gaps that allegedly motivate grammatical change would be rare. A comparison of the languages of the world shows that this view cannot be maintained. There are many functions that are expressed grammatically in some languages which in others have no grammatical expression. An example is *tense*, which is expressed inflectionally in less than half of the languages of the world. A substantial number of inflectional languages do not have tense markers, and show no movement toward developing them.

Second, the view that the development of inflection is motivated primarily by unfulfilled communicative needs predicts that there will not be developments by which two or more markers arise to fulfill the same or similar functions. Such situations do arise, however: periphrastic progressives arise in languages in which a simple present can express progressive, as for example in Spanish; English has at least three modal auxiliaries that express *probability* — *may, might* and *could*.

Third, the view that inflection develops to fill certain communicative needs is not consistent with the fact that many of the uses of inflectional morphology are redundant in context. Agreement markers are often redundant, as are tense and aspect markers. Inflections for subordinating moods usually co-occur with other markers of subordination, and are also redundant. It would be difficult to argue that such markers are fulfilling specific communicative needs.

Finally, when actual cases of change in inflectional markers are studied in progress, it can be seen that the cause and effect relation is not that proposed by Givón. The case studied by Silva-Corvalán 1984 shows that no prior erosion of old inflections is required before newer inflections take over their functions. Silva-Corvalán reports on certain Castilian dialects in which the Conditional inflection (formed by the suffixation of the Imperfect form of the auxiliary verb *haber* "to have" to the infinitive), is replacing the Past Subjunctive in many of its functions. For example, in the following two sentences from Silva-Corvalán's corpus, the underlined Conditional forms would, in the Standard or more conservative dialects, be Past Subjunctive forms:

¿Sabe lo que hacíamos para que no se *caerían* de la cama?
You know what we did so that they *wouldn't fall off* the bed?

Si yo *tendría* alguna persona que les *interesaría* de ir a ver como están...
If I *had* someone who *might be interested* in going to see them...

The Past Subjunctive forms that would fit in these sentences are *cayera*, *tuviera* and *interesara*, respectively. These forms are distinct from all other inflected verb forms in Spanish, they are not phonologically eroded, nor are they opaque or ambiguous in any way. There is no sense in which it can be said that the Conditional is moving into these environments to fulfill some communcative need, for that "need" is adequately met by the Past Subjunctive. In fact, the replacement of the Past Subjunctive with the Conditional in one context *creates* ambiguity. In the complements to verbs of saying, the Conditional is used if the complement proposition is to be taken as a report (first example) below, but the Past Subjunctive is used if the complement is to be taken as a request or command (second example below):

Dijo que irías mañana.   "He said you would go tomorrow"
Dijo que fueras mañana.   "He said for you to go tomorrow"

If the Conditional replaces the Past Subjunctive in sentences such as the second one, then ambiguity is created. However, Silva-Corvalán reports that this is precisely what is happening in these dialects. The Conditional is expanding its sphere of usage despite what might be considered to be a *loss* in communicative efficiency.

If communicative need does not motivate the generalization of grammatical markers to new functions, then what does? I suggest that grammatical generalization is motivated by positive forces, rather than called into play for remedial purposes. Certain semantic functions are very similar, and generalization of grammatical markers to subsume closely related functions is a spontaneous process that attends not at all to "needs". It was noted above that some languages use a subordinate verb form for *if*-clauses, while other languages use the same "conditional" form for both *if*- and *then*- clauses of conditional sentences. For instance, Tiwi uses the Future and the Past prefixes together on the verb forms of both clauses of counterfactual conditionals. So there is nothing specific to Spanish about the development that

Silva-Corvalán reports, rather what is observed there is only another instance of a universal tendency for grammatical change.

NOTES

1. Languages such as Garo, in which aspect, tense and mood affixes *all* appear in the same position are of course not to be counted here.

2. The following discussion is based on work done in collaboration with William Pagliuca. Further discussion and examples can be found in Bybee and Pagliuca 1984.

3. In Tiwi the usual order for prefixes is for tense to follow mood, with the exception of the Compulsional, which is preceded by the Non-Past prefix. The examples cited in Chapter 8 indicate that the Compulsional is an agent-oriented modality, so this ordering is to be expected, as indicated in the discussion below.

4. Bickerton 1977 expresses considerable doubt about the "irrealis" reading of the *bin* plus *go* combination in Hawaiian, since the only informant who produced these combinations denies that this was the intended meaning.

CHAPTER 10: CONCLUSION

The study of language is the study of the relation of meaning to form. The search for a linguistic theory is the search for the language-specific and universal principles that govern this relation. Many factors complicate this enterprise; many approaches to the problem are possible. The current endeavor has been offered as a contribution to the data that must be input to linguistic theorizing, and to the theorizing itself. The data presented here are innovative in the sense that a wide variety of types — cross-linguistic, experimental and diachronic — has been drawn together in an attempt to create a coherent picture. The cross-linguistic data are innovative because they are drawn from a stratified random sample of languages, and because they present an exhaustive survey of verbal inflection. The theory is innovative in the sense that it proposes principles to predict the properties of morphological systems that have previously seemed arbitrary, e.g. the occurrence of suppletion and allomorphy, and the meaning of morphological categories. Furthermore, the theory brings together both the psychological and the diachronic in an attempt to explain the recurrent properties of morphological systems in terms of the dynamic processes that create them.

Whether or not the data presented here turn out to be useful to others, and regardless of the correctness of the details of the particular principles and analyses, there are two main theoretical points that have been implicit in all the discussion, and which I consider to be essential to further progress in theoretical morphology. I would like to restate these two points here in reviewing the main conclusions of the book. The first is that morphology must be viewed as an interaction of rule and rote processing. The second is that no explanation for linguistic phenomena is complete until a causal relation can be shown to exist between the principle proposed as explanation and the linguisic phenomena to be explained.

1.   *The interaction of rules and rote processing*

In the literature on morphology, there has always been a great deal of emphasis placed on the optimality of morphological transparency or analyzability or the "one meaning - one form" principle.[1] From the point of view of transparency, regular rules are good and natural, and irregularities, allomorphy and suppletion are undesirable and unnatural. However, if we expand our perspectives beyond morphology, and consider all the modes of expression that natural languages have at their disposal, we can see that the "one meaning - one form" principle is actually used very sparingly. If the "one meaning - one form" principle were applied rigorously in a language, there would be very few monomorphemic words, for nearly every concept that is named with a word in a language can be broken down into smaller semantic components each of which could have separate formal expression. If there were separate morphemes to indicate humanness, animacy, color, size, number of legs, ability to fly, and so on, nearly every animal in nature could be named by combinations of these features and the arbitrariness and opacity of language would be considerably reduced.

However, this is not the way natural languages work. Concepts, entities, states and events that are perceived by humans as distinguishable are given separate, unanalyzable labels. Even combinations of morphemes that begin as transparent tend to become opaque and arbitrary if they name a cognitively distinguishable concept. Rather than having a very small arbitrary lexical component and a large number of combinatory possibilities, natural languages tend to have a large arbitrary lexical component and a small number of combinatory possibilities.[2]

Since lexical expression is such a highly utilized option in natural language, it is not surprising that some morphological processes will have characteristics of lexical expression, such as suppletion, allomorphy and fusion. The task of the linguist, then, is to predict the distribution of such expression properties, to explore the boundaries between morphology and lexicon. In this book, I have proposed principles based on the semantic relation between stem and affix that make some predictions about the occurrence of these properties. In particular, I have proposed that the *relevance* of the meaning of the affix to the stem determines the degree of fusion between affix and stem. Further, the relevance of the morphological notion to the stem detemines how cognitively distinguishable or discrete the resulting concept is. This semantic discreteness determines the degree of relatedness of a particular inflected form to the rest of the paradigm. I have argued that the formal expression properties diagram the semantic relations, so that suppletion and allomorphy tend to co-occur with the most highly relevant inflectional categories.

Another factor that I have often mentioned as a determinant of suppletion and allomorphy is word frequency. While it seems clear that the *maintenance* of morphological irregularities depends on sufficient frequency for rote learning, it is perhaps more interesting that word frequency actually contributes to the *creation* of suppletion. This follows from the fact that highly frequent and salient combinations of semantic features will, simply because of their frequency, be highly distinguishable cognitively, and susceptible to being treated as unanalyzable wholes. Thus for high frequency verbs such as *be, do* and *have*, suppletive expression is just as natural as regular morphological expression. Even if they do have regular forms, they are just as likely to be treated in the mental lexicon as though they were suppletive.

The *basic / derived* relation is based on a very similar principle. Zero expression represents another divergence from the "one meaning - one form" principle, but again a predictable one. The most usual and frequent combination of semantic elements is taken to be a unitary concept and not a combination at all. The less usual combinations are formally analyzable. This view predicts both the unmarked status of *dog* in the singular versus *dogs*, as well as the unmarked *cattle* versus *a head of cattle*.

Given the pervasiveness of fused or lexical expression and the universal availability of syntactic combination or periphrastic expression, what is there left for morphological expression to do? Actually, the role of morphology in natural language is a very restricted one. Of course, many languages have virtually no inflectional morphology, and some of these have very little derivational morphology as well. This leads us to ask why morphology develops at all, and what notions are coded morphologically. This book presents data that bear on this question, but has not answered the question. I have tried to explicate one factor that obviously is essential to morphological expression. This factor is *generality of semantic content*. We have seen that generality must be achieved on two planes for a morpheme to be inflectional. On the one hand, a morphological process must be *lexically general* in the sense that it can apply to any stem of the proper semantic and syntactic categories, and on the other hand, it must be general in the sense that it can occur in a wide variety of contexts at the clause level, e.g. in clauses with different sorts of participants and participant roles, with verbs of different inherent valence or aspect, etc. What sorts of semantic notions can achieve this generality? Cross-linguistic data indicate that particular notions within the categories of aspect, tense and mood occur over and over again in unrelated languages, but I have no explanation for why these notions become general while other logical possibilities do not.

2.   *Diachronic mechanisms*

We owe to the many works by Joseph Greenberg the idea that there must be a diachronic component to any explanation of language universals. That is, it is not enough to find cross-linguistic correlations and to propose principles to account for them: it must also be shown that the proposed principles also drive the diachronic mechanisms that create the observed correlation. I have not been completely successful in achieving explanation at this level for all the principles that I have proposed, but I would like to outline here the degree of success I have managed.

A good case to begin with is the *basic / derived* relation, since the correlation of zero expression to the unmarked member of a category is well-established. One could argue that there is a psychological principle behind this correlation, a principle that says that conceptually basic semantic material seeks the simplest expression. This principle is articulated by Vennemann 1972, and later by Clark and Clark 1978.[3] However, the principle cannot be said to explain the correlation unless it can be shown that the psychological principle is the moving force in the creation of the correlation. If the correlation is created diachronically by some unrelated concurrence of factors, then the proposed principle is not the explanation for the correlation.

What, then, is the diachronic source of zero expression? Zeroes appear where non-zero inflections have developed to cover a part of some semantic domain, leaving the other part formally unmarked. Thus in a language where there is a future inflection, and the present is zero-marked, the cause for this might be that there was a good source for the development of a future marker, but no good source for a present marker. If this were the case, then the fact that the present is zero-marked would have nothing to do with the proposed psychological principle. However, this is not the case. There are two diachronic mechanisms (that I know of) that create zeros, and in both cases the proposed principle can be seen as a force behind these mechanisms. First, the fact that future inflections develop so much more often than present inflections stems from the fact that explicit expression of the future is more often necessary than explicit expression of the present, and this is itself a result of the proposed psychological principle, if the following is true. In a language which does not have grammatical expression of the future, an untensed verb, in the absence of context, will be taken to refer to the present, while a reference to a future prediction, intention or probability will require an explicit statement, an added marker. This marker may eventually develop into an inflection, and when it does, the present will remain formally unmarked. The fact that no explicit indicator is necessary to refer to the present is a consequence of the general principle behind zero-expression: the basic concept needs no explicit marker.

The second diachronic implementation of this principle is in morphological reanalysis, by which a form that has a mark for a conceptually-basic concept (such as 3s) is reanalyzed as having zero expression for that concept. Examples of this type of reanalysis are given in Chapter 3, section 1.3. The existence of two independent diachronic implementations of the psychological principle is strong evidence that this is indeed the principle behind the cross-linguistic correlation.

Now consider the *relevance* principle. This principle is proposed to explain the cross-linguistic regularities in the meaning of verbal affixes, and in their order, as well as the degree of fusion of an affix with a stem (which includes the morpho-phonemic effect the affix has on the stem). The meaning and the ordering of affixes is not freely decided by each generation of speakers, so any proposed explanation must be an explanation of the creation of affixes and their particular order. The relevance principle applies here because it also applies to elements before they are bound, and while they are still movable in the clause: elements that belong together conceptually will occur together in the clause. So the more a concept has to do with the content of the verb, the closer it will occur to the verb stem. Thus when these elements become bound to the verb stem, their order will be the same. I have also suggested another way that the relevance principle can be implemented diachronically: a highly relevant notion may be more easily analyzed as fused with the verb stem than one of lesser relevance. But I do not have any strong evidence that this is the case, other than the cross-linguistic evidence, which is what I am trying to explain.

The degree of fusion of an affix to a stem could be the simple consequence of the length of time an affix has been attached to a stem, and thus only rather indirectly explained by the relevance principle. But there is also evidence for relevance as a positive force in the distribution of stem allomorphy, which is one of the indicators of degree of fusion. The more relevant a notion is to the verb, the more semantically distinguishable the resulting concept is. Thus two forms of the same verb that differ in aspect are more semantically distinct than two forms of the same verb that differ in person. They are thus more likely to have separate lexical representation, and consequently more likely to differ in form and to resist morpho-phonemic leveling. On the other hand, a form that is distinguished from the basic form only by a category of lower relevance, such as person agreement, is more likely to be reformed morpho-phonemically, and thus less likely to differ morpho-phonemically from the base. Further, two forms distinguished by a highly relevant category are more likely to drift apart semantically and create a suppletive paradigm. In this way, the relevance principle contributes directly to the diachronic changes that create the correlations associated with relevance.

A third correlation, long noted and discussed by others, is the correlation between irregular inflected forms and word frequency. The psychological principle behind this corelation is that highly frequent forms are learned by rote memorization, and stored and processed as unanalyzed units. This psychological principle contributes to the observed correlation in a preventive way, in that highly frequent forms are protected from regularization, and in a positive way, since high frequency contributes to the formation of suppletive paradigms.

A final correlation that I have discussed at some length is the correlation of inflectional expression with generality of semantic content. In this case, the level of explanation achieved here is inadequate, for although the dia-chronic phenomenon of semantic generalization, which is behind this corre-lation, is well-known, the psychological principle that drives this process is as yet undiscovered. We do not know why meanings tend to generalize and increase in frequency and contexts of usage over time. This is the fundamental question that must be answered for an understanding of the nature of gram-matical meaning, and as such, deserves our full attention.

NOTES

1. This principle is discussed by Vennemann 1972, and after that appealed to in a great many works. A recent example of the overapplication of this principle is Dressler 1984.

2. Of course, languages differ along just this parameter. Some languages appear to have a small number of roots out of which a large number of combinations are possible. However, even

in these languages, many of the combinations must be considered lexicalized, since their meanings are not transparently derivable from the combination of the meanings of the parts.

3. When Vennemann proposed this principle, he also proposed and gave evidence for the diachronic mechanism behind the synchronic correlation.

APPENDIX: LANGUAGES OF PERKINS' SAMPLE

ACOMA (Keresan) Miller 1965.

AINU (undetermined) Batchelor 1938, Simeon 1968.

ANDAMANESE (Andamanese) Basu 1952, 1955.

APINAYE (Ge-Pano-Carib) Callow 1962.

BASQUE (undetermined) N'Diaye-Correard 1970.

BURUSHASKI (undetermined) Lorimer 1935-1938.

CAR (undetermined) Braine 1970.

DIEGUEÑO (Hokan) Langdon 1970.

GARO (Sino-Tibetan) Burling 1961.

GEORGIAN (Caucasian) Aronson 1982, Vogt 1971

GILYAK (undetermined) Austerlitz 1958, 1959, Beffa 1982, Jakobson 1957a.

GOAJIRO (Arawakan) Holmer 1949.

HAITIAN (none) Hall 1970.

IATMUL (Central New Guinea) Staalsen 1969, 1972.

KARANKAWA (undetermined) Gatschet 1891.

KHASI (undetermined) Rabel 1961.

KHMER (Mon-Khmer) Huffman 1967.

KIWAI (Kiwai) Ray 1933.

KOREAN (Altaic) Martin 1960, Ramstedt 1939.

!KUNG (Khoisan) Snyman 1970.

KUTENAI (undetermined) Garvin 1948, 1951.

KWAKIUTL (Wakashan) Boas 1947.

LOGBARA (Nilo-Saharan) Crazzolara 1960.

MAASAI (Nilo-Hamitic) Tucker and Mpaayei 1955.

MALAYALAM (Dravidian) Andrewskutty 1971, George 1971.

MIWOK (Penutian) Freeland 1951.

NAHUATL (Aztec Tanoan) Andrew 1975.

NAVAHO (Na-Dene) Young and Morgan 1980.

OJIBWA (Macro-Algonquin) Bloomfield 1957, Todd 1970.

PALAUNG (Palaung-Wa) Milne 1921.

PAWNEE (Macro-Siouan) Parks 1976.
QUILEUTE (Chimakuan) Andrade 1933.
SANTA CRUZ (Papuan) Wurm 1969.
TEMIAR (Semang) Carey 1961.
SERBIAN (Indo-European) Partridge 1972.
SONGHAI (undetermined) Prost 1956.
SUSU (Niger-Congo) Houis 1963, Sangster and Faber 1968, 1969.
TARASCAN (undetermined) Foster 1969.
TASMANIAN (undetermined) Schmidt 1952.
TIMUCUA (undetermined) Granberry 1956.
TIWI (Australian) Osborne 1974.
TOBELORESE (West Papuan) Hueting 1936.
TONGAN (Austronesian) Churchward 1953.
TOUAREG (Afro-Asiatic) Prasse 1972-1975.
VIETNAMESE (Vietmanese) Thompson 1965.
WAPPO (Yukian) Thompson, Sandra A. Personal communication.
YANOMAMA (Macro-Chibchan) Migliazza 1972.
YUKAGHIR (undetermined) Jochelson 1905.
YUPIK (Am. Paleosiberian) Jacobson 1977.
ZAPOTEC (Oto-Manguen) Pickett 1953.

REFERENCES

Aksu, Ayhan, and Dan Slobin. 1984. The acquisition of Turkish morphology. In D. Slobin (ed.) *The cross-linguistic study of language acquisition*. Hillsdale, NJ: Lawrence Erlbaum.

Andersen, Henning. 1969. A study in diachronic morphophonemics: the Ukrainian prefixes. *Language* 45. 807-830.

Andersen, Henning. 1980. Morphological change: toward a typology. In J. Fisiak (ed.) *Historical morphology*. The Hague: Mouton.

Anderson, Lloyd. 1982. The 'Perfect' as a universal and as a language particular category. In P. Hopper (ed.) *Tense and aspect*. Amsterdam: John Benjamins.

Anderson, Stephen. 1982. Where's morphology? *Linguistic Inquiry* 13. 571-612.

Andrade, M. J. 1933. *Quileute*. In F. Boas (ed.) *Handbook of American Indian Languages III*. New York: Columbia University Press.

Andrew, J. Richard. 1975. *Introduction to Classical Nahuatl*. Austin: University of Texas Press.

Andrewskutty, A. P. 1971. *Malayalam: an intensive course*. Trivandrum, India: Department of Linguistics, University of Kerala.

Antinucci, Francesco and Ruth Miller. 1976. How children learn to talk about what happened. *Journal of child language* 3.169-189.

Ard, Josh. n.d. Using morpheme order to reconstruct syntax: a Ukrainian counter-example. San José State Occasional Papers in Linguistics, 1.

Arnott, D. W. 1970. *The nominal and verbal systems of Fula*. Oxford: Clarendon Press.

Aronoff, Mark. 1976. *Word formation in generative grammar*. Cambridge, MA: MIT Press.

Aronson, Howard I. 1982. *Georgian: a reading grammar*. Columbus, OH: Slavica.

Ashton, E. O. et al. 1954. *A Luganda grammar*. London: Longmans, Green.

Austerlitz, Robert. 1958. Vocatif et imperatif en ghiliak. *Orbis* 7. 477-481.

Austerlitz, Robert. 1959. Semantic components of pronoun systems: Gilyak.

Word 15. 102-109.

Barber, E. J. W. 1975. Voice--beyond the passive. BLS 1.16-24.

Basu, D. N. 1952. A general note on the Andamanese languages. Indian Linguistics 16. 214-225.

Basu, D. N. 1955. A linguistic introduction to Andamanese. Bulletin of the Department of Anthropology 1. 55-70. Government of India Press.

Batchelor, John O. B. E. 1938. *A grammar of the Ainu language.* Memoir V. Tokyo.

Baxter, A. R. W. 1975. Some aspects of naturalness in phonological theory. Oxford University Thesis.

Beard, Robert E. 1981. The plural as a lexical derivation (word formation). Paper presented at the Annual Meeting of the Linguistic Society of America, New York.

Beffa, Marie-Lise. 1982. Présentation de la langue Nivx. *Études mongoles et sibériennes* 13. 49-98.

Bell, Alan. 1978. Language samples. In J. Greenberg et al. (eds.), Vol. 1.

Bellugi, Ursula. 1967. *The acquisition of negation.* Harvard Dissertation.

Berman, Ruth Aronson. 1978. *Modern Hebrew structure.* Tel-Aviv: University Publishing Projects.

Bickerton, Derek. 1974. Creolization, linguistic universals, natural semantax and the brain. University of Hawaii Working Papers in Linguistics 6.3. 124-141.

Bickerton, Derek. 1977. Pidginization and creolization: Language acquisition and language universals. In A. Valdman (ed.) *Pidgin and creole linguistics.* Bloomington: Indiana University Press.

Bloom, Lois, Karin Lifter and Jeremy Hafitz. 1980. Semantics of verbs and the development of verb inflection in child language. *Language* 56. 386-412.

Bloomfield, Leonard. 1933. *Language.* New York: Holt, Rinehart and Winston.

Bloomfield, Leonard. 1957. *Eastern Ojibwa: Grammatical sketch, texts and word list.* Ann Arbor: University of Michigan Press.

Boas, Franz. 1947. *Kwakiutl grammar, with a glossary of the suffixes.* Transactions of the American Philosophical Society, vol. 37, part 3.

Bolozky, Shmuel. 1980. Paradigm coherence: evidence from Modern Hebrew. *Afroasiatic linguistics* 7/4.2-24.

Braine, Jean Critchfield. 1970. *Nicobarese grammar - Car dialect.* University of California at Berkeley Dissertation.

Burling, Robbins. 1961. *A Garo grammar*. Indian Linguistics, Monograph series 21. Poona, India: Linguistic Society of India.

Burrow, T. and S. Bhattacharya. 1970. *The Pengo language*. Oxford: Clarendon Press.

Bybee, Joan L. 1984. Diagrammatic iconicity in stem / inflection relations. In J. Haiman (ed.) *Iconicity in syntax*. Amsterdam: John Benjamins.

Bybee, Joan L. and Mary Alexandra Brewer. 1980. Explanation in morphophonemics: changes in Provençal and Spanish preterite forms. *Lingua* 52.201-242.

Bybee, Joan L. and Carol Lynn Moder. 1983. Morphological classes as natural categories. *Language* 59.251-270.

Bybee, Joan L. and William Pagliuca. 1984. Cross-linguistic comparison and the evolution of grammatical meaning. Paper presented at the Conference on Historical Semantics and Word-Formation, Błażejewko, Poland.

Bybee, Joan L. and Elly Pardo. 1981. Morphological and lexical conditioning of rules: experimental evidence from Spanish. *Linguistics* 19.937-968.

Bybee, Joan L. and Dan I. Slobin. 1982. Rules and schemas in the development and use of the English Past Tense. *Language* 58. 265-289.

Callow, John. 1962. *The Apinaye language: phonology and grammar*. London University Dissertation.

Carey, Iskander. 1961. *Tengleq Kui Serok*. Kuala Lumpur: Dewan Bahasa Dan Pustaka.

Cazden, Courtney. 1968. The acquisition of noun and verb inflection. *Child development* 39.433-438.

Chomsky, Noam. 1957. *Syntactic structures*. The Hague: Mouton.

Chomsky, Noam and Morris Halle. 1968. *The sound pattern of English*. New York: Harper and Row.

Churchward, Clark Maxwell. 1953. *Tongan grammar*. London: Oxford University Press.

Clark, Eve V. and Herbert H. Clark. 1978. Universals, relativity and language processing. In J. Greenberg et al. (eds.), Vol. 1.

Clark, Eve V. and Herbert H. Clark. 1979. When nouns surface as verbs. *Language* 55. 767-811.

Coates, Jennifer. 1983. *The semantics of the modal auxiliaries*. London: Croom Helm.

Comrie, Bernard. 1976. *Aspect*. Cambridge: Cambridge University Press.

Comrie, Bernard. 1984. *Tense*. Cambridge: Cambridge University Press.

Cowgill, Warren. 1963. A search for universals in Indo-European diachronic morphology. In J. Greenberg (ed.) *Universals of Language*. Cambridge, MA: MIT Press.

Crazzolara, J. P. 1960. *A study of the Logbara (Ma'di) language*. London: Oxford University Press.

Dahl, Östen. 1979. Typology of sentence negation. *Linguistics* 17.79-106.

Dillon, Myles and D. O. O'Croinin. 1961. *Teach yourself Irish*. New York: McKay.

Dressler, Wolfgang U. 1984. Suppletion in word formation. Paper presented at the Conference on Historical Semantics and Word Formation, Błażejewko, Poland.

Fidelholtz, James L. 1975. Word frequency and vowel reduction in English. *Papers from the Parasession on Natural Phonology*. Chicago Linguistic Society.

Fleischman, Suzanne. 1982. *The future in thought and language*. Cambridge: Cambridge University Press.

Fleischman, Suzanne. 1983. From pragmatics to grammar: diachronic reflections on complex pasts and futures in Romance. *Lingua* 60.183-214.

Foley, William and Robert Van Valin. 1984. *Functional syntax and universal grammar*. Cambridge: Cambridge University Press.

Forsyth, J. 1970. *A grammar of aspect: usage and meaning in the Russian verb*. Cambridge: Cambridge University Press.

Foster, Mary Lecron. 1969. *The Tarascan language*. Berkeley: University of California Press.

Francis, W. Nelson, and Henry Kučera. 1982. *Frequency analysis of English Usage*. Boston: Houghton Mifflin.

Freeland, L. S. 1951. *Language of the Sierra Miwok*. Memoirs of IJAL or Indiana University Publications in Anthropology and Linguistics VI.

Friedrich, Paul. 1974. On aspect theory and Homeric aspect. IJAL 40. 4. Part 2.

Garvin, Paul L. 1948, 1951. Kutenai. IJAL XIV. 37-47, 87-90, 171-87, XVII. 84-97.

Gatschet, Albert S. 1891. The Karankawa Indians. Peabody Museum of American Ethnology: Archaeological and Ethnological Papers, vol. 1, no. 2. Harvard University.

George, K. M. 1971. *Malayalam grammar and reader*. Kottayam, India: National Book Stall.

Gili Gaya, S. 1960. *Funciones gramaticales en el habla enfantil*. Publicaciones pedagógicas, serie II, no. 24. Río Piedras: Univerity of Puerto Rico.

Givón, Talmy. 1971. Historical syntax and synchronic morphology: an archaeologist's field trip. CLS 7. 349-415.

Givón, Talmy. 1973. The time-axis phenomenon. *Language* 49.800-925.

Givón, Talmy. 1978. *On understanding grammar*. New York: Academic Press.

Givón, Talmy. 1982. Tense-aspect-modality: the creole prototype and beyond. In P. Hopper (ed.) *Tense and aspect*. Amsterdam: John Benjamins.

Granberry, Julian. 1956. Timucua I. IJAL XXII. 97-105.

Greenberg, Joseph. 1954 [1960]. A quantitative approach to the morphological typology of language. IJAL 26. 178-194.

Greenberg, Joseph. 1963. Some universals of grammar with particular reference to the order of meaningful elements. In J. Greenberg (ed.) *Universals of language*. Cambridge, MA: MIT Press.

Greenberg, Joseph. 1966. *Language universals*. The Hague: Mouton.

Greenberg, Joseph. 1969. Some methods of dynamic comparison in linguistics. In J. Puhvel (ed.) *Substance and structure of language*. Berkeley and Los Angeles: University of California Press.

Greenberg, Joseph, Charles Ferguson and Edith Moravcsik (eds.). 1978. *Universals of human language*. 4 Volumes. Stanford: Stanford University Press.

Guillaume, Paul. 1927 [1973]. The development of formal elements in the child's speech. In C. Ferguson and D. Slobin (eds.) *Studies in child language development*. New York: Holt, Rinehart and Winston.

Haiman, John. 1983. Iconic and economic motivation. *Language* 59. 781-819.

Hall, Robert A., Jr. et al. 1970. *Haitian Creole: grammar, texts and vocabulary*. Memoirs of the American Folklore Society, v. 43. Mamaroneck, NY: Kraus Reprint Corp.

Hare, R. M. 1971. *Practical inferences*. London: Macmillan.

Harris, James W. 1978. Two theories of nonautomatic alternation. *Language* 54. 41-60.

Harris, Martin. 1982. The 'past simple' and 'present perfect' in Romance. In N. Vincent and M. Harris (eds.) *Studies in the Romance verb*. London: Croom Helm.

Hockett, Charles. 1954. Two models of grammatical description. *Word* 10. 210-231.

Hooper, Joan B. 1976a. *An introduction to natural generative phonology*. New York: Academic Press.

Hooper, Joan B. 1976b. Word frequency in lexical diffusion and the source of morpho-phonemic change. In W. Christie (ed.) *Current trends in historical linguistics*. Amsterdam: North Holland.

Hooper, Joan Bybee. 1979a. Child morphology and morphophonemic change. *Linguistics* 17.21-50. Also in J. Fisiak (ed.) *Historical Morphology*. The Hague: Mouton.

Hooper, Joan B. 1979b. Substantive principles in natural generative phonology. In D. Dinnsen (ed.) *Current phonological theories*. Bloomington: Indiana University Press.

Holmer, Nils M. 1949. Goajiro. IJAL XV. 45-56, 110-120, 145-157, 232-235.

Hope, Edward R. 1974. *The deep syntax of Lisu sentences*. Pacific Linguistics, Series B, No. 34.

Hopper, Paul J. 1977. Observations on the typology of focus and aspect in narrative language. NUSA 4. Jakarta. Reprinted in *Studies in Language* 3.37-64, 1979.

Horn, Lawrence. 1975. *On the semantic properties of logical operators in English*. UCLA Dissertation.

Houis, Maurice. 1963. *Étude descriptive de la langue susu*. Ifan, Dakar.

Huffman, Franklin E. 1967. *An outline of Cambodian grammar*. Cornell University Dissertation.

Hueting, A. 1936. Iets over de Spraakkunst van de Tobeloreesche-taal. Bijdragen Tot De Taal-Land-en Volkenkunde. 94.295-407.

Ingram, David. 1978. Typology and universals of personal pronouns. In J. Greenberg et al. (eds.) *Universals of human language*, Vol. 3. Stanford: Stanford University Press.

Jacobson, Steven A. 1977. *A grammatical sketch of Siberian Yupik Eskimo as spoken on St. Lawrence Island, Alaska*. Fairbanks: Alaska Native Language Center, University of Alaska.

Jakobson, Roman. 1939. Signe zéro. Reprinted in *Roman Jakobson, Selected Writings, III*. The Hague: Mouton.

Jakobson, Roman. 1957a. Notes on Gilyak. In Studies Presented to Yuen Ren Chao. The Bulletin of the Institute of History and Philology, Academia Sinica.

Jakobson, Roman. 1957b. Shifters, verbal categories and the Russian verb. Reprinted in *Roman Jakobson, Selected Writings, III*. The Hague: Mouton.

Jochelson, Vladimir I. 1905. Essay on the grammar of the Yukaghir language. *American Anthropologist* 7. 369-424.

Juilland, A. and E. Chang-Rodríguez. 1964. *Frequency dictionary of Spanish words*. The Hague: Mouton.

Kempley, S. T. and John Morton. 1982. The effects of priming with regularly and irregularly related words in auditory word recognition. *British Journal of Psychology* 73. 441-454.

Kenny, J. 1974. A numerical taxomony of ethnic units using Murdock's 1967 world sample. Ann Arbor: University Microfilms.

Kernan, K. T. and B. G. Blount. 1966. The acquisition of Spanish grammar by Mexican children. *Anthropological Linguistics* 8.1-14.

Kiparsky, Paul and Lise Menn. 1977. On the acquisition of phonology. In J. Macnamara (ed.) *Language learning and thought*. New York: Academic Press.

Klausenburger, Jürgen. 1981. The velar insert in Romance. MS. University of Washington. To appear in E. Pulgram (ed.) *Michigan Romance Studies*, Vol. 4.

Kroeber, A. L. and W. G. Grace. 1960. *The Sparkman grammar of Luiseño*. Berkeley and Los Angeles: University of California Press.

Kuryłowicz, Jerzy. 1964. *The inflectional categories of Indo-European*. Heidelberg.

Kuryłowicz, Jerzy. 1968. The notion of morpho(pho)neme. In W. Lehmann and Y. Malkiel (eds.) *Directions in historical linguistics*. Austin: University of Texas Press.

Langacker, Ronald. 1972. *Fundamentals of linguistic analysis*. New York: Harcourt Brace.

Langdon, Margaret. 1970. *A grammar of Diegueño: the Mesa Grande dialect*. Berkeley: University of California Press.

Lehmann, Winfred P. 1973. A structural principle of language and its implications. *Language* 49.47-66.

Lewis, G. L. 1967. *Turkish grammar*. Oxford: Clarendon Press.

Li, Charles N., Sandra A. Thompson and R. McMillan Thompson. 1982. The discourse motivation for the perfect aspect: The Mandarin particle LE. In P. Hopper (ed.) *Tense and aspect*. Amsterdam: John Benjamins.

Linell, Per. 1979. *Psychological reality in phonology*. Cambridge: Cambridge University Press.

Lorimer, David L. R. 1935-1938. *The Burushaski language*. Three volumes. Cambridge, MA: Harvard University Press.

Lukatela, G., B. Gligorijevic, A. Kostić and M. T. Turvey. 1980. Representation of inflected nouns in the internal lexicon. *Memory and cognition*

8. 415-423.

Lyons, John. 1977. *Semantics*. Cambridge: Cambridge University Press.

MacWhinney, Brian. 1974. *The acquisition of Hungarian*. University of California at Berkeley Dissertation.

MacWhinney, Brian. 1978. *The acquisition of morphophonology*. Monographs of the Society for Research in Child Development, no 174, vol. 43.

Malkiel, Yakov. 1974. New problems in romance interfixation (I): the velar insert in the present tense. *Romance Philology* 27:304-355.

Malkiel, Yakov. 1978. Derivational categories. In J. Greenberg, et al. (eds.) Vol 3.

Mańczak, Witold. 1978. Sporadic sound change. In J. Fisiak (ed.) *Recent developments in historical phonology*. The Hague: Mouton.

Mańczak, Witold. 1980. Laws of analogy. In J. Fisiak (ed.) *Historical morphology*. The Hague: Mouton.

Marchese, Lynell. 1979. *Tense / aspect and the development of auxiliaries in the Kru language family*. UCLA Dissertation. To appear. Summer Institute of Linguistics.

Martin, Samuel E. 1960. *Korean reference grammar*. Research and Studies in Uralic and Altaic Languages, Project no. 19. Cleveland: Bell and Howell.

Matthews, Peter. 1974. *Morphology*. Cambridge: Cambridge Univerity Press.

McCawley, James D. 1971. Tense and time in English. In C. Fillmore and D. Langendoen (eds.) *Studies in linguistic semantics*. New York: Holt, Rinehart and Winston.

McDonald, Betsy H. 1982. *Aspects of the American Sign Language predicate system*. SUNY/Buffalo Dissertation.

Menéndez García, Manuel. 1963. *El cuarto de los valles de Oviedo*. Instituto de estudios asturianos.

Menéndez-Pidal, Ramón. 1904 [1968]. *Manual de gramatica historica espanola*. Madrid: Espasa-Calpe.

Meyer-Lübke, W. 1923. *Grammaire des langues romanes*. New York: Stechert.

Migliazza, Ernest Cesar. 1972. *Yanomama grammar and intelligibility*. Indiana University Dissertation.

Miller, Wick R. 1965. *Acoma grammar and texts*. Berkeley: University of California Press.

Milne, Mary Lewis. 1921. *An elementary Palaung grammar*. Oxford: The

Clarendon Press.

Moore, Samuel and Albert H. Marckwardt. 1968. *Historical outline of English sounds and inflections.* Ann Arbor: George Wahr Publishing Co.

Moravcsik, Edith. 1978. Reduplicative constructions. In J. Greenberg et al. (eds). *Universals of human language.* Vol. 3. Stanford: Stanford University Press.

Mosel, Ulrike. 1980. *Tolai and Tok Pisin: the influence of the substratum on the development of New Guinea Pidgin.* Pacific Linguistics, Series B, No. 73.

Mülhäusler, Peter. 1980. Structural expansion and the process of creolization. In Valdman and Highfield (eds.) *Theoretical contributions in creole studies.* New York: Academic Press.

Murdock, George P. 1967. *Atlas of world cultures.* Pittsburgh: University of Pittsburgh Press.

N'Diaye-Correard, Genevieve. 1970. *Structure du dialecte basque de Maya.* The Hague: Mouton.

Nida, Eugene. 1946. *Morphology.* Ann Arbor: University of Michigan Press.

Noonan, Michael. 1981. Complementation. To appear in T. Shopen et al. (eds.) *Language typology and syntactic fieldwork.*

Osborne, C. R. 1974. *The Tiwi language.* Canberra: Australian Institute of Aboriginal Studies.

Ó Siadhail, Míchaél. 1980. *Learning Irish.* Dublin: Dublin Institute for Advanced Studies.

Pagliuca, William. 1976. PRE-fixing. MS. SUNY/Buffalo.

Pagliuca, William. 1982. *Prolegomena to a theory of articulatory evolution.* SUNY/Buffalo Dissertation.

Parks, Douglas R. 1976. *A grammar of Pawnee.* Garland Studies in American Indian Linguistics. New York: Garland Publishing.

Partridge, Monica. 1972. *Serbo-Croatian practical grammar and reader.* Belgrade.

Penny, R. J. 1969. *El habla Pasiega.* London: Tamersis Books.

Perkins, Revere D. 1980. *The evolution of culture and grammar.* SUNY/Buffalo Dissertation.

Peters, Ann M. 1983. *The units of language acquisition.* Cambridge: Cambridge University Press.

Phillips, Judith W. 1983. *A partial grammar of the Haitian Creole verb system: forms, functions and syntax.* SUNY/Buffalo Dissertation.

Pickett, Velma Bernice. 1953, 1955. Isthmus Zapotec verb analysis I. IJAL

19. 292-296. Isthmus Zapotec verb analysis II. IJAL 21. 217-232.

Prost, André. 1956. *La langue Sonay et ses dialectes*. Memoires, no. 47. Dakar, Senegal: Institut Fonamental D'Afrique Noire.

Rabel, Lili. 1961. *Khasi, a language of Assam*. Baton Rouge: Louisiana State University.

Ramstedt, G. J. 1939. *A Korean grammar*. Helsinki: Suomalais-Ugrilainen Seura.

Ray, Sidney H. 1933. *A grammar of the Kiwai language, Fly Delta, with a Kiwai vocabulary by E. B. Riley*. Port Moresby, Australia: Government Printer.

Rodríguez Bou, Ismael. 1952. *Recuento de vocabulario español*. Vol. III. Rio Piedras: University of Puerto Rico.

Ronjat, J. 1937. *Grammaire historique des parlers provençaux modernes*. Vol.3. Montpellier: Société des langues romanes.

Rudes, Blair A. 1980. On the nature of verbal suppletion. *Linguistics* 18. 655-676.

Rudes, Blair A. 1984. Reconstructing word order in a polysynthetic language: from SOV to SVO in Iroquoian. In J. Fisiak (ed.), *Historical syntax*. The Hague: Mouton.

Sadock, Jerrold. 1980. Noun incorporation in Greenlandic. *Language* 56. 300-319.

Sadock, Jerrold M. and Carl Chr. Olsen. 1976. Phonological processes across word-boundary in West Greenlandic. *Papers in Eskimo and Aleut Linguistics*. Chicago Linguisitic Society.

Sangster, Linda and Emmanuel Faber. 1968. *Susu basic course*. Bloomington: Indiana University Intensive Language Training Center.

Sangster, Linda and Emmanuel Faber. 1969. *Susu intermediate course*. Bloomington: Indiana University Intensive Language Training Center.

Sapir, Edward. 1911. The problem of noun incorporation in American languages. *American Anthropologist* 13. 250-252.

Sapir, Edward. 1921. *Language*. New York: Harcourt, Brace and World.

Schmidt, V. W. 1952. *Die Tasmanischen Sprachen: Quellen, Gruppierungen, Grammatik, Wörterbücher*. Utrecht-Anvers: Publication 8, Commission d'Enquete Linguistique, CIPL.

Silva-Corvalán, Carmen. 1984. Modality and semantic change. Paper presented at the Conference on Historical Semantics and Word Formation, Błażejewko, Poland.

Simeon, George John. 1968. *The phonemics and morphology of Hokkaido*

Ainu. University of Southern California Dissertation.

Simões, Maria C. P. and Carol Stoel-Gammon. 1979. The acquisition of inflections in Portuguese: a study of the development of person markers on verbs. *Journal of child language* 6.53-67.

Slobin, Dan I. 1973. Cognitive prerequisites for the development of grammar. In C. Ferguson and D. Slobin (eds.) *Studies of child language development*. New York: Holt, Rinehart and Winston.

Snyman, J. W. 1970. *An introduction to the !Xũ (!Kung) language*. Universtiy of Cape Town, School of African Studies, Communications no. 34. Cape Town, South Africa: Balkema.

Staalsen, Philip. 1969. The dialects of Iatmul. Pacific Linguistics A. 22.69-84.

Staalsen, Philip. 1972. Clause relationships in Iatmul. Pacific Linguistics A. 31. 45-69.

Stanners, R., J. Neiser, W. Hernon, and R. Hall. 1979. Memory representation for morphologically related words. *Journal of verbal learning and verbal behavior* 18.399-412.

Steele, Susan. 1975. Is it possible? Working Papers on Language Universals 18.35-58.

Stephany, Ursula. 1981. Verbal grammar in Modern Greek early child language. In P. Dale and D. Ingram (eds.) *Child language: an international perspective*. Baltimore: University Park Press.

Subrahmanyam, P. S. 1971. *Dravidian verb morphology*. Tamilnadu: Annamalai University.

Talmy, Leonard. 1978. The relation of grammar to cognition -- a synopsis. In D. Waltz (ed.) Proceedings of TINLAP 2.

Talmy, Leonard. 1980. Lexicalization patterns in language. To appear in Shopen et al. (eds.) *Language typology and syntactic fieldwork*.

Thompson, Laurence C. 1965. *A Vietnamese grammar*. Seattle: University of Washington Press.

Thompson, Sandra A. 1975. On the issue of productivity in the lexikon (sic). *Kritikon Litterarum* 4. 332-349.

Thorndike, Edward and Irving Lorge. 1944. *The teacher's word book of 30,000 words*. New York: Columbia University.

Tiersma, Peter M. 1982. Local and general markedness. *Language* 58.832-849.

Todd, Evelyn Mary. 1970. *A grammar of the Ojibwa language: the Severin dialect*. University of North Carolina Dissertation.

Tucker, A. N. and J. T. Mpaayei. 1955. *A Maasai grammar*. London:

Longmans.

Ultan, Russell. 1978. The nature of future tenses. In J. Greenberg et al. (eds.) Vol. 3.

Vennemann, Theo. 1972. Rule inversion. *Lingua* 29. 209-242.

Vennemann, Theo. 1973. Explanation in syntax. In J. Kimball (ed.) *Syntax and Semantics II*. New York: Academic Press.

Vennemann, Theo. 1974. Words and syllables in natural generative phonology. *Papers from the Parasession on Natural Phonology*. Chicago Linguistic Society.

Vennemann, Theo. 1978. Rule inversion and lexical storage: the case of Sanskrit visarga. In J. Fisiak (ed.) *Recent developments in historical phonology*. The Hague: Mouton.

Vincent, Nigel. 1980. Words versus morphemes in morphological change: the case of Italian *-iamo*. In J. Fisiak (ed.) *Historical morphology*. The Hague: Mouton.

Voegelin, Charles F. and Florence M. Voegelin. 1966. *Index to the languages of the world*. Anthropological linguistics, vols. 6 and 7.

Vogt, Hans. 1971. *Grammaire de la langue georgiénne*. Oslo, Norway: Universitetsforlaget.

Watkins, Calvert. 1962. *Indo-European origins of the Celtic verb*. Dublin: Dublin Institute for Advanced Studies.

Weinreich, Uriel. 1963. On the semantic structure of language. In J. Greenberg (ed.) *Universals of language*. Cambridge, Mass: MIT Press.

Whorf, Benjamin Lee. 1938. Some verbal categories of Hopi. *Language* 14. 275-286.

Woodbury, Hanni. 1975. Onondaga noun incorporation. IJAL 41.1. 10-20.

Wurm, S. A. 1969. The linguistic situation in the Reef and Santa Cruz Islands. *Pacific Linguistics* A. 21. 47-105.

Yates, Alan. 1975. *Teach yourself Catalan*. London: Hodder & Stoughton.

Young, Robert and William Morgan. 1980. *The Navajo Language: a grammar and colloquial dictionary*. Albuquerque: University of New Mexico Press.

Zager, David. 1980. *A real time process model of morphological change*. SUNY/Buffalo Dissertation.

Zager, David. 1983. Morphology as an activity. MS.

Zimmer, Karl. 1964. *Affixal negation in English and other languages*. Supplement to *Word* 20:2, Monograph 5. New York: Linguistic Circle of New York.

Zwicky, Arnold, and Geoffrey Pullum. 1983. Cliticization vs. inflection: English *n't*. *Language* 59.502-513.

INDEX

In the TYPOLOGICAL STUDIES IN LANGUAGE (TSL) series the following volumes have been published thus far, and will be published during 1985:

1. HOPPER, Paul (ed.): *TENSE-ASPECT: BETWEEN SEMANTICS & PRAGMATICS.* Amsterdam, 1982.

2. HAIMAN, John & Pam MUNRO (eds.): *PROCEEDINGS OF A SYMPOSIUM ON SWITCH REFERENCE, Winnipeg, May 1981.* Amsterdam, 1983.

3. GIVÓN, T. (ed.): *TOPIC CONTINUITY IN DISCOURSE: A QUANTITATIVE CROSS-LANGUAGE STUDY.* Amsterdam, 1983.

4. CHISHOLM, William, Louis T. MILIC & John GREPPIN (eds.): *INTERROGATIVITY: A COLLOQUIUM ON THE GRAMMAR, TYPOLOGY AND PRAGMATICS OF QUESTIONS IN SEVEN DIVERSE LANGUAGES, Cleveland, Ohio, October 5th 1981 - May 3rd 1982.* Amsterdam, 1984.

5. RUTHERFORD, William E. (ed.): *LANGUAGE UNIVERSALS AND SECOND LANGUAGE ACQUISITION.* Amsterdam, 1984.

6. HAIMAN, John (ed.): *ICONICITY IN SYNTAX. Proceedings of a Symposium on Iconicity in Syntax, Stanford, June 24-6, 1983.* Amsterdam, 1985.

7. CRAIG, Colette (ed.): *NOUN CLASSES AND CATEGORIZATION. Proceedings of a Symposium on Categorization and Noun Classification, Eugene, Ore. October 1983.* Amsterdam, 1985.

8. SLOBIN, Dan I. (ed.): *ASPECTS OF SYNTAX, SEMANTICS, AND DISCOURSE STRUCTURE IN TURKISH* (working title). *Proceedings of a Conference on Turkish Linguistics, held at Berkeley, May 1982.* Amsterdam, 1985.

9. BYBEE, Joan L.: *Morphology. A Study of the Relation between Meaning and Form.* Amsterdam, 1985.